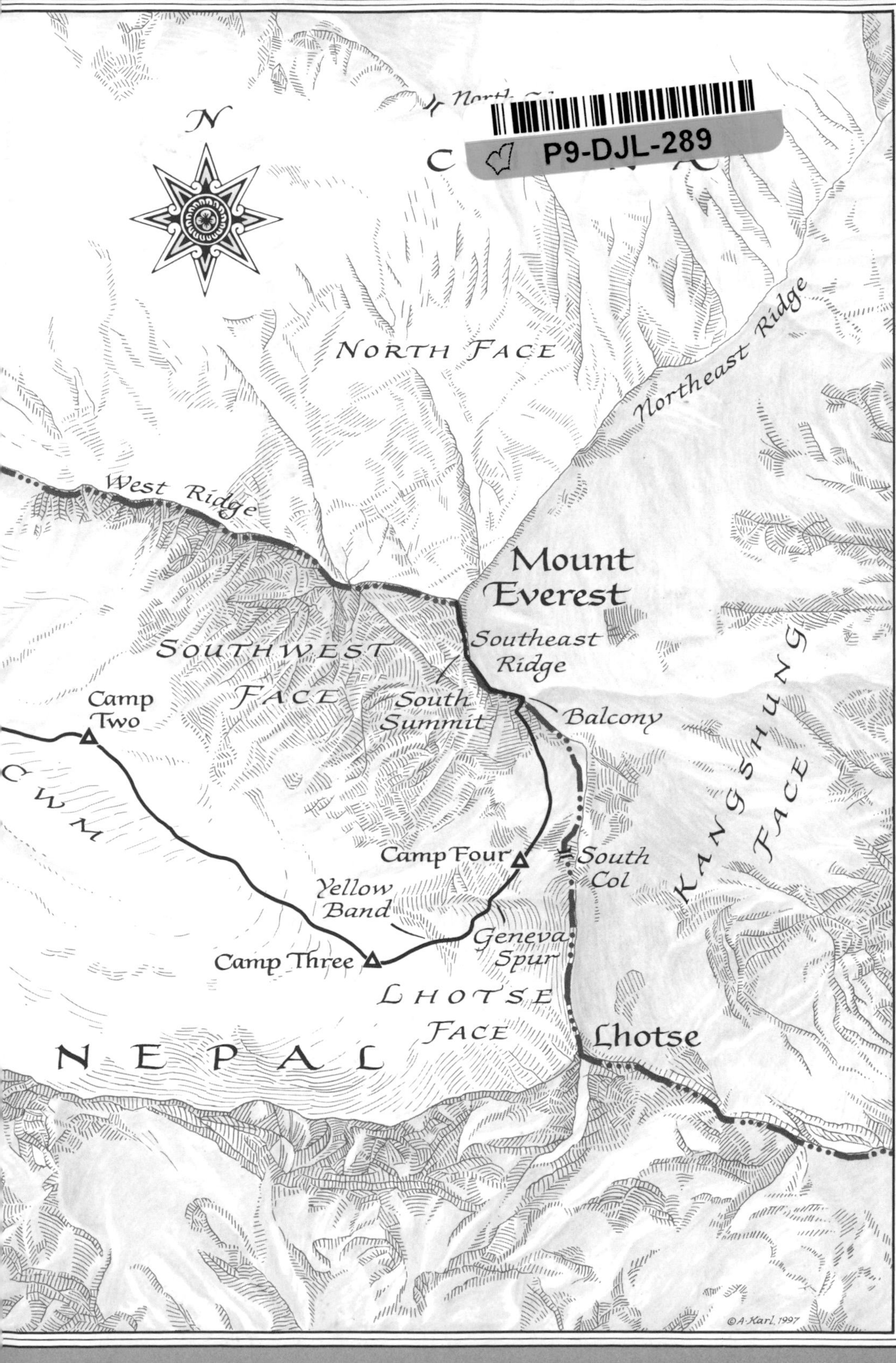
N
NORTH FACE
Northeast Ridge
West Ridge
Mount Everest
SOUTHWEST FACE
Southeast Ridge
South Summit
Balcony
Camp Two
CWM
KANGSHUNG FACE
Camp Four
South Col
Yellow Band
Geneva Spur
Camp Three
LHOTSE FACE
Lhotse
NEPAL
©A. Karl, 1997

P9-DJL-289

Also by Jon Krakauer

Iceland

Eiger Dreams

Into the Wild

INTO THIN AIR

INTO THIN AIR

A Personal Account of the Mount Everest Disaster

Jon Krakauer

VILLARD NEW YORK

Copyright © 1997 by Jon Krakauer
Illustrations copyright © 1997 by Randy Rackliff
Endpaper maps copyright © 1997 by Anita Karl

All rights reserved under International and Pan-American Copyright Conventions.
Published in the United States by Villard Books, a division of Random House, Inc., New York, and simultaneously in Canada by Random House of Canada Limited, Toronto.

Villard Books is a registered trademark of Random House, Inc.

Portions of this work were originally published in *Outside.*

Grateful acknowledgment is made to the following for permission to reprint previously published material:

BÂTON WICKS PUBLICATIONS: Excerpts from *Upon That Mountain* by Eric Shipton (Hodder, London, 1943). This title is now collected in the omnibus *Eric Shipton—The Six Mountain Travel Books* (Diadem, London, and the Mountaineers, Seattle, 1995). Reprinted by permission of Nick Shipton and Bâton Wicks Publications, Macclesfield, Cheshire, England.
HAYNES PUBLISHING: Excerpts from *Everest* by Walt Unsworth. Published by Oxford Illustrated Press, an imprint of Haynes Publishing, Sparkford, Nr Yeovil, Somerset, BA22 7JJ. Reprinted by permission of the author and publisher.
SIMON AND SCHUSTER AND A. P. WATT LTD: Six lines from "The Second Coming" by William Butler Yeats, from *The Collected Works of W. B. Yeats, Volume 1: The Poems* revised and edited by Richard J. Finneran. Copyright © 1924 by Macmillan Publishing Company. Copyright renewed 1952 by Bertha Georgie Yeats. Reprinted by permission of Simon and Schuster and A. P. Watt Ltd. on behalf of Michael Yeats.

Library of Congress Cataloging-in-Publication Data
Krakauer, Jon.
Into thin air: a personal account of the Mount Everest disaster / Jon Krakauer.
p. cm.
Includes bibliographical references.
ISBN 0-679-45752-6
1. Mountaineering accidents—Everest, Mount (China and Nepal).
2. Mount Everest Expedition (1996). 3. Krakauer, Jon. I. Title.
GV199.44.E85K725 1997 796.5'22'095496—dc21 96-30031

Random House website address: http://www.randomhouse.com/

Printed in the United States of America on acid-free paper

6 8 9 7

Book design by Caroline Cunningham

For Linda;

and in memory of Andy Harris, Doug Hansen, Rob Hall,
Yasuko Namba, Scott Fischer, Ngawang Topche Sherpa, Chen Yu-Nan,
Bruce Herrod, and Lopsang Jangbu Sherpa

Men play at tragedy because they do not believe in the reality of the tragedy which is actually being staged in the civilised world.

José Ortega y Gasset

Introduction

In March 1996, *Outside* magazine sent me to Nepal to participate in, and write about, a guided ascent of Mount Everest. I went as one of eight clients on an expedition led by a well-known guide from New Zealand named Rob Hall. On May 10 I arrived on top of the mountain, but the summit came at a terrible cost.

Among my five teammates who reached the top, four, including Hall, perished in a rogue storm that blew in without warning while we were still high on the peak. By the time I'd descended to Base Camp nine climbers from four expeditions were dead, and three more lives would be lost before the month was out.

The expedition left me badly shaken, and the article was difficult to write. Nevertheless, five weeks after I returned from Nepal I delivered a manuscript to *Outside,* and it was published in the September issue of the magazine. Upon its completion I attempted to put Everest out of my mind and get on with my life, but that turned out to be impossible. Through a fog of messy emotions, I continued trying to make sense of what had happened up there, and I obsessively mulled the circumstances of my companions' deaths.

The *Outside* piece was as accurate as I could make it under the circumstances, but my deadline had been unforgiving, the sequence of events had been frustratingly complex, and the memories of the survivors had been badly distorted by exhaustion, oxygen depletion, and shock. At one point during my research I asked three other people to recount an incident all four of us had witnessed high on the mountain, and none of us could agree on such crucial facts as the time, what had been said, or even who had been present. Within days after the *Outside* article went to press, I discovered that a few of the details I'd reported were in error. Most were minor inaccuracies of the sort that inevitably creep into works of deadline journalism, but one of my blunders was in no sense minor, and it had a devastating impact on the friends and family of one of the victims.

Only slightly less disconcerting than the article's factual errors was the material that necessarily had to be omitted for lack of space. Mark Bryant, the editor of *Outside,* and Larry Burke, the publisher, had given me an extraordinary amount of room to tell the story: they ran the piece at 17,000 words—four or five times as long as a typical magazine feature. Even so, I felt that it was much too abbreviated to do justice to the tragedy. The Everest climb had rocked my life to its core, and it became desperately important for me to record the events in complete detail, unconstrained by a limited number of column inches. This book is the fruit of that compulsion.

The staggering unreliability of the human mind at high altitude made the research problematic. To avoid relying excessively on my own perceptions, I interviewed most of the protagonists at great length and on multiple occasions. When possible I also corroborated details with radio logs maintained by people at Base Camp, where clear thought wasn't in such short supply. Readers familiar with the *Outside* article may notice discrepancies between certain details (primarily matters of time) reported in the magazine and those reported in the book; the revisions reflect new information that has come to light since publication of the magazine piece.

Several authors and editors I respect counseled me not to write the book as quickly as I did; they urged me to wait two or three years and put some distance between me and the expedition in order to gain some crucial perspective. Their advice was sound, but in the end I ignored it—mostly because what happened on the mountain was gnawing my guts out. I thought that writing the book might purge Everest from my life.

It hasn't, of course. Moreover, I agree that readers are often poorly served when an author writes as an act of catharsis, as I have done here. But I hoped something would be gained by spilling my soul in the calamity's immediate aftermath, in the roil and torment of the moment. I wanted my account to have a raw, ruthless sort of honesty that seemed in danger of leaching away with the passage of time and the dissipation of anguish.

Some of the same people who warned me against writing hastily had also cautioned me against going to Everest in the first place. There were many, many fine reasons not to go, but attempting to climb Everest is an intrinsically irrational act—a triumph of desire over sensibility. Any person who would seriously consider it is almost by definition beyond the sway of reasoned argument.

The plain truth is that I knew better but went to Everest anyway. And in doing so I was a party to the death of good people, which is something that is apt to remain on my conscience for a very long time.

Jon Krakauer
Seattle
November 1996

Dramatis Personæ

*Mount Everest Spring 1996**

Adventure Consultants Guided Expedition

Rob Hall	New Zealand, leader and head guide
Mike Groom	Australia, guide
Andy "Harold" Harris	New Zealand, guide
Helen Wilton	New Zealand, Base Camp manager
Dr. Caroline Mackenzie	New Zealand, Base Camp doctor
Ang Tshering Sherpa	Nepal, Base Camp sirdar
Ang Dorje Sherpa	Nepal, climbing sirdar
Lhakpa Chhiri Sherpa	Nepal, climbing Sherpa
Kami Sherpa	Nepal, climbing Sherpa
Tenzing Sherpa	Nepal, climbing Sherpa
Arita Sherpa	Nepal, climbing Sherpa
Ngawang Norbu Sherpa	Nepal, climbing Sherpa
Chuldum Sherpa	Nepal, climbing Sherpa
Chhongba Sherpa	Nepal, Base Camp cook
Pemba Sherpa	Nepal, Base Camp Sherpa
Tendi Sherpa	Nepal, cook boy
Doug Hansen	USA, client
Dr. Seaborn Beck Weathers	USA, client
Yasuko Namba	Japan, client
Dr. Stuart Hutchison	Canada, client
Frank Fischbeck	Hong Kong, client
Lou Kasischke	USA, client
Dr. John Taske	Australia, client
Jon Krakauer	USA, client and journalist

*Not everyone present on Mt. Everest in the spring of 1996 is listed.

Susan Allen	Australia, trekker
Nancy Hutchison	Canada, trekker

Mountain Madness Guided Expedition

Scott Fischer	USA, leader and head guide
Anatoli Boukreev	Russia, guide
Neal Beidleman	USA, guide
Dr. Ingrid Hunt	USA, Base Camp manager, team doctor
Lopsang Jangbu Sherpa	Nepal, climbing sirdar
Ngima Kale Sherpa	Nepal, Base Camp sirdar
Ngawang Topche Sherpa	Nepal, climbing Sherpa
Tashi Tshering Sherpa	Nepal, climbing Sherpa
Ngawang Dorje Sherpa	Nepal, climbing Sherpa
Ngawang Sya Kya Sherpa	Nepal, climbing Sherpa
Ngawang Tendi Sherpa	Nepal, climbing Sherpa
Tendi Sherpa	Nepal, climbing Sherpa
"Big" Pemba Sherpa	Nepal, climbing Sherpa
Pemba Sherpa	Nepal, Base Camp cook boy
Sandy Hill Pittman	USA, client and journalist
Charlotte Fox	USA, client
Tim Madsen	USA, client
Pete Schoening	USA, client
Klev Schoening	USA, client
Lene Gammelgaard	Denmark, client
Martin Adams	USA, client
Dr. Dale Kruse	USA, client
Jane Bromet	USA, journalist

MacGillivray Freeman IMAX/IWERKS Expedition

David Breashears	USA, leader and film director
Jamling Norgay Sherpa	India, deputy leader and film talent
Ed Viesturs	USA, climber and film talent
Araceli Segarra	Spain, climber and film talent
Sumiyo Tsuzuki	Japan, climber and film talent

Robert Schauer	Austria, climber and cinematographer
Paula Barton Viesturs	USA, Base Camp manager
Audrey Salkeld	U.K., journalist
Liz Cohen	USA, film production manager
Liesl Clark	USA, film producer and writer

Taiwanese National Expedition

"Makalu" Gau Ming-Ho	Taiwan, leader
Chen Yu-Nan	Taiwan, climber
Kami Dorje Sherpa	Nepal, climbing sirdar
Ngima Gombu Sherpa	Nepal, climbing Sherpa
Mingma Tshering Sherpa	Nepal, climbing Sherpa

Johannesburg *Sunday Times* Expedition

Ian Woodall	U.K., leader
Bruce Herrod	U.K., deputy leader and photographer
Cathy O'Dowd	South Africa, climber
Deshun Deysel	South Africa, climber
Edmund February	South Africa, climber
Andy de Klerk	South Africa, climber
Andy Hackland	South Africa, climber
Ken Woodall	South Africa, climber
Tierry Renard	France, climber
Ken Owen	South Africa, sponsor and trekker
Philip Woodall	U.K., Base Camp manager
Alexandrine Gaudin	France, administrative assistant
Dr. Charlotte Noble	South Africa, team doctor
Ken Vernon	South Africa, journalist
Richard Shorey	South Africa, photographer
Patrick Conroy	South Africa, radio operator
Ang Dorje Sherpa	Nepal, climbing sirdar
Pemba Tendi Sherpa	Nepal, climbing Sherpa
Jangbu Sherpa	Nepal, climbing Sherpa

Ang Babu Sherpa	Nepal, climbing Sherpa
Dawa Sherpa	Nepal, climbing Sherpa

Alpine Ascents International Guided Expedition

Todd Burleson	USA, leader and guide
Pete Athans	USA, guide
Jim Williams	USA, guide
Dr. Ken Kamler	USA, client and team doctor
Charles Corfield	USA, client
Becky Johnston	USA, trekker and screenwriter

International Commercial Expedition

Mal Duff	U.K., leader
Mike Trueman	Hong Kong, deputy leader
Michael Burns	U.K., Base Camp manager
Dr. Henrik Jessen Hansen	Denmark, expedition doctor
Veikka Gustafsson	Finland, climber
Kim Sejberg	Denmark, climber
Ginge Fullen	U.K., climber
Jaakko Kurvinen	Finland, climber
Euan Duncan	U.K., climber

Himalayan Guides Commercial Expedition

Henry Todd	U.K., leader
Mark Pfetzer	USA, climber
Ray Door	USA, climber

Swedish Solo Expedition

Göran Kropp	Sweden, climber
Frederic Bloomquist	Sweden, filmmaker
Ang Rita Sherpa	Nepal, climbing Sherpa and film crew member

Norwegian Solo Expedition

Petter Neby	Norway, climber

New Zealand–Malaysian Guided Pumori Expedition

Guy Cotter	New Zealand, leader and guide
Dave Hiddleston	New Zealand, guide
Chris Jillet	New Zealand, guide

American Commercial Pumori/Lhotse Expedition

Dan Mazur	USA, leader
Jonathan Pratt	U.K., co-leader
Scott Darsney	USA, climber and photographer
Chantal Mauduit	France, climber
Stephen Koch	USA, climber and snowboarder
Brent Bishop	USA, climber
Diane Taliaferro	USA, climber
Dave Sharman	U.K., climber
Tim Horvath	USA, climber
Dana Lynge	USA, climber
Martha Lynge	USA, climber

Nepali Everest Cleaning Expedition

Sonam Gyalchhen Sherpa	Nepal, leader

Himalayan Rescue Association Clinic

(in Pheriche Village)

Dr. Jim Litch	USA, staff doctor
Dr. Larry Silver	USA, staff doctor
Laura Ziemer	USA, staff member

Indo-Tibetan Border Police Everest Expedition

(climbing from the Tibetan side of the mountain)

Mohindor Singh	India, leader
Harbhajan Singh	India, deputy leader and climber
Tsewang Smanla	India, climber
Tsewang Paljor	India, climber
Dorje Morup	India, climber
Hira Ram	India, climber
Tashi Ram	India, climber
Sange Sherpa	India, climbing Sherpa
Nadra Sherpa	India, climbing Sherpa
Koshing Sherpa	India, climbing Sherpa

Japanese-Fukuoka Everest Expedition

(climbing from the Tibetan side of the mountain)

Koji Yada	Japan, leader
Hiroshi Hanada	Japan, climber
Eisuke Shigekawa	Japan, climber
Pasang Tshering Sherpa	Nepal, climbing Sherpa
Pasang Kami Sherpa	Nepal, climbing Sherpa
Any Gyalzen	Nepal, climbing Sherpa

JON KRAKAUER

The Balcony, 27,600 feet, May 10, 7:20 A.M. Two Sherpas on Scott Fischer's team lean over their ice axes to catch their breath as Andy Harris comes up behind them. Other climbers rest a short distance below.

SCOTT FISCHER/WOODFIN CAMP & ASSOCIATES

The summit ridge from the South Summit, May 10, 1:00 P.M. When Fischer took this photo he was at the end of the line, gazing up at the crowd pushing for the top. Three climbers are visible just above the Hillary Step; a fourth can be seen in the middle of the Step.

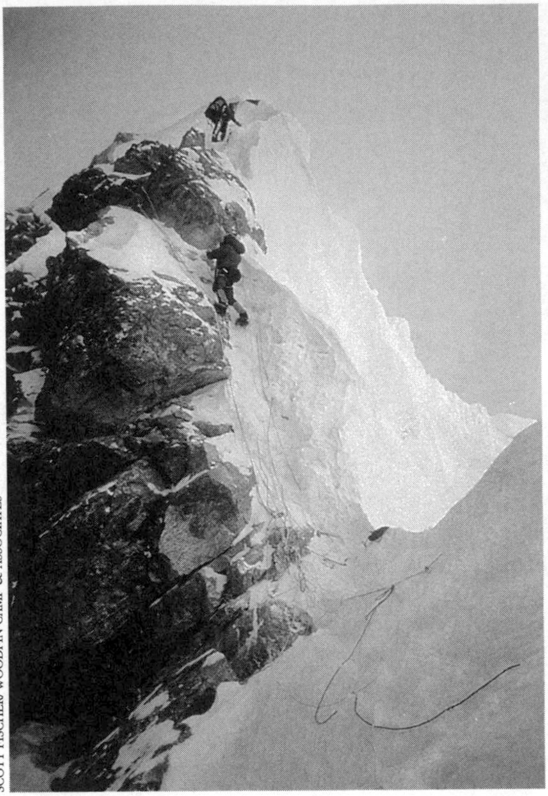

SCOTT FISCHER/WOODFIN CAMP & ASSOCIATES

The Hillary Step This steep notch in the summit ridge, which lies some 200 vertical feet below the top of the peak, presents some of the most technically demanding climbing on the standard route up Everest.

SCOTT FISCHER/WOODFIN CAMP & ASSOCIATES

Bottleneck at the Hillary Step, May 10, approximately 2:10 P.M. Scott Fischer took this photo from the base of the Step, looking up. Doug Hansen is the left-most figure in the foreground, standing in right profile, as he awaits his turn to ascend the fixed rope.

SCOTT FISCHER/WOODFIN CAMP & ASSOCIATES

Looking down the summit ridge, May 10, approximately 4:10 P.M. Fischer was looking down from the top of the Hillary Step at *(left to right)* Lene Gammelgaard, Tim Madsen, and Charlotte Fox as they descended ahead of him. Neal Beidleman and Sandy Pittman are visible as small figures in the upper right corner of the frame.

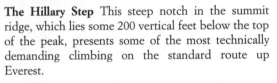

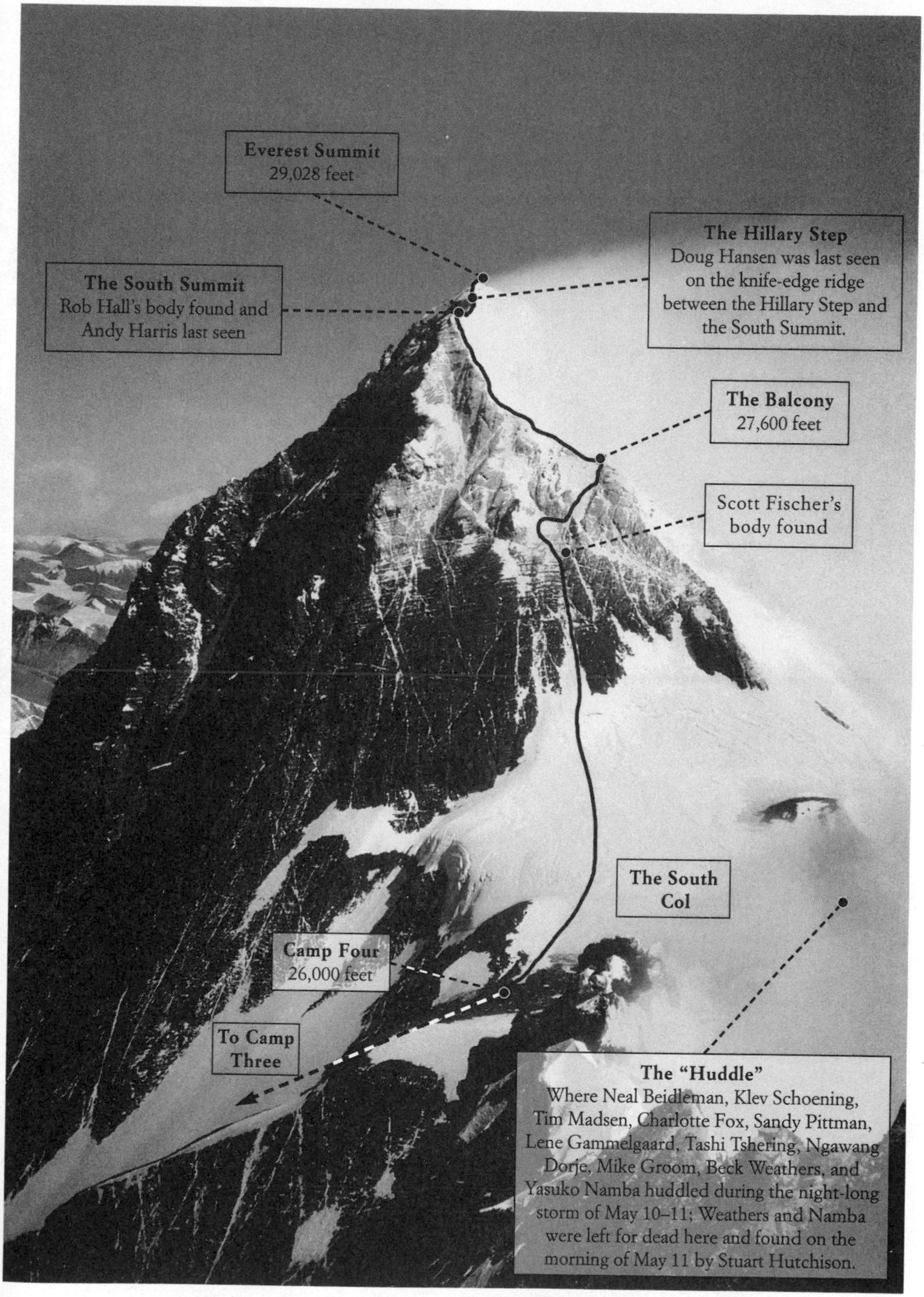
Everest Summit
29,028 feet
The Hillary Step
Doug Hansen was last seen on the knife-edge ridge between the Hillary Step and the South Summit.
The South Summit
Rob Hall's body found and Andy Harris last seen
The Balcony
27,600 feet
Scott Fischer's body found
The South Col
Camp Four
26,000 feet
To Camp Three
The "Huddle"
Where Neal Beidleman, Klev Schoening, Tim Madsen, Charlotte Fox, Sandy Pittman, Lene Gammelgaard, Tashi Tshering, Ngawang Dorje, Mike Groom, Beck Weathers, and Yasuko Namba huddled during the night-long storm of May 10–11; Weathers and Namba were left for dead here and found on the morning of May 11 by Stuart Hutchison.

The upper slopes of Mt. Everest from the summit of Lhotse Everest's trademark plume of cloud can be seen blowing from the crest of the Southeast Ridge, the standard route up the peak.

JON KRAKAUER

Rob Hall, age thirty-five, from New Zealand, leader of the Adventure Consultants expedition.

SCOTT FISCHER/WOODFIN CAMP & ASSOCIATES

Scott Fischer, age forty, American, leader of the Mountain Madness expedition.

KYODO NEWS INTERNATIONAL

Yasuko Namba, Japanese, member of Hall's team; at forty-seven the oldest woman to reach the summit of Everest.

PHOTOSOUTH

LEFT: Andy Harris, age thirty-one, from New Zealand, guide on Hall's team.

RIGHT: Doug Hansen, age forty-six, American, member of Hall's team; a postal worker who held down two jobs to pay for his dream to climb Everest.

AP/WIDE WORLD PHOTOS

JON KRAKAUER

High wind rakes the summit of Everest, May 12 Descending from Camp Four after the storm, at 25,000 feet, Krakauer turned to look back at the upper reaches of the peak, where his friends Hall, Harris, Hansen, and Fischer had lost their lives. Namba had perished on the South Col, just twenty minutes from shelter.

INTO THIN AIR

Chapter One

EVEREST SUMMIT   MAY 10, 1996   29,028 FEET

It would seem almost as though there were a cordon drawn round the upper part of these great peaks beyond which no man may go. The truth of course lies in the fact that, at altitudes of 25,000 feet and beyond, the effects of low atmospheric pressure upon the human body are so severe that really difficult mountaineering is impossible and the consequences even of a mild storm may be deadly, that nothing but the most perfect conditions of weather and snow offers the slightest chance of success, and that on the last lap of the climb no party is in a position to choose its day. . . .

No, it is not remarkable that Everest did not yield to the first few attempts; indeed, it would have been very surprising and not a little sad if it had, for that is not the way of great mountains. Perhaps we had become a little arrogant with our fine new technique of ice-claw and rubber slipper, our age of easy mechanical conquest. We had forgotten that the mountain still holds the master card, that it will grant success only in its own good time. Why else does mountaineering retain its deep fascination?

Eric Shipton, in 1938
Upon That Mountain

Straddling the top of the world, one foot in China and the other in Nepal, I cleared the ice from my oxygen mask, hunched a shoulder against the wind, and stared absently down at the vastness of Tibet. I understood on some dim, detached level that the sweep of earth beneath my feet was a spectacular sight. I'd been fantasizing about this moment, and the release of emotion that would accompany it, for many months. But now that I was finally here, actually standing on the summit of Mount Everest, I just couldn't summon the energy to care.

It was early in the afternoon of May 10, 1996. I hadn't slept in fifty-seven hours. The only food I'd been able to force down over the preceding three days was a bowl of ramen soup and a handful of peanut M&Ms. Weeks of violent coughing had left me with two separated ribs that made ordinary breathing an excruciating trial. At 29,028 feet up in the troposphere, so little oxygen was reaching my brain that my mental capacity was that of a slow child. Under the circumstances, I was incapable of feeling much of anything except cold and tired.

I'd arrived on the summit a few minutes after Anatoli Boukreev, a Russian climbing guide working for an American commercial expedition, and just ahead of Andy Harris, a guide on the New Zealand–based team to which I belonged. Although I was only slightly acquainted with Boukreev, I'd come to know and like Harris well during the preceding six weeks. I snapped four quick photos of Harris and Boukreev striking summit poses, then turned and headed down. My watch read 1:17 P.M. All told, I'd spent less than five minutes on the roof of the world.

A moment later, I paused to take another photo, this one looking down the Southeast Ridge, the route we had ascended. Training my lens on a pair of climbers approaching the summit, I noticed something that until that moment had escaped my attention. To the south, where the sky had been perfectly clear just an hour earlier, a blanket of clouds now hid Pumori, Ama Dablam, and the other lesser peaks surrounding Everest.

Later—after six bodies had been located, after a search for two others had been abandoned, after surgeons had amputated the gangrenous right hand of my teammate Beck Weathers—people would ask why, if the weather had begun to deteriorate, had climbers on the upper mountain not heeded the signs? Why did veteran Himalayan guides keep moving upward, ushering a gaggle of relatively inexperienced amateurs—each of whom had paid as much as $65,000 to be taken safely up Everest—into an apparent death trap?

Nobody can speak for the leaders of the two guided groups involved, because both men are dead. But I can attest that nothing I saw early on the afternoon of May 10 suggested that a murderous storm was bearing down. To my oxygen-depleted mind, the clouds drifting up the grand valley of ice known as the Western Cwm* looked innocuous, wispy, insubstantial. Gleaming in the brilliant midday sun, they appeared no different from the harmless puffs of convection condensation that rose from the valley almost every afternoon.

As I began my descent I was extremely anxious, but my concern had little to do with the weather: a check of the gauge on my oxygen tank had revealed that it was almost empty. I needed to get down, fast.

The uppermost shank of Everest's Southeast Ridge is a slender, heavily corniced fin of rock and wind-scoured snow that snakes for a quarter mile between the summit and a subordinate pinnacle known as the South Summit. Negotiating the serrated ridge presents no great technical hurdles, but the route is dreadfully exposed. After leaving the summit, fifteen minutes of cautious shuffling over a 7,000-foot abyss brought me to the notorious Hillary Step, a pronounced notch in the ridge that demands some technical maneuvering. As I clipped into a fixed rope and prepared to rappel over the lip, I was greeted with an alarming sight.

Thirty feet below, more than a dozen people were queued up at the base of the Step. Three climbers were already in the process of hauling themselves up the rope that I was preparing to descend. Exercising my only option, I unclipped from the communal safety line and stepped aside.

The traffic jam was comprised of climbers from three expeditions: the team I belonged to, a group of paying clients under the leadership of the celebrated New Zealand guide Rob Hall; another guided party headed by the American Scott Fischer; and a noncommercial Taiwanese team. Moving at the snail's pace that is the norm above 26,000 feet, the throng labored up the Hillary Step one by one, while I nervously bided my time.

* The Western Cwm, pronounced *koom,* was named by George Leigh Mallory, who first saw it during the initial Everest expedition of 1921 from the Lho La, a high pass on the border between Nepal and Tibet. *Cwm* is a Welsh term for valley or cirque.

Harris, who'd left the summit shortly after I did, soon pulled up behind me. Wanting to conserve whatever oxygen remained in my tank, I asked him to reach inside my backpack and turn off the valve on my regulator, which he did. For the next ten minutes I felt surprisingly good. My head cleared. I actually seemed less tired than I had with the gas turned on. Then, abruptly, I sensed that I was suffocating. My vision dimmed and my head began to spin. I was on the brink of losing consciousness.

Instead of turning my oxygen off, Harris, in his hypoxically impaired state, had mistakenly cranked the valve open to full flow, draining the tank. I'd just squandered the last of my gas going nowhere. There was another tank waiting for me at the South Summit, 250 feet below, but to get there I would have to descend the most exposed terrain on the entire route without the benefit of supplemental oxygen.

And first I had to wait for the mob to disperse. I removed my now useless mask, planted my ice ax into the mountain's frozen hide, and hunkered on the ridge. As I exchanged banal congratulations with the climbers filing past, inwardly I was frantic: "Hurry it up, hurry it up!" I silently pleaded. "While you guys are fucking around here, I'm losing brain cells by the millions!"

Most of the passing crowd belonged to Fischer's group, but near the back of the parade two of my teammates eventually appeared, Rob Hall and Yasuko Namba. Demure and reserved, the forty-seven-year-old Namba was forty minutes away from becoming the oldest woman to climb Everest and the second Japanese woman to reach the highest point on each continent, the so-called Seven Summits. Although she weighed just ninety-one pounds, her sparrowlike proportions disguised a formidable resolve; to an astounding degree, Yasuko had been propelled up the mountain by the unwavering intensity of her desire.

Later still, Doug Hansen arrived atop the Step. Another member of our expedition, Doug was a postal worker from a Seattle suburb who'd become my closest friend on the mountain. "It's in the bag!" I yelled over the wind, trying to sound more upbeat than I felt. Exhausted, Doug mumbled something from behind his oxygen mask that I didn't catch, shook my hand weakly, then continued plodding upward.

At the very end of the line was Scott Fischer, whom I knew casually from Seattle, where we both lived. Fischer's strength and drive were legendary—in 1994 he'd climbed Everest without using bottled oxygen—so I was surprised at how slowly he was moving and how hammered he looked when he pulled his mask aside to say hello. "Bruuuuuuce!" he wheezed with forced cheer, employing his trademark frat-boyish greeting. When I asked how he was doing, Fischer insisted that he was feeling fine: "Just dragging ass a little today for some reason. No big deal." With the Hillary Step finally clear, I clipped into the strand of orange rope, swung quickly around Fischer as he slumped over his ice ax, and rappelled over the edge.

It was after three o'clock when I made it down to the South Summit. By now tendrils of mist were streaming over the 27,923-foot top of Lhotse and lapping at Everest's summit pyramid. No longer did the weather look so benign. I grabbed a fresh oxygen cylinder, jammed it onto my regulator, and hurried down into the gathering cloud. Moments after I dropped below the South Summit, it began to snow lightly and visibility went to hell.

Four hundred vertical feet above, where the summit was still washed in bright sunlight under an immaculate cobalt sky, my compadres dallied to memorialize their arrival at the apex of the planet, unfurling flags and snapping photos, using up precious ticks of the clock. None of them imagined that a horrible ordeal was drawing nigh. Nobody suspected that by the end of that long day, every minute would matter.

Chapter Two

DEHRA DUN, INDIA 1852 2,234 FEET

Far from the mountains in winter, I discovered the blurred photo of Everest in Richard Halliburton's Book of Marvels. *It was a miserable reproduction in which the jagged peaks rose white against a grotesquely blackened and scratched sky. Everest itself, sitting back from the front ones, didn't even appear highest, but it didn't matter. It was; the legend said so. Dreams were the key to the picture, permitting a boy to enter it, to stand at the crest of the windswept ridge, to climb toward the summit, now no longer far above. . . .*

This was one of those uninhibited dreams that come free with growing up. I was sure that mine about Everest was not mine alone; the highest point on earth, unattainable, foreign to all experience, was there for many boys and grown men to aspire toward.

Thomas F. Hornbein
Everest: The West Ridge

The actual particulars of the event are unclear, obscured by the accretion of myth. But the year was 1852, and the setting was the offices of the Great Trigonometrical Survey of India in the northern hill station of Dehra Dun. According to the most plausible version of what transpired, a clerk rushed into the chambers of Sir Andrew Waugh, India's surveyor general, and exclaimed that a Bengali computer named Radhanath Sikhdar, working out of the Survey's Calcutta bureau, had "discovered the highest mountain in the world." (In Waugh's day a computer was a job description rather than a machine.) Designated Peak XV by surveyors in the field who'd first measured the angle of its rise with a twenty-four-inch theodolite three years earlier, the mountain in question jutted from the spine of the Himalaya in the forbidden kingdom of Nepal.

Until Sikhdar compiled the survey data and did the math, nobody had suspected that there was anything noteworthy about Peak XV.

The six survey sites from which the summit had been triangulated were in northern India, more than a hundred miles from the mountain. To the surveyors who shot it, all but the summit nub of Peak XV was obscured by various high escarpments in the foreground, several of which gave the illusion of being much greater in stature. But according to Sikhdar's meticulous trigonometric reckoning (which took into account such factors as curvature of the earth, atmospheric refraction, and plumb-line deflection) Peak XV stood 29,002* feet above sea level, the planet's loftiest point.

In 1865, nine years after Sikhdar's computations had been confirmed, Waugh bestowed the name Mount Everest on Peak XV, in honor of Sir George Everest, his predecessor as surveyor general. As it happened, Tibetans who lived to the north of the great mountain already had a more mellifluous name for it, Jomolungma, which translates to "goddess, mother of the world," and Nepalis who resided to the south called the peak Sagarmatha, "goddess of the sky." But Waugh pointedly chose to ignore these native appellations (as well as official policy encouraging the retention of local or ancient names), and Everest was the name that stuck.

Once Everest was determined to be the highest summit on earth, it was only a matter of time before people decided that Everest needed to be climbed. After the American explorer Robert Peary claimed to have reached the North Pole in 1909 and Roald Amundsen led a Norwegian party to the South Pole in 1911, Everest—the so-called Third Pole—became the most coveted object in the realm of terrestrial exploration. Getting to the top, proclaimed Gunther O. Dyrenfurth, an influential alpinist and chronicler of early Himalayan mountaineering, was "a matter of universal human endeavor, a cause from which there is no withdrawal, whatever losses it may demand."

Those losses, as it turned out, would not be insignificant. Following Sikhdar's discovery in 1852, it would require the lives of twenty-

* Modern surveys using lasers and state-of-the-art Doppler satellite transmissions have revised this measurement upward a mere 26 feet—to the currently accepted altitude of 29,028 feet, or 8,848 meters.

four men, the efforts of fifteen expeditions, and the passage of 101 years before the summit of Everest would finally be attained.

| | |

Among mountaineers and other connoisseurs of geologic form, Everest is not regarded as a particularly comely peak. Its proportions are too chunky, too broad of beam, too crudely hewn. But what Everest lacks in architectural grace, it makes up for with sheer, overwhelming mass.

Demarcating the Nepal-Tibet border, towering more than 12,000 feet above the valleys at its base, Everest looms as a three-sided pyramid of gleaming ice and dark, striated rock. The first eight expeditions to Everest were British, all of which attempted the mountain from the northern, Tibetan, side—not so much because it presented the most obvious weakness in the peak's formidable defenses but rather because in 1921 the Tibetan government opened its long-closed borders to foreigners, while Nepal remained resolutely off limits.

The first Everesters were obliged to trek 400 arduous miles from Darjeeling across the Tibetan plateau simply to reach the foot of the mountain. Their knowledge of the deadly effects of extreme altitude was scant, and their equipment was pathetically inadequate by modern standards. Yet in 1924 a member of the third British expedition, Edward Felix Norton, reached an elevation of 28,126 feet—just 900 feet below the summit—before being defeated by exhaustion and snow blindness. It was an astounding achievement that was probably not surpassed for twenty-nine years.

I say "probably" because of what transpired four days after Norton's summit assault. At first light on June 8, two other members of the 1924 British team, George Leigh Mallory and Andrew Irvine, departed the highest camp for the top.

Mallory, whose name is inextricably linked to Everest, was the driving force behind the first three expeditions to the peak. While on a lantern-slide lecture tour of the United States, it was he who so notoriously quipped, "Because it is there" when an irritating newspaperman demanded to know why he wanted to climb Everest. In 1924

Mallory was thirty-eight, a married schoolmaster with three young children. A product of upper-tier English society, he was also an aesthete and idealist with decidedly romantic sensibilities. His athletic grace, social charm, and striking physical beauty had made him a favorite of Lytton Strachey and the Bloomsbury crowd. While tent-bound high on Everest, Mallory and his companions would read aloud to one another from *Hamlet* and *King Lear.*

As Mallory and Irvine struggled slowly toward the summit of Everest on June 8, 1924, mist billowed across the upper pyramid, preventing companions lower on the mountain from monitoring the two climbers' progress. At 12:50 P.M., the clouds parted momentarily, and teammate Noel Odell caught a brief but clear glimpse of Mallory and Irvine high on the peak, approximately five hours behind schedule but "moving deliberately and expeditiously" toward the top.

The two climbers failed to return to their tent that night, however, and neither Mallory nor Irvine was ever seen again. Whether one or both of them reached the summit before being swallowed by the mountain and into legend has been fiercely debated ever since. The balance of the evidence suggests not. Lacking tangible proof, they were not credited with the first ascent, in any case.

In 1949, after centuries of inaccessibility, Nepal opened its borders to the outside world, and a year later the new Communist regime in China closed Tibet to foreigners. Those who would climb Everest therefore shifted their attention to the south side of the peak. In the spring of 1953 a large British team, organized with the righteous zeal and overpowering resources of a military campaign, became the third expedition to attempt Everest from Nepal. On May 28, following two and a half months of prodigious effort, a high camp was dug tenuously into the Southeast Ridge at 27,900 feet. Early the following morning Edmund Hillary, a rangy New Zealander, and Tenzing Norgay, a highly skilled Sherpa mountaineer, set out for the top breathing bottled oxygen.

By 9:00 A.M. they were at the South Summit, gazing across the dizzyingly narrow ridge that led to the summit proper. Another hour brought them to the foot of what Hillary described as "the most formidable-looking problem on the ridge—a rock step some forty feet high. . . . The rock itself, smooth and almost holdless, might have been an interesting Sunday afternoon problem to a group of expert climbers in the Lake District, but here it was a barrier beyond our feeble strength to overcome."

With Tenzing nervously paying out rope from below, Hillary wedged himself into a cleft between the rock buttress and a fin of vertical snow at its edge, then began to inch his way up what would thereafter be known as the Hillary Step. The climbing was strenuous and sketchy, but Hillary persisted until, as he would later write,

> I could finally reach over the top of the rock and drag myself out of the crack on to a wide ledge. For a few moments I lay regaining my breath and for the first time really felt the fierce determination that nothing now could stop us reaching the top. I took a firm stance on the ledge and signaled to Tenzing to come on up. As I heaved hard on the rope Tenzing wriggled his way up the crack and finally collapsed exhausted at the top like a giant fish when it has just been hauled from the sea after a terrible struggle.

Fighting exhaustion, the two climbers continued up the undulating ridge above. Hillary wondered,

> rather dully, whether we would have enough strength left to get through. I cut around the back of another hump and saw that the ridge ahead dropped away and we could see far into Tibet. I looked up and there above us was a rounded snow cone. A few whacks of the ice-axe, a few cautious steps, and Tensing [sic] and I were on top.

And thus, shortly before noon on May 29, 1953, did Hillary and Tenzing become the first men to stand atop Mount Everest.

Three days later, word of the ascent reached Queen Elizabeth on the eve of her coronation, and the *Times* of London broke the news on the morning of June 2 in its early edition. The dispatch had been filed from Everest via a coded radio message (to prevent competitors from scooping the *Times*) by a young correspondent named James Morris who, twenty years later, having earned considerable esteem as a writer, would famously change his gender to female and his Christian name to Jan. As Morris wrote four decades after the momentous climb in *Coronation Everest: The First Ascent and the Scoop That Crowned the Queen,*

> It is hard to imagine now the almost mystical delight with which the coincidence of the two happenings [the coronation and the Everest ascent] was greeted in Britain. Emerging at last from the austerity which had plagued them since the second world war, but at the same time facing the loss of their great empire and the inevitable decline of their power in the world, the British had half-convinced themselves that the accession of the young Queen was a token of a fresh start—a new Elizabethan age, as the newspapers like to call it. Coronation Day, June 2, 1953, was to be a day of symbolical hope and rejoicing, in which all the British patriotic loyalties would find a supreme moment of expression: and marvel of marvels, on that very day there arrived the news from distant places—from the frontiers of the old Empire, in fact—that a British team of mountaineers . . . had reached the supreme remaining earthly objective of exploration and adventure, the top of the world. . . .
>
> The moment aroused a whole orchestra of rich emotions among the British—pride, patriotism, nostalgia for the lost past of the war and derring do, hope for a rejuvenated future. . . . People of a certain age remember vividly to this day the moment when, as they waited on a drizzly June morning for the Coronation procession to pass by in London, they heard the magical news that the summit of the world was, so to speak, theirs.

Tenzing became a national hero throughout India, Nepal, and Tibet, each of which claimed him as one of their own. Knighted by the queen, Sir Edmund Hillary saw his image reproduced on postage stamps, comic strips, books, movies, magazine covers—overnight, the hatchet-faced beekeeper from Auckland had been transformed into one of the most famous men on earth.

| | |

Hillary and Tenzing climbed Everest a month before I was conceived, so I didn't share in the collective sense of pride and wonder that swept the world—an event that an older friend says was comparable, in its visceral impact, to the first manned landing on the moon. A decade later, however, a subsequent ascent of the mountain helped establish the trajectory of my life.

On May 22, 1963, Tom Hornbein, a thirty-two-year-old doctor from Missouri, and Willi Unsoeld, thirty-six, a professor of theology from Oregon, reached the summit of Everest via the peak's daunting West Ridge, previously unclimbed. By then the summit had already been achieved on four occasions, by eleven men, but the West Ridge was considerably more difficult than either of the two previously established routes: the South Col and Southeast Ridge or the North Col and Northeast Ridge. Hornbein's and Unsoeld's ascent was—and continues to be—deservedly hailed as one of the great feats in the annals of mountaineering.

Late in the day on their summit push, the two Americans climbed a stratum of steep, crumbly rock—the infamous Yellow Band. Surmounting this cliff demanded tremendous strength and skill; nothing so technically challenging had ever been climbed at such extreme altitude. Once on top of the Yellow Band, Hornbein and Unsoeld doubted they could safely descend it. Their best hope for getting off the mountain alive, they concluded, was to go over the top and down the well-established Southeast Ridge route, an extremely audacious plan, given the late hour, the unknown terrain, and their rapidly diminishing supply of bottled oxygen.

Hornbein and Unsoeld arrived on the summit at 6:15 P.M., just as the sun was setting, and were forced to spend the night in the open above 28,000 feet—at the time, the highest bivouac in history. It was a cold night, but mercifully without wind. Although Unsoeld's toes froze and would later be amputated, both men survived to tell their tale.

I was nine years old at the time and living in Corvallis, Oregon, where Unsoeld also made his home. He was a close friend of my father's, and I sometimes played with the oldest Unsoeld children—Regon, who was a year older than me, and Devi, a year younger. A few months before Willi Unsoeld departed for Nepal, I reached the summit of my first mountain—an unspectacular 9,000-foot volcano in the Cascade Range that now sports a chairlift to the top—in the company of my dad, Willi, and Regon. Not surprisingly, accounts of the 1963 epic on Everest resonated loud and long in my preadolescent imagination. While my friends idolized John Glenn, Sandy Koufax, and Johnny Unitas, my own heroes were Hornbein and Unsoeld.

Secretly, I dreamed of ascending Everest myself one day; for more than a decade it remained a burning ambition. By the time I was in my early twenties climbing had become the focus of my existence to the exclusion of almost everything else. Achieving the summit of a mountain was tangible, immutable, concrete. The incumbent hazards lent the activity a seriousness of purpose that was sorely missing from the rest of my life. I thrilled in the fresh perspective that came from tipping the ordinary plane of existence on end.

And climbing provided a sense of community as well. To become a climber was to join a self-contained, rabidly idealistic society, largely unnoticed and surprisingly uncorrupted by the world at large. The culture of ascent was characterized by intense competition and undiluted machismo, but for the most part, its constituents were concerned with impressing only one another. Getting to the top of any given mountain was considered much less important than *how* one got there: prestige was earned by tackling the most unforgiving routes with minimal equipment, in the boldest style imaginable. Nobody was admired more than so-called free soloists: visionaries who ascended alone, without rope or hardware.

In those years I lived to climb, existing on five or six thousand dollars a year, working as a carpenter and a commercial salmon fisherman just long enough to fund the next trip to the Bugaboos or Tetons or Alaska Range. But at some point in my midtwenties I abandoned my boyhood fantasy of climbing Everest. By then it had become fashionable among alpine cognoscenti to denigrate Everest as a "slag heap"—a peak lacking sufficient technical challenges or aesthetic appeal to be a worthy objective for a "serious" climber, which I desperately aspired to be. I began to look down my nose at the world's highest mountain.

Such snobbery was rooted in the fact that by the early 1980s, Everest's easiest line—via South Col and the Southeast Ridge—had been climbed more than a hundred times. My cohorts and I referred to the Southeast Ridge as the "Yak Route." Our contempt was only reinforced in 1985, when Dick Bass—a wealthy fifty-five-year-old Texan with limited climbing experience—was ushered to the top of Everest by an extraordinary young climber named David Breashears, an event that was accompanied by a blizzard of uncritical media attention.

Previously, Everest had by and large been the province of elite mountaineers. In the words of Michael Kennedy, the editor of *Climbing* magazine, "To be invited on an Everest expedition was an honor earned only after you served a long apprenticeship on lower peaks, and to actually reach the summit elevated a climber to the upper firmament of mountaineering stardom." Bass's ascent changed all that. In bagging Everest, he became the first person to climb all of the Seven Summits,* a feat that brought him worldwide renown, spurred

* The highest peaks on each of the seven continents are: Everest, 29,028 feet (Asia); Aconcagua, 22,834 feet (South America); McKinley (also known as Denali), 20,320 feet (North America); Kilimanjaro, 19,340 feet (Africa); Elbrus, 18,510 feet (Europe); Vinson Massif, 16,067 feet (Antarctica); Kosciusko, 7,316 feet (Australia). After Dick Bass climbed all seven, a Canadian climber named Patrick Morrow argued that because the highest point in Oceania, the group of lands that includes Australia, is not Kosciusko but rather the much more difficult summit of Carstensz Pyramid (16,535 feet) in the Indonesian province of Irian Barat, Bass wasn't the first to bag the Seven Summits—he, Morrow, was. More than one critic of the Seven Summits concept has pointed out that a considerably more difficult challenge than ascending the highest peak on each continent would be to climb the second-highest peak on each continent, a couple of which happen to be very demanding climbs.

a swarm of other weekend climbers to follow in his guided bootprints, and rudely pulled Everest into the postmodern era.

"To aging Walter Mitty types like myself, Dick Bass was an inspiration," Seaborn Beck Weathers explained in a thick East Texas twang during the trek to Everest Base Camp last April. A forty-nine-year-old Dallas pathologist, Beck was one of eight clients on Rob Hall's 1996 guided expedition. "Bass showed that Everest was within the realm of possibility for regular guys. Assuming you're reasonably fit and have some disposable income, I think the biggest obstacle is probably taking time off from your job and leaving your family for two months."

For a great many climbers, the record shows, stealing time away from the daily grind has not been an insurmountable obstacle, nor has the hefty outlay of cash. Over the past half decade, the traffic on all of the Seven Summits, but especially Everest, has multiplied at an astonishing rate. And to meet the demand, the number of commercial enterprises peddling guided ascents of the Seven Summits, especially Everest, has multiplied correspondingly. In the spring of 1996, thirty distinct expeditions were on the flanks of Everest, at least ten of them organized as money-making ventures.

The government of Nepal recognized that the throngs flocking to Everest created serious problems in terms of safety, aesthetics, and impact to the environment. While grappling with the issue, Nepalese ministers came up with a solution that seemed to hold the dual promise of limiting the crowds while increasing the flow of hard currency into the impoverished national coffers: raise the fee for climbing permits. In 1991 the Ministry of Tourism charged $2,300 for a permit that allowed a team of any size to attempt Everest. In 1992 the fee was increased to $10,000 for a team of up to nine climbers, with another $1,200 to be paid for each additional climber.

But climbers continued to swarm to Everest despite the higher fees. In the spring of 1993, on the fortieth anniversary of the first ascent, a record fifteen expeditions, comprising 294 climbers, attempted to scale the peak from the Nepalese side. That autumn the ministry raised the permit fee yet again—to a staggering $50,000 for as many as five climbers, plus $10,000 for each additional climber, up to a maximum of seven. Additionally, the government decreed that no more than four expeditions would be allowed on the Nepalese flanks each season.

What the Nepalese ministers didn't take into consideration, however, was that China charged only $15,000 to allow a team of any size to climb the mountain from Tibet and placed no limit on the number of expeditions each season. The flood of Everesters therefore shifted from Nepal to Tibet, leaving hundreds of Sherpas out of work. The ensuing hue and cry persuaded Nepal, in the spring of 1996, to abruptly cancel the four-expedition limit. And while they were at it, the government ministers jacked up the permit fee once again—this time to $70,000 for up to seven climbers, plus another $10,000 for each additional climber. Judging from the fact that sixteen of the thirty expeditions on Everest last spring were climbing on the Nepalese side of the mountain, the high cost of obtaining a permit doesn't seem to have been a significant deterrent.

Even before the calamitous outcome of the 1996 premonsoon climbing season, the proliferation of commercial expeditions over the past decade was a touchy issue. Traditionalists were offended that the world's highest summit was being sold to rich parvenus—some of who, if denied the services of guides, would probably have difficulty making it to the top of a peak as modest as Mount Rainier. Everest, the purists sniffed, had been debased and profaned.

Such critics also pointed out that, thanks to the commercialization of Everest, the once hallowed peak has now even been dragged into the swamp of American jurisprudence. Having paid princely sums to be escorted up Everest, some climbers have then sued their guides when the summit eluded them. "Occasionally you'll get a client who thinks he's bought a guaranteed ticket to the summit," laments Peter Athans, a highly respected guide who's made eleven trips to Everest and reached the top four times. "Some people don't understand that an Everest expedition can't be run like a Swiss train."

Sadly, not every Everest lawsuit is unwarranted. Inept or disreputable companies have on more than one occasion failed to deliver crucial logistical support—oxygen, for instance—as promised. On some expeditions guides have gone to the summit without any of their paying customers, prompting the bitter clients to conclude that they were brought along simply to pick up the tab. In 1995, the leader of a commercial expedition absconded with tens of thousands of dollars of his clients' money before the trip even got off the ground.

| | |

In March 1995 I received a call from an editor at *Outside* magazine proposing that I join a guided Everest expedition scheduled to depart five days hence and write an article about the mushrooming commercialization of the mountain and the attendant controversies. The magazine's intent was not that I climb the peak; the editors simply wanted me to remain in Base Camp and report the story from the East Rongbuk Glacier, at the foot of the Tibetan side of the mountain. I considered the offer seriously—I went so far as to book a flight and get the required immunizations—and then bowed out at the last minute.

Given the disdain I'd expressed for Everest over the years, one might reasonably assume that I declined to go on principle. In truth, the call from *Outside* had unexpectedly aroused a powerful, long-buried desire. I said no to the assignment only because I thought it would be unbearably frustrating to spend two months in the shadow of Everest without ascending higher than Base Camp. If I were going to travel to the far side of the globe and spend eight weeks away from my wife and home, I wanted an opportunity to climb the mountain.

I asked Mark Bryant, the editor of *Outside,* if he would consider postponing the assignment for twelve months (which would give me time to train properly for the physical demands of the expedition). I also inquired if the magazine would be willing to book me with one of the more reputable guide services—and cover the $65,000 fee—thus giving me a shot at actually reaching the summit. I didn't really expect him to say yes to this plan. I'd written more than sixty pieces for *Outside* over the previous fifteen years, and seldom had the travel budget for any of these assignments exceeded two or three thousand dollars.

Bryant called back a day later after conferring with *Outside*'s publisher. He said that the magazine wasn't prepared to shell out $65,000 but that he and the other editors thought the commercialization of Everest was an important story. If I was serious about trying to climb the mountain, he insisted, *Outside* would figure out a way to make it happen.

I I I

During the thirty-three years I'd called myself a climber, I'd undertaken some difficult projects. In Alaska I'd put up a hairy new route on the Mooses Tooth, and pulled off a solo ascent of the Devils Thumb that involved spending three weeks alone on a remote ice cap. I'd done a number of fairly extreme ice climbs in Canada and Colorado. Near the southern tip of South America, where the wind sweeps the land like "the broom of God"—"*la escoba de Dios,*" as the locals say—I'd scaled a frightening, mile-high spike of vertical and overhanging granite called Cerro Torre; buffeted by hundred-knot winds, plastered with frangible atmospheric rime, it was once (though no longer) thought to be the world's hardest mountain.

But these escapades had occurred years earlier, in some cases decades earlier, when I was in my twenties and thirties. I was forty-one now, well past my climbing prime, with a graying beard, bad gums, and fifteen extra pounds around my midriff. I was married to a woman I loved fiercely—and who loved me back. Having stumbled upon a tolerable career, for the first time in my life I was actually living above the poverty line. My hunger to climb had been blunted, in short, by a bunch of small satisfactions that added up to something like happiness.

None of the climbs I'd done in the past, moreover, had taken me to even moderately high altitude. Truth be told, I'd never been higher than 17,200 feet—not even as high as Everest Base Camp.

As an avid student of mountaineering history, I knew that Everest had killed more than 130 people since the British first visited the mountain in 1921—approximately one death for every four climbers who'd reached the summit—and that many of those who died had been far stronger and possessed vastly more high-altitude experience than I. But boyhood dreams die hard, I discovered, and good sense be damned. In late February 1996, Bryant called to say that there was a place waiting for me on Rob Hall's upcoming Everest expedition. When he asked if I was sure I wanted to go through with this, I said yes without even pausing to catch my breath.

Chapter Three

OVER NORTHERN INDIA   MARCH 29, 1996   30,000 FEET

Speaking abruptly I gave them a parable. I said, it's the planet Neptune I'm talking about, just plain ordinary Neptune, not Paradise, because I don't happen to know about Paradise. So you see this means you, nothing more, just you. Now there happens to be a big spot of rock I said, up there, and I must warn you that people are pretty stupid up in Neptune, chiefly because they each lived tied up in their own string. And some of them, whom I had wanted to mention in particular, some of them had got themselves absolutely determined about that mountain. You wouldn't believe it, I said, life or death, use or no use, these people had got the habit, and they now spent their spare time and all their energies in chasing the clouds of their own glory up and down all the steepest faces in the district. And one and all they came back uplifted. And well they might, I said, for it was amusing that even in Neptune most of them made shift to chase themselves pretty safely up the easier faces. But anyhow there was uplift, and indeed it was observable, both in the resolute set of their faces and in the gratification that shone in their eyes. And as I had pointed out, this was in Neptune not Paradise, where, it may be, there perhaps is nothing else to be done.

John Menlove Edwards
Letter from a Man

Two hours into Thai Air flight 311 from Bangkok to Kathmandu, I left my seat and walked to the rear of the airplane. Near the bank of lavatories on the starboard side I crouched to peer through a small, waist-level window, hoping to catch a glimpse of some mountains. I was not disappointed: there, raking the horizon, stood the jagged incisors of the Himalaya. I stayed at the window for the rest of the flight, spellbound, hunkered over a trash bag full of empty soda cans and half-eaten meals, my face pressed against the cold Plexiglas.

Immediately I recognized the huge, sprawling bulk of Kanchenjunga, at 28,169 feet above sea level the third-highest mountain on earth. Fifteen minutes later, Makalu, the world's fifth-highest peak, came into view—and then, finally, the unmistakable profile of Everest itself.

The ink-black wedge of the summit pyramid stood out in stark relief, towering over the surrounding ridges. Thrust high into the jet stream, the mountain ripped a visible gash in the 120-knot hurricane, sending forth a plume of ice crystals that trailed to the east like a long silk scarf. As I gazed across the sky at this contrail, it occurred to me that the top of Everest was precisely the same height as the pressurized jet bearing me through the heavens. That I proposed to climb to the cruising altitude of an Airbus 300 jetliner struck me, at that moment, as preposterous, or worse. My palms felt clammy.

Forty minutes later I was on the ground in Kathmandu. As I walked into the airport lobby after clearing customs, a big-boned, clean-shaven young man took note of my two huge duffels and approached. "Would you be Jon, then?" he inquired in a lilting New Zealand accent, glancing at a sheet of photocopied passport photos depicting Rob Hall's clients. He shook my hand and introduced himself as Andy Harris, one of Hall's guides, come to deliver me to our hotel.

Harris, who was thirty-one, said there was supposed to be another client arriving on the same flight from Bangkok, a fifty-three-year-old attorney from Bloomfield Hills, Michigan, named Lou Kasischke. It ended up taking an hour for Kasischke to locate his bags, so while we waited Andy and I compared notes on some hard climbs we'd both survived in western Canada and discussed the merits of skiing versus snowboarding. Andy's palpable hunger for climbing, his unalloyed enthusiasm for the mountains, made me wistful for the period in my own life when climbing was the most important thing imaginable, when I charted the course of my existence in terms of mountains I'd ascended and those I hoped one day to ascend.

Just before Kasischke—a tall, athletic, silver-haired man with patrician reserve—emerged from the airport customs queue, I asked Andy how many times he'd been on Everest. "Actually," he confessed cheerfully, "this will be my first time, same as you. It should be interesting to see how I do up there."

Hall had booked us at the Garuda Hotel, a friendly, funky establishment in the heart of Thamel, Kathmandu's frenetic tourist district, on a narrow avenue choked with cycle rickshas and street hustlers. Long popular with expeditions bound for the Himalaya, the Garuda's walls were covered with signed photographs of famous alpinists who'd slept there over the years: Reinhold Messner, Peter Habeler, Kitty Calhoun, John Roskelley, Jeff Lowe. Ascending the stairs to my room I passed a large four-color poster titled "Himalayan Trilogy," depicting Everest, K2, and Lhotse—the planet's highest, second-highest, and fourth-highest mountains, respectively. Superimposed against the images of these peaks, the poster showed a grinning, bearded man in full alpine regalia. A caption identified this climber as Rob Hall; the poster, intended to drum up business for Hall's guiding company, Adventure Consultants, commemorated his rather impressive feat of ascending all three peaks during two months in 1994.

An hour later I met Hall in the flesh. He stood six foot three or four and was skinny as a pole. There was something cherubic about his face, yet he looked older than his thirty-five years—perhaps it was the sharply etched creases at the corners of his eyes, or the air of authority he projected. He was dressed in a Hawaiian shirt and faded Levis patched on one knee with an embroidered yin-yang symbol. An unruly thatch of brown hair corkscrewed across his forehead. His shrublike beard was in need of a trim.

Gregarious by nature, Hall proved to be a skillful raconteur with a caustic Kiwi wit. Launching into a long story involving a French tourist, a Buddhist monk, and a particularly shaggy yak, Hall delivered the punch line with an impish squint, paused a beat for effect, then threw his head back in a booming, contagious laugh, unable to contain his delight in his own yarn. I liked him immediately.

Hall was born into a working-class Catholic family in Christchurch, New Zealand, the youngest of nine children. Although he had a quick, scientific mind, at the age of fifteen he dropped out of school after butting heads with an especially autocratic teacher, and in 1976 he went to work for Alp Sports, a local manufacturer of climbing equipment. "He started out doing odd jobs, working a sewing machine, things like that," remembers Bill Atkinson, now an accomplished climber and guide, who also worked at Alp Sports at the time. "But because of Rob's impressive organizational skills, which were apparent even when he was sixteen and seventeen, he was soon running the entire production side of the company."

Hall had for some years been an avid hill walker; about the same time he went to work for Alp Sports, he took up rock and ice climbing as well. He was a fast learner, says Atkinson, who became Hall's most frequent climbing partner, "with the ability to soak up skills and attitudes from anybody."

In 1980, when Hall was nineteen, he joined an expedition that climbed the demanding North Ridge of Ama Dablam, a 22,294-foot peak of incomparable beauty fifteen miles south of Everest. During that trip, Hall's first to the Himalaya, he made a side excursion to Everest Base Camp and resolved that one day he would climb the world's highest mountain. It required ten years and three attempts, but in May 1990, Hall finally reached the summit of Everest as the leader of an expedition that included Peter Hillary, the son of Sir Edmund. On the summit Hall and Hillary made a radio transmission that was broadcast live throughout New Zealand, and at 29,028 feet received congratulations from Prime Minister Geoffrey Palmer.

By this time Hall was a full-time professional climber. Like most of his peers, he sought funding from corporate sponsors to pay for his expensive Himalayan expeditions. And he was savvy enough to understand that the more attention he got from the news media, the easier it would be to coax corporations to open their checkbooks. As it happened, he proved to be extremely adept at getting his name into print and his mug on the telly. "Yeah," Atkinson allows, "Rob always did have a bit of a flair for publicity."

In 1988, a guide from Auckland named Gary Ball became Hall's primary climbing partner and closest friend. Ball reached the summit of Everest with Hall in 1990, and soon after returning to New Zealand they concocted a scheme to climb the highest summits on each of the seven continents, à la Dick Bass—but to raise the bar by doing all seven of them in seven months.* With Everest, the most difficult of the septet, already taken care of, Hall and Ball wangled backing from a big electrical utility, Power Build, and were on their way. On December 12, 1990, mere hours before their seven-month deadline was due to expire, they reached the crest of the seventh summit—the Vinson Massif, at 16,067 feet the highest point in Antarctica—to considerable fanfare throughout their homeland.

Despite their success, Hall and Ball were concerned about their long-term prospects in the professional climbing racket. "To continue receiving sponsorship from companies," explains Atkinson, "a climber has to keep upping the ante. The next climb has to be harder and more spectacular than the last. It becomes an ever-tightening spiral; eventually you're not up to the challenge anymore. Rob and Gary understood that sooner or later they wouldn't be up to performing at the cutting edge, or they'd have an unlucky accident and get killed.

"So they decided to switch direction and get into high-altitude guiding. When you're guiding you don't get to do the climbs you necessarily most want to do; the challenge comes from getting clients up and down, which is a different sort of satisfaction. But it's a more sustainable career than endlessly chasing after sponsorships. There's a limitless supply of clients out there if you offer them a good product."

During the "seven summits in seven months" extravaganza, Hall and Ball formulated a plan to go into business together guiding clients up the Seven Summits. Convinced that an untapped market of dreamers existed with ample cash but insufficient experience to climb the world's great mountains on their own, Hall and Ball launched an enterprise they christened Adventure Consultants.

* It took Bass four years to ascend the Seven Summits.

Almost immediately, they racked up an impressive record. In May 1992 Hall and Ball led six clients to the summit of Everest. A year later they guided another group of seven to the top on an afternoon when forty people reached the summit in a single day. They came home from that expedition, however, to unanticipated public criticism from Sir Edmund Hillary, who decried Hall's role in the growing commercialization of Everest. The crowds of novices being escorted to the top for a fee, huffed Sir Edmund, "were engendering disrespect for the mountain."

In New Zealand, Hillary is one of the most honored figures in the nation; his craggy visage even stares out from the face of the five-dollar bill. It saddened and embarrassed Hall to be publicly castigated by this demigod, this ur-climber who had been one of his childhood heroes. "Hillary is regarded as a living national treasure here in New Zealand," says Atkinson. "What he says carries a lot of weight, and it must have really hurt to be criticized by him. Rob wanted to make a public statement to defend himself, but he realized that going up against such a venerated figure in the media was a no-win situation."

Then, five months after the Hillary brouhaha flared, Hall was rocked by an even greater blow: in October 1993, Gary Ball died of cerebral edema—swelling of the brain brought on by high altitude—during an attempt on 26,795-foot Dhaulagiri, the world's sixth-tallest mountain. Ball drew his last, labored breaths in Hall's arms, lying comatose in a small tent high on the peak. The next day Hall buried his friend in a crevasse.

In a New Zealand television interview following the expedition, Hall somberly described how he took their favorite climbing rope and lowered Ball's body into the depths of the glacier. "A climbing rope is designed to sort of attach you together, and you never let go of it," he said. "And I had to let it just sort of slip through me hands."

"Rob was devastated when Gary died," says Helen Wilton, who worked as Hall's Base Camp manager on Everest in 1993, '95, and '96. "But he dealt with it very quietly. That was Rob's way—to get on with things." Hall resolved to carry on alone with Adventure Consultants. In his systematic fashion he continued to refine the company's infrastructure and services—and continued to be extraordinarily successful at escorting amateur climbers to the summits of big, remote mountains.

Between 1990 and 1995, Hall was responsible for putting thirty-nine climbers on the summit of Everest—three more ascents than had been made in the first twenty years after Sir Edmund Hillary's inaugural climb. With justification, Hall advertised that Adventure Consultants was "the world leader in Everest Climbing, with more ascents than any other organisation." The brochure he sent to prospective clients declared,

> So, you have a thirst for adventure! Perhaps you dream of visiting seven continents or standing on top of a tall mountain. Most of us never dare act on our dreams and scarcely venture to share them or admit to great inner yearnings.
>
> Adventure Consultants specialises in organising and guiding mountain climbing adventures. Skilled in the practicalities of developing dreams into reality, we work with you to reach your goal. We will not drag you up a mountain—you will have to work hard—but we guarantee to maximise the safety and success of your adventure.
>
> For those who dare to face their dreams, the experience offers something special beyond the power of words to describe. We invite you to climb your mountain with us.

By 1996 Hall was charging $65,000 a head to guide clients to the top of the world. By any measure this is a lot of money—it equals the mortgage on my Seattle home—and the quoted price did not include airfare to Nepal or personal equipment. No company's fee was higher—indeed, some of his competitors charged a third as much. But thanks to Hall's phenomenal success rate he had no trouble filling the roster for this, his eighth expedition to Everest. If you were hell-bent on climbing the peak and could somehow come up with the dough, Adventure Consultants was the obvious choice.

| | |

On the morning of March 31, two days after arriving in Kathmandu, the assembled members of the 1996 Adventure Consultants Everest Expedition walked across the tarmac of Tribhuvan International Airport and climbed aboard a Russian-built Mi-17 helicopter operated by Asian Airlines. A dented relic of the Afghan war, it was as big as a school bus, seated twenty-six passengers, and looked like it had been riveted together in somebody's backyard. The flight engineer latched the door and handed out wads of cotton to stuff in our ears, and the behemoth chopper lumbered into the air with a head-splitting roar.

The floor was piled high with duffels, backpacks, and cardboard boxes. Jammed into jump seats around the perimeter of the aircraft was the human cargo, facing inward, knees wedged against chests. The deafening whine of the turbines made conversation out of the question. It wasn't a comfortable ride, but nobody complained.

In 1963, Tom Hornbein's expedition began the long trek to Everest from Banepa, a dozen miles outside Kathmandu, and spent thirty-one days on the trail before arriving at Base Camp. Like most modern Everesters, we'd elected to leapfrog over the majority of those steep, dusty miles; the chopper was supposed to set us down in the distant village of Lukla, 9,200 feet up in the Himalaya. Assuming we didn't crash en route, the flight would trim some three weeks from the span of Hornbein's trek.

Glancing around the helicopter's capacious interior, I tried to fix the names of my teammates in my memory. In addition to guides Rob Hall and Andy Harris there was Helen Wilton, a thirty-nine-year-old mother of four, who was returning for her third season as Base Camp manager. Caroline Mackenzie—an accomplished climber and physician in her late twenties—was the expedition doctor and, like Helen, would be going no higher than Base Camp. Lou Kasischke, the gentlemanly lawyer I'd met at the airport, had climbed six of the Seven

Summits—as had Yasuko Namba, forty-seven, a taciturn personnel director who worked at the Tokyo branch of Federal Express. Beck Weathers, forty-nine, was a garrulous pathologist from Dallas. Stuart Hutchison, thirty-four, attired in a Ren and Stimpy T-shirt, was a cerebral, somewhat wonkish Canadian cardiologist on leave from a research fellowship. John Taske, at fifty-six the oldest member of our group, was an anesthesiologist from Brisbane who'd taken up climbing after retiring from the Australian army. Frank Fischbeck, fifty-three, a dapper, genteel publisher from Hong Kong, had attempted Everest three times with one of Hall's competitors; in 1994 he'd gotten all the way to the South Summit, just 330 vertical feet below the top. Doug Hansen, forty-six, was an American postal worker who'd gone to Everest with Hall in 1995 and, like Fischbeck, had reached the South Summit before turning back.

I wasn't sure what to make of my fellow clients. In outlook and experience they were nothing like the hard-core climbers with whom I usually went into the mountains. But they seemed like nice, decent folks, and there wasn't a certifiable asshole in the entire group—at least not one who was showing his true colors at this early stage of the proceedings. Nevertheless, I didn't have much in common with any of my teammates except Doug. A wiry, hard-partying man with a prematurely weathered face that brought to mind an old football, he'd been a postal worker for more than twenty-seven years. He told me that he'd paid for the trip by working the night shift and doing construction jobs by day. Because I'd earned my living as a carpenter for eight years before becoming a writer—and because the tax bracket we shared set us conspicuously apart from the other clients—I already felt comfortable around Doug in a way that I didn't with the others.

For the most part I attributed my growing unease to the fact that I'd never climbed as a member of such a large group—a group of complete strangers, no less. Aside from one Alaska trip I'd done twenty-one years earlier, all my previous expeditions had been undertaken with one or two trusted friends, or alone.

In climbing, having confidence in your partners is no small concern. One climber's actions can affect the welfare of the entire team.

The consequences of a poorly tied knot, a stumble, a dislodged rock, or some other careless deed are as likely to be felt by the perpetrator's colleagues as the perpetrator. Hence it's not surprising that climbers are typically wary of joining forces with those whose bona fides are unknown to them.

But trust in one's partners is a luxury denied those who sign on as clients on a guided ascent; one must put one's faith in the guide instead. As the helicopter droned toward Lukla, I suspected that each of my teammates hoped as fervently as I that Hall had been careful to weed out clients of dubious ability, and would have the means to protect each of us from one another's shortcomings.

Chapter Four

PHAKDING MARCH 31, 1996 9,186 FEET

For those who didn't dally, our daily treks ended early in the afternoon, but rarely before the heat and aching feet forced us to ask each passing Sherpa, "How much farther to camp?" The reply, we soon were to discover, was invariable: "Only two mile more, Sah'b. . . ."

Evenings were peaceful, smoke settling in the quiet air to soften the dusk, lights twinkling on the ridge we would camp on tomorrow, clouds dimming the outline of our pass for the day after. Growing excitement lured my thoughts again and again to the West Ridge. . . .

There was loneliness, too, as the sun set, but only rarely now did doubts return. Then I felt sinkingly as if my whole life lay behind me. Once on the mountain I knew (or trusted) that this would give way to total absorption with the task at hand. But at times I wondered if I had not come a long way only to find that what I really sought was something I had left behind.

Thomas F. Hornbein
Everest: The West Ridge

From Lukla the way to Everest led north through the crepuscular gorge of the Dudh Kosi, an icy, boulder-choked river that churned with glacial runoff. We spent the first night of our trek in the hamlet of Phakding, a collection of a half dozen homes and lodges crowded onto a shelf of level ground on a slope above the river. The air took on a wintry sting as night fell, and in the morning, as I headed up the trail, a glaze of frost sparkled from the rhododendron leaves. But the Everest region lies at 28 degrees north latitude—just beyond the tropics—and as soon as the sun rose high enough to penetrate the depths of the canyon the temperature soared. By noon, after we'd crossed a wobbly footbridge suspended high over the river—the fourth river crossing of the day—rivulets of sweat were dripping off my chin, and I peeled down to shorts and a T-shirt.

Beyond the bridge, the dirt path abandoned the banks of the Dudh Kosi and zigzagged up the steep canyon wall, ascending through aromatic stands of pine. The spectacularly fluted ice pinnacles of Thamserku and Kusum Kangru pierced the sky more than two vertical miles above. It was magnificent country, as topographically imposing as any landscape on earth, but it wasn't wilderness, and hadn't been for hundreds of years.

Every scrap of arable land had been terraced and planted with barley, bitter buckwheat, or potatoes. Strings of prayer flags were strung across the hillsides, and ancient Buddhist *chortens*[*] and walls of exquisitely carved *mani*[†] stones stood sentinel over even the highest passes. As I made my way up from the river, the trail was clogged with trekkers, yak[‡] trains, red-robed monks, and barefoot Sherpas straining beneath back-wrenching loads of firewood and kerosene and soda pop.

Ninety minutes above the river, I crested a broad ridge, passed a matrix of rock-walled yak corrals, and abruptly found myself in downtown Namche Bazaar, the social and commercial hub of Sherpa society. Situated 11,300 feet above sea level, Namche occupies a huge, tilting bowl proportioned like a giant satellite television dish, midway up a precipitous mountainside. More than a hundred buildings nestled dramatically on the rocky slope, linked by a maze of narrow paths and catwalks. Near the lower edge of town I located the Khumbu Lodge, pushed aside the blanket that functioned as a front door, and found my teammates drinking lemon tea around a table in the corner.

* A *chorten* is a religious monument, usually made of rock and often containing sacred relics; it is also called a stupa.

† *Mani* stones are small, flat rocks that have been meticulously carved with Sanskrit symbols denoting the Tibetan Buddhist invocation *Om mani padme hum* and are piled along the middle of trails to form long, low *mani* walls. Buddhist protocol dictates that travelers always pass *mani* walls on the left.

‡ Technically speaking, the great majority of the "yaks" one sees in the Himalaya are actually *dzopkyo*—male crossbreeds of yaks and cattle—or *dzom,* female crossbreeds. Additionally, female yaks, when purebred, are correctly termed *naks.* Most Westerners, however, have a hard time telling any of these shaggy beasts apart and refer to all of them as yaks.

When I approached, Rob Hall introduced me to Mike Groom, the expedition's third guide. A thirty-three-year-old Australian with carrot-colored hair and the lean build of a marathon runner, Groom was a Brisbane plumber who worked as a guide only occasionally. In 1987, forced to spend a night in the open while descending from the 28,169-foot summit of Kanchenjunga, he froze his feet and had to have all his toes amputated. This setback had not put a damper on his Himalayan career, however: he'd gone on to climb K2, Lhotse, Cho Oyu, Ama Dablam, and, in 1993, Everest without supplementary oxygen. An exceedingly calm, circumspect man, Groom was pleasant company but seldom spoke unless spoken to and replied to questions tersely, in a barely audible voice.

Dinner conversation was dominated by the three clients who were doctors—Stuart, John, and especially Beck, a pattern that would be repeated for much of the expedition. Fortunately, both John and Beck were wickedly funny and had the group in stitches. Beck, however, was in the habit of turning his monologues into scathing, Limbaughesque rants against bed-wetting liberals, and at one point that evening I made the mistake of disagreeing with him: in response to one of his comments I suggested that raising the minimum wage seemed like a wise and necessary policy. Well informed and a very skilled debater, Beck made hash out of my fumbling avowal, and I lacked the wherewithal to rebut him. All I could do was to sit on my hands, tongue-tied and steaming.

As he continued to hold forth in his swampy, East Texas drawl about the numerous follies of the welfare state, I got up and left the table to avoid humiliating myself further. When I returned to the dining room, I approached the proprietress to ask for a beer. A small, graceful Sherpani, she was in the midst of taking an order from a group of American trekkers. "We hungry," a ruddy-cheeked man announced to her in overly loud pidgin, miming the act of eating. "Want eat po-ta-toes. Yak bur-ger. Co-ca Co-la. You have?"

"Would you like to see the menu?" the Sherpani replied in clear, sparkling English that carried a hint of a Canadian accent. "Our selection is actually quite large. And I believe there is still some freshly baked apple pie available, if that interests you, for dessert."

The American trekker, unable to comprehend that this brown-skinned woman of the hills was addressing him in perfectly enunciated King's English, continued to employ his comical pidgin argot: "Men-u. Good, good. Yes, yes, we like see men-u."

Sherpas remain an enigma to most foreigners, who tend to regard them through a romantic scrim. People unfamiliar with the demography of the Himalaya often assume that all Nepalese are Sherpas, when in fact there are no more than 20,000 Sherpas in all of Nepal, a nation the size of North Carolina that has some 20 million residents and more than fifty distinct ethnic groups. Sherpas are a mountain people, devoutly Buddhist, whose forebears migrated south from Tibet four or five centuries ago. There are Sherpa villages scattered throughout the Himalaya of eastern Nepal, and sizable Sherpa communities can be found in Sikkim and Darjeeling, India, but the heart of Sherpa country is the Khumbu, a handful of valleys draining the southern slopes of Mount Everest—a small, astonishingly rugged region completely devoid of roads, cars, or wheeled vehicles of any kind.

Farming is difficult in the high, cold, steep-walled valleys, so the traditional Sherpa economy revolved around trading between Tibet and India, and herding yaks. Then, in 1921, the British embarked on their first expedition to Everest, and their decision to engage Sherpas as helpers sparked a transformation of Sherpa culture.

Because the Kingdom of Nepal kept its borders closed until 1949, the initial Everest reconnaissance, and the next eight expeditions to follow, were forced to approach the mountain from the north, through Tibet, and never passed anywhere near the Khumbu. But those first nine expeditions embarked for Tibet from Darjeeling, where many Sherpas had emigrated, and where they had developed a reputation among the resident colonialists for being hardworking, affable, and intelligent. Additionally, because most Sherpas had lived for generations in villages situated between 9,000 and 14,000 feet, they were physiologically adapted to the rigors of high altitude. Upon the recommendation of A. M. Kellas, a Scottish physician who'd climbed and traveled extensively with Sherpas, the 1921 Everest expedition hired a large corps of them as load bearers and camp helpers, a practice that's been followed by all but a smattering of expeditions in the seventy-five years since.

For better and worse, over the past two decades the economy and culture of the Khumbu has become increasingly and irrevocably tied to the seasonal influx of trekkers and climbers, some 15,000 of whom visit the region annually. Sherpas who learn technical climbing skills and work high on the peaks—especially those who have summitted Everest—enjoy great esteem in their communities. Those who become climbing stars, alas, also stand a fair chance of losing their lives: ever since 1922, when seven Sherpas were killed in an avalanche during the second British expedition, a disproportionate number of Sherpas have died on Everest—fifty-three all told. Indeed, they account for more than a third of all Everest fatalities.

Despite the hazards, there is stiff competition among Sherpas for the twelve to eighteen staff positions on the typical Everest expedition. The most sought-after jobs are the half dozen openings for skilled climbing Sherpas, who can expect to earn $1,400 to $2,500 for two months of hazardous work—attractive pay in a nation mired in grinding poverty and with an annual per capita income of around $160.

To handle the growing traffic from Western climbers and trekkers, new lodges and teahouses are springing up across the Khumbu region, but the new construction is especially evident in Namche Bazaar. On the trail to Namche I passed countless porters headed up from the lowland forests, carrying freshly cut wood beams that weighed in excess of one hundred pounds—crushing physical toil, for which they were paid about three dollars a day.

Longtime visitors to the Khumbu are saddened by the boom in tourism and the change it has wrought on what early Western climbers regarded as an earthly paradise, a real-life Shangri-La. Entire valleys have been denuded of trees to meet the increased demand for firewood. Teens hanging out in Namche *carrom* parlors are more likely to be wearing jeans and Chicago Bulls T-shirts than quaint traditional robes. Families are apt to spend their evenings huddled around video players viewing the latest Schwarzenegger opus.

The transformation of the Khumbu culture is certainly not all for the best, but I didn't hear many Sherpas bemoaning the changes. Hard currency from trekkers and climbers, as well as grants from international relief organizations supported by trekkers and climbers, have funded schools and medical clinics, reduced infant mortality, built footbridges, and brought hydroelectric power to Namche and other villages. It seems more than a little patronizing for Westerners to lament the loss of the good old days when life in the Khumbu was so much simpler and more picturesque. Most of the people who live in this rugged country seem to have no desire to be severed from the modern world or the untidy flow of human progress. The last thing Sherpas want is to be preserved as specimens in an anthropological museum.

| | |

A strong walker, pre-acclimatized to the altitude, could cover the distance from the Lukla airstrip to Everest Base Camp in two or three long days. Because most of us had just arrived from sea level, however, Hall was careful to keep us to a more indolent pace that gave our bodies time to adapt to the increasingly thin air. Seldom did we walk more than three or four hours on any given day. On several days, when Hall's itinerary called for additional acclimatization, we walked nowhere at all.

On April 3, after an acclimatization day in Namche, we resumed the trek toward Base Camp. Twenty minutes beyond the village I rounded a bend and arrived at a breathtaking overlook. Two thousand feet below, slicing a deep crease through the surrounding bedrock, the Dudh Kosi appeared as a crooked strand of silver glinting from the shadows. Ten thousand feet above, the huge backlit spike of Ama Dablam hovered over the head of the valley like an apparition. And seven thousand feet higher still, dwarfing Ama Dablam, was the icy thrust of Everest itself, all but hidden behind Nuptse. As always seemed to be the case, a horizontal plume of condensation streamed from the summit like frozen smoke, betraying the violence of the jet-stream winds.

I stared at the peak for perhaps thirty minutes, trying to apprehend what it would be like to be standing on that gale-swept vertex. Although I'd ascended hundreds of mountains, Everest was so different from anything I'd previously climbed that my powers of imagination were insufficient for the task. The summit looked so cold, so high, so impossibly far away. I felt as though I might as well be on an expedition to the moon. As I turned away to continue walking up the trail, my emotions oscillated between nervous anticipation and a nearly overwhelming sense of dread.

Late that afternoon I arrived at Tengboche,* the largest, most important Buddhist monastery in the Khumbu. Chhongba Sherpa, a wry, thoughtful man who had joined our expedition as Base Camp cook, offered to arrange a meeting with the *rimpoche*—"the head lama of all Nepal," Chhongba explained, "a very holy man. Just yesterday he has finished a long period of silent meditation—for the past three months he has not spoken. We will be his first visitors. This is most auspicious." Doug, Lou, and I each gave Chhongba one hundred rupees (approximately two dollars) to buy ceremonial *katas*—white silk scarves to be presented to the rimpoche—and then we removed our shoes and Chhongba led us to a small, drafty chamber behind the main temple.

Seated cross-legged on a brocade pillow, wrapped in burgundy robes, was a short, rotund man with a shiny pate. He looked very old and very tired. Chhongba bowed reverently, spoke briefly to him in the Sherpa tongue, and indicated for us to come forward. The rimpoche then blessed each of us in turn, placing the katas we had purchased around our necks as he did so. Afterward he smiled beatifically and offered us tea. "This kata you should wear to the top of Everest,"† Chhongba instructed me in a solemn voice. "It will please God and keep you from harm."

* Unlike Tibetan, to which it is closely related, Sherpa is not a written language, so Westerners are forced to resort to phonetic renderings. As a consequence there is little uniformity in the spelling of Sherpa words or names; Tengboche, for instance, is written variously as Tengpoche or Thyangboche, and similar incongruities crop up in spelling most other Sherpa words.

† Although the Tibetan name for the peak is Jomolungma and the Nepali name is Sagarmatha, most Sherpas seem to refer to the mountain as "Everest" in daily conversation—even when speaking with other Sherpas.

Unsure how to act in the company of a divine presence, this living reincarnation of an ancient and illustrious lama, I was terrified of unwittingly giving offense or committing some irredeemable faux pas. As I sipped sweet tea and fidgeted, his Holiness rooted around in an adjacent cabinet, brought out a large, ornately decorated book, and handed it to me. I wiped my dirty hands on my pants and opened it nervously. It was a photo album. The rimpoche, it turned out, had recently traveled to America for the first time, and the book held snapshots from this trip: his Holiness in Washington standing before the Lincoln Memorial and the Air and Space Museum; his Holiness in California on the Santa Monica Pier. Grinning broadly, he excitedly pointed out his two favorite photos in the entire album: his Holiness posing beside Richard Gere, and another shot of him with Steven Seagal.

| | |

The first six days of the trek went by in an ambrosial blur. The trail took us past glades of juniper and dwarf birch, blue pine and rhododendron, thundering waterfalls, enchanting boulder gardens, burbling streams. The Valkyrian skyline bristled with peaks that I'd been reading about since I was a child. Because most of our gear was carried by yaks and human porters, my own backpack held little more than a jacket, a few candy bars, and my camera. Unburdened and unhurried, caught up in the simple joy of walking in exotic country, I fell into a kind of trance—but the euphoria seldom lasted for long. Sooner or later I'd remember where I was headed, and the shadow Everest cast across my mind would snap me back to attention.

We all trekked at our own pace, pausing often for refreshment at trailside teahouses and to chat with passersby. I frequently found myself traveling in the company of Doug Hansen, the postal worker, and Andy Harris, Rob Hall's laid-back junior guide. Andy—called "Harold" by Rob and all his Kiwi friends—was a big, sturdy lad, built like an NFL quarterback, with rugged good looks of the sort that earn men roles in cigarette advertisements. During the antipodal winter he was employed as a much-in-demand helicopter-skiing guide. Summers he worked for scientists conducting geologic research in Antarctica or escorted climbers into New Zealand's Southern Alps.

As we walked up the trail Andy spoke longingly of the woman with whom he lived, a physician named Fiona McPherson. As we rested on a rock he pulled a picture out of his pack to show me. She was tall, blond, athletic-looking. Andy said he and Fiona were in the midst of building a house together in the hills outside of Queenstown. Waxing ardent about the uncomplicated pleasures of sawing rafters and pounding nails, Andy admitted that when Rob had first offered him this Everest job he'd been ambivalent about accepting it: "It was quite hard to leave Fi and the house, actually. We'd only just gotten the roof on, yeah? But how can you turn down a chance to climb Everest? Especially when you have an opportunity to work alongside somebody like Rob Hall."

Although Andy had never been to Everest before, he was no stranger to the Himalaya. In 1985 he climbed a difficult 21,927-foot peak called Chobutse, about thirty miles west of Everest. And in the fall of 1994 he spent four months helping Fiona run the medical clinic in Pheriche, a gloomy, wind-battered hamlet 14,000 feet above sea level, where we stayed the nights of April 4 and 5.

The clinic was funded by a foundation called the Himalayan Rescue Association primarily to treat altitude-related illnesses (although it also offered free treatment to the local Sherpas) and to educate trekkers about the insidious hazards of ascending too high, too fast. It had been established in 1973 after four members of a single Japanese trekking group succumbed to the altitude and died in the vicinity. Prior to the clinic's existence, acute altitude illness killed approximately one or two out of every 500 trekkers who passed through Pheriche. Laura Ziemer—an upbeat American lawyer who, at the time of our visit, was working at the four-room facility with her physician husband, Jim Litch, and another young physician named Larry Silver—emphasized that this alarming death rate hadn't been skewed upward by mountaineering accidents; the victims had been "just ordinary trekkers who never ventured beyond the established trails."

Now, thanks to the educational seminars and emergency care provided by the clinic's volunteer staff, that mortality rate has been cut to less than one death per 30,000 trekkers. Although idealistic Westerners like Ziemer who work at the Pheriche clinic receive no remuneration and must even pay their own travel expenses to and from Nepal, it is a prestigious posting that attracts highly qualified applicants from around the world. Caroline Mackenzie, Hall's expedition doctor, had worked at the HRA Clinic with Fiona McPherson and Andy in the autumn of 1994.

In 1990, the year Hall first summitted Everest, the clinic was run by an accomplished, self-confident physician from New Zealand named Jan Arnold. Hall met her as he passed through Pheriche on his way to the mountain, and he was immediately smitten. "I asked Jan to go out with me as soon as I got down from Everest," Hall reminisced during our first night in the village. "For our first date I proposed going to Alaska and climbing Mount McKinley together. And she said yes." They were married two years later. In 1993 Arnold climbed to the summit of Everest with Hall; in 1994 and 1995 she traveled to Base Camp to work as the expedition doctor. Arnold would have returned to the mountain again this year, except that she was seven months pregnant with their first child. So the job went to Dr. Mackenzie.

After dinner on Thursday, our first night in Pheriche, Laura Ziemer and Jim Litch invited Hall, Harris, and Helen Wilton, our Base Camp manager, over to the clinic to raise a glass and catch up on gossip. Over the course of the evening, the conversation drifted to the inherent risks of climbing—and guiding—Everest, and Litch remembers the discussion with chilling clarity: Hall, Harris, and Litch were in complete agreement that sooner or later a major disaster involving a large number of clients was "inevitable." But, said Litch—who had climbed Everest from Tibet the previous spring—"Rob's feeling was that it wouldn't be him; he was just worried about 'having to save another team's ass,' and that when the unavoidable calamity struck, he was 'sure it would occur on the more dangerous north side' " of the peak—the Tibetan side.

| | |

On Saturday, April 6, a few hours above Pheriche, we arrived at the lower end of the Khumbu Glacier, a twelve-mile tongue of ice that flows down from the south flank of Everest and would serve as our highway—I hoped mightily—to the summit. At 16,000 feet now, we'd left behind the last trace of green. Twenty stone monuments stood in a somber row along the crest of the glacier's terminal moraine, overlooking the mist-filled valley: memorials to climbers who had died on Everest, most of them Sherpa. From this point forward our world would be a barren, monochromatic expanse of rock and wind-blown ice. And despite our measured pace I had begun to feel the effects of the altitude, which left me light-headed and constantly fighting for breath.

The trail here remained buried beneath a head-high winter snowpack in many places. As the snow softened in the afternoon sun, the hoofs of our yaks punched through the frozen crust, and the beasts wallowed to their bellies. The grumbling yak drivers thrashed their animals to force them onward and threatened to turn around. Late in the day we reached a village called Lobuje, and there sought refuge from the wind in a cramped, spectacularly filthy lodge.

A collection of low, tumbledown buildings huddled against the elements at the edge of the Khumbu Glacier, Lobuje was a grim place, crowded with Sherpas and climbers from a dozen different expeditions, German trekkers, herds of emaciated yaks—all bound for Everest Base Camp, still a day's travel up the valley. The bottleneck, Rob explained, was due to the unusually late and heavy snowpack, which until just yesterday had kept any yaks at all from reaching Base Camp. The hamlet's half dozen lodges were completely full. Tents were jammed side by side on the few patches of muddy earth not covered with snow. Scores of Rai and Tamang porters from the low foothills—dressed in thin rags and flip-flops, they were working as load bearers for various expeditions—were bivouacked in caves and under boulders on the surrounding slopes.

The three or four stone toilets in the village were literally overflowing with excrement. The latrines were so abhorrent that most people, Nepalese and Westerners alike, evacuated their bowels outside on the open ground, wherever the urge struck. Huge stinking piles of human feces lay everywhere; it was impossible not to walk in it. The river of snowmelt meandering through the center of the settlement was an open sewer.

The main room of the lodge where we stayed was furnished with wooden bunk platforms for some thirty people. I found an unoccupied bunk on the upper level, shook as many fleas and lice as possible from the soiled mattress, and spread out my sleeping bag. Against the near wall was a small iron stove that supplied heat by burning dried yak dung. After sunset the temperature dropped well below freezing, and porters flocked in from the cruel night to warm themselves around the stove. Because dung burns poorly under the best of circumstances, and especially so in the oxygen-depleted air of 16,200 feet, the lodge filled with dense, acrid smoke, as if the exhaust from a diesel bus were being piped directly into the room. Twice during the night, coughing uncontrollably, I had to flee outside for air. By morning my eyes were burning and bloodshot, my nostrils were clogged with black soot, and I'd developed a dry, persistent hack that would stay with me until the end of the expedition.

Rob had intended for us to spend just one day acclimatizing in Lobuje before traveling the final six or seven miles to Base Camp, which our Sherpas had reached some days earlier in order to ready the site for our arrival and begin establishing a route up the lower slopes of Everest itself. On the evening of April 7, however, a breathless runner arrived in Lobuje with a disturbing message from Base Camp: Tenzing, a young Sherpa employed by Rob, had fallen 150 feet into a crevasse—a gaping crack in the glacier. Four other Sherpas had hauled him out alive, but he was seriously injured, possibly with a broken femur. Rob, ashen-faced, announced that he and Mike Groom would hurry to Base Camp at dawn to coordinate Tenzing's rescue. "I regret to have to tell you this," he continued, "but the rest of you will need to wait here in Lobuje with Harold until we get the situation under control."

Tenzing, we later learned, had been scouting the route above Camp One, climbing a relatively gentle section of the Khumbu Glacier with four other Sherpas. The five men were walking single file, which was smart, but they weren't using a rope—a serious violation of mountaineering protocol. Tenzing was moving closely behind the other four, stepping exactly where they had stepped, when he broke through a thin veneer of snow spanning a deep crevasse. Before he even had time to yell, he dropped like a rock into the Cimmerian bowels of the glacier.

At 20,500 feet, the altitude was deemed too high for safe evacuation by helicopter—the air was too insubstantial to provide much lift for a helicopter's rotors, making landing, taking off, or merely hovering unreasonably hazardous—so he would have to be carried 3,000 vertical feet to Base Camp down the Khumbu Icefall, some of the steepest, most treacherous ground on the entire mountain. Getting Tenzing down alive would require a massive effort.

Rob was always especially concerned about the welfare of the Sherpas who worked for him. Before our group departed Kathmandu, he had sat all of us down and given us an uncommonly stern lecture about the need to show our Sherpa staff gratitude and proper respect. "The Sherpas we've hired are the best in the business," he told us. "They work incredibly hard for not very much money by Western standards. I want you all to remember we would have absolutely *no* chance of getting to the summit of Everest without their help. I'm going to repeat that: Without the support of our Sherpas none of us has any chance of climbing the mountain."

In a subsequent conversation, Rob confessed that in past years he'd been critical of some expedition leaders for being careless with their Sherpa staff. In 1995 a young Sherpa had died on Everest; Hall speculated that the accident may have occurred because the Sherpa had been "allowed to climb high on the mountain without proper training. I believe that it's the responsibility of those of us who run these trips to prevent that sort of thing from happening."

The previous year a guided American expedition had hired a Sherpa named Kami Rita as a cook boy. Strong and ambitious, twenty-one or twenty-two years old, he lobbied hard to be allowed to work on the upper mountain as a climbing Sherpa. In appreciation for Kami's enthusiasm and dedication, some weeks later his wish was granted—despite the fact that he had no climbing experience and had received no formal training in proper techniques.

From 22,000 feet to 25,000 feet the standard route ascends a sheer, treacherous ice slope known as the Lhotse Face. As a safety measure, expeditions always attach a series of ropes to this slope from bottom to top, and climbers are supposed to protect themselves by clipping a short safety tether to the fixed ropes as they ascend. Kami, being young and cocky and inexperienced, didn't think it was really necessary to clip into the rope. One afternoon as he was carrying a load up the Lhotse Face he lost his purchase on the rock-hard ice and fell more than 2,000 feet to the bottom of the wall.

My teammate Frank Fischbeck had witnessed the whole episode. In 1995 he was making his third attempt on Everest as a client of the American company that had hired Kami. Frank was ascending the ropes on the upper Lhotse Face, he said in a troubled voice, "when I looked up and saw a person tumbling down from above, falling head over heels. He was screaming as he went past, and left a trail of blood."

Some climbers rushed to where Kami came to rest at the bottom of the face, but he had died from the extensive injuries he'd suffered on the way down. His body was brought down to Base Camp, where, in the Buddhist tradition, his friends brought meals to feed the corpse for three days. Then he was carried to a village near Tengboche and cremated. As the body was consumed by flames, Kami's mother wailed inconsolably and struck her head with a sharp rock.

Kami was very much in Rob's mind at first light on April 8, when he and Mike hurried toward Base Camp to try and get Tenzing off Everest alive.

Chapter Five

LOBUJE APRIL 8, 1996 16,200 FEET

Passing through the towering ice pinnacles of Phantom Alley we entered the rock-strewn valley floor at the bottom of a huge amphitheater. . . . Here [the Icefall] turned sharply to flow southward as the Khumbu Glacier. We set up our Base Camp at 17,800 feet on the lateral moraine that formed the outer edge of the turn. Huge boulders lent an air of solidity to the place, but the rolling rubble underfoot corrected the misimpression. All that one could see and feel and hear—of Icefall, moraine, avalanche, cold—was of a world not intended for human habitation. No water flowed, nothing grew—only destruction and decay. . . . This would be home for the next several months, until the mountain was climbed.

Thomas F. Hornbein
Everest: The West Ridge

On April 8, just after dark, Andy's hand-held radio crackled to life outside the lodge in Lobuje. It was Rob, calling from Base Camp, and he had good news. It had taken a team of thirty-five Sherpas from several different expeditions the entire day, but they'd gotten Tenzing down. Strapping him to an aluminum ladder, they managed to lower, drag, and carry him through the Icefall, and he was now resting from the ordeal at Base Camp. If the weather held, a helicopter would arrive at sunrise to fly him to a hospital in Kathmandu. With audible relief, Rob gave us the go-ahead to leave Lobuje in the morning and proceed to Base Camp ourselves.

We clients were also immensely relieved that Tenzing was safe. And we were no less relieved to be getting out of Lobuje. John and Lou had picked up some kind of virulent intestinal ailment from the unclean surroundings. Helen, our Base Camp manager, had a grinding altitude-induced headache that wouldn't go away. And my cough had worsened considerably after a second night in the smoke-filled lodge.

For this, our third night in the village, I decided to escape the noxious smudge by moving into a tent, pitched just outside, that Rob and Mike had vacated when they went to Base Camp. Andy elected to move in with me. At 2:00 A.M. I was awakened when he bolted into a sitting position beside me and began to moan. "Yo, Harold," I inquired from my sleeping bag, "are you O.K.?"

"I'm not sure, actually. Something I ate for dinner doesn't seem to be sitting too well just now." A moment later Andy desperately pawed the zippered door open and barely managed to thrust his head and torso outside before vomiting. After the retching subsided, he hunkered motionless on his hands and knees for several minutes, half out of the tent. Then he sprang to his feet, sprinted a few meters away, yanked his trousers down, and succumbed to a loud attack of diarrhea. He spent the rest of the night out in the cold, violently discharging the contents of his gastrointestinal tract.

In the morning Andy was weak, dehydrated, and shivering violently. Helen suggested he remain in Lobuje until he regained some strength, but Andy refused to consider it. "There's no way in bloody hell I'm spending another night in this shit hole," he announced, grimacing, with his head between his knees. "I'm going on to Base Camp today with the rest of you. Even if I have to bloody crawl."

By 9:00 A.M. we'd packed up and gotten under way. While the rest of the group moved briskly up the trail, Helen and I stayed behind to walk with Andy, who had to exert a monumental effort just to put one foot in front of the other. Again and again he would stop, hunch over his ski poles to collect himself for several minutes, then summon the energy to struggle onward.

The route climbed up and down the unsettled rocks of the Khumbu Glacier's lateral moraine for several miles, then dropped down onto the glacier itself. Cinders, coarse gravel, and granite boulders covered much of the ice, but every now and then the trail would cross a patch of bare glacier—a translucent, frozen medium that glistened like polished onyx. Meltwater sluiced furiously down innumerable surface and subterranean channels, creating a ghostly harmonic rumble that resonated through the body of the glacier.

In midafternoon we reached a bizarre procession of freestanding ice pinnacles, the largest nearly 100 feet high, known as Phantom Alley. Sculpted by the intense solar rays, glowing a radioactive shade of turquoise, the towers reared like giant shark's teeth out of the surrounding rubble as far as the eye could see. Helen—who'd been over this ground numerous times—announced that we were getting close to our destination.

A couple of miles farther, the glacier made a sharp turn to the east, we plodded to the crest of a long slope, and spread before us was a motley city of nylon domes. More than three hundred tents, housing as many climbers and Sherpas from fourteen expeditions, speckled the boulder-strewn ice. It took us twenty minutes to locate our compound among the sprawling settlement. As we climbed the final rise, Rob strode down to greet us. "Welcome to Everest Base Camp," he grinned. The altimeter on my wristwatch read 17,600 feet.

| | |

The ad hoc village that would serve as our home for the next six weeks sat at the head of a natural amphitheater delineated by forbidding mountain walls. The escarpments above camp were draped with hanging glaciers, from which calved immense ice avalanches that thundered down at all hours of the day and night. A quarter mile to the east, pinched between the Nuptse Wall and the West Shoulder of Everest, the Khumbu Icefall spilled through a narrow gap in a chaos of frozen shards. The amphitheater opened to the southwest, so it was flooded with sunlight; on clear afternoons when there was no wind it was warm enough to sit comfortably outside in a T-shirt. But the moment the sun dipped behind the conical summit of Pumori—a 23,507-foot peak immediately west of Base Camp—the temperature plummeted into the teens. Retiring to my tent at night, I was serenaded by a madrigal of creaks and percussive cracks, a reminder that I was lying on a moving river of ice.

In striking contrast to the harshness of our surroundings stood the myriad creature comforts of the Adventure Consultants camp, home to fourteen Westerners—the Sherpas referred to us collectively as "members" or "sahibs"—and fourteen Sherpas. Our mess tent, a cavernous canvas structure, was furnished with an enormous stone table, a stereo system, a library, and solar-powered electric lights; an adjacent communications tent housed a satellite phone and fax. A shower had been improvised from a rubber hose and a bucket filled with water heated by the kitchen staff. Fresh bread and vegetables arrived every few days on the backs of yaks. Continuing a Raj-era tradition established by expeditions of yore, every morning Chhongba and his cook boy, Tendi, came to each client's tent to serve us steaming mugs of Sherpa tea in our sleeping bags.

I had heard many stories about how Everest had been turned into a garbage dump by the ever-increasing hordes, and commercial expeditions were reputed to be the primary culprits. Although in the 1970s and '80s Base Camp was indeed a big rubbish heap, in recent years it had been turned into a fairly tidy place—certainly the cleanest human settlement I'd seen since leaving Namche Bazaar. And the commercial expeditions actually deserved much of the credit for the cleanup.

Bringing clients back to Everest year after year, the guides had a stake in this that one-time visitors did not. As part of their expedition in 1990, Rob Hall and Gary Ball spearheaded an effort that removed five tons of garbage from Base Camp. Hall and some of his fellow guides also began working with government ministries in Kathmandu to formulate policies that encouraged climbers to keep the mountain clean. By 1996, in addition to their permit fee, expeditions were required to post a $4,000 bond that would be refunded only if a predetermined amount of trash were carried back to Namche and Kathmandu. Even the barrels collecting the excrement from our toilets had to be removed and hauled away.

Base Camp bustled like an anthill. In a certain sense, Hall's Adventure Consultants compound served as the seat of government for the entire Base Camp, because nobody on the mountain commanded more respect than Hall. Whenever there was a problem—a labor dispute with the Sherpas, a medical emergency, a critical decision about climbing strategy—people trudged over to our mess tent to seek Hall's advice. And he generously dispensed his accumulated wisdom to the very rivals who were competing with him for clients, most notably Scott Fischer.

Previously, Fischer had successfully guided one 8,000-meter mountain:* 26,400-foot Broad Peak in the Karakoram Range of Pakistan, in 1995. He'd also attempted Everest four times and reached the top once, in 1994, but not in the role of a guide. The spring of 1996 marked his first visit to the mountain as the leader of a commercial expedition; like Hall, Fischer had eight clients in his group. His camp, distinguished by a huge Starbucks Coffee promotional banner suspended from a house-size block of granite, was situated just five minutes' walk down the glacier from ours.

The sundry men and women who make careers out of scaling the world's highest peaks constitute a small, ingrown club. Fischer and Hall were business rivals, but as prominent members of the high-altitude fraternity their paths frequently crossed, and on a certain level they considered themselves friends. Fischer and Hall met in the 1980s in the Russian Pamir, and they subsequently spent considerable time in each other's company in 1989 and 1994 on Everest. They had firm plans to join forces and attempt Manaslu—a difficult 26,781-foot peak in central Nepal—immediately after guiding their respective clients up Everest in 1996.

The bond between Fischer and Hall had been cemented back in 1992, when they had bumped into each other on K2, the world's second-highest mountain. Hall was attempting the peak with his *compañero* and business partner, Gary Ball; Fischer was climbing with an elite American climber named Ed Viesturs. On their way down from the summit in a howling storm, Fischer, Viesturs, and a third American, Charlie Mace, encountered Hall struggling to cope with a barely conscious Ball, who had been stricken with a life-threatening case of altitude sickness and was unable to move under his own power.

* There are fourteen so-called 8,000-meter peaks: mountains that stand more than 8,000 meters (26,246 feet) above sea level. Although it is a somewhat arbitrary designation, mountaineers have always attached special prestige to ascents of 8,000-meter peaks. The first person to climb all fourteen of them was Reinhold Messner, in 1986. To date, only four other climbers have repeated the feat.

Fischer, Viesturs, and Mace helped drag Ball down the avalanche-swept lower slopes of the mountain through the blizzard, saving his life. (A year later Ball would die of a similar ailment on the slopes of Dhaulagiri.)

Fischer, forty, was a strapping, gregarious man with a blond ponytail and a surfeit of manic energy. As a fourteen-year-old schoolboy in Basking Ridge, New Jersey, he had chanced upon a television program about mountaineering and was enthralled. The next summer he traveled to Wyoming and enrolled in an Outward Bound–style wilderness course run by the National Outdoor Leadership School (NOLS). As soon as he graduated from high school he moved west permanently, found seasonal employment as a NOLS instructor, placed climbing at the center of his cosmos, and never looked back.

When Fischer was eighteen and working at NOLS, he fell in love with a student in his course named Jean Price. They were married seven years later, settled in Seattle, and had two children, Andy and Katie Rose (who were nine and five, respectively, when Scott went to Everest in 1996). Price earned her commercial pilot's license and became a captain for Alaska Airlines—a prestigious, well-paying career that allowed Fischer to climb full-time. Her income also permitted Fischer to launch Mountain Madness in 1984.

If the name of Hall's business, Adventure Consultants, mirrored his methodical, fastidious approach to climbing, Mountain Madness was an even more accurate reflection of Scott's personal style. By his early twenties, he had developed a reputation for a harrowing, damn-the-torpedoes approach to ascent. Throughout his climbing career, but especially during those early years, he survived a number of frightening mishaps that by all rights should have killed him.

On at least two occasions while rock climbing—once in Wyoming, another time in Yosemite—he crashed into the ground from more than 80 feet up. While working as a junior instructor on a NOLS course in the Wind River Range he plunged 70 feet, unroped, to the bottom of a crevasse on the Dinwoody Glacier. Perhaps his most infamous tumble, though, occurred when he was a novice ice climber: despite his inexperience, Fischer had decided to attempt the coveted first ascent of a difficult frozen cascade called Bridal Veil Falls, in Utah's Provo Canyon. Racing two expert climbers up the ice, Fischer lost his purchase 100 feet off the deck and plummeted to the ground.

To the amazement of those who witnessed the incident, he picked himself up and walked away with relatively minor injuries. During his long plunge to earth, however, the tubular pick of an ice tool impaled his calf and came out the other side. When he extracted the hollow pick it removed a core sample of tissue, leaving a hole in his leg big enough to stick a pencil through. Fischer saw no reason to waste his limited supply of cash on medical treatment for such a minor injury, so he climbed for the next six months with an open, suppurating wound. Fifteen years later he proudly showed me the permanent scar inflicted by that fall: a pair of shiny, dime-size marks bracketing his Achilles tendon.

"Scott would push himself beyond any physical limitation," recalls Don Peterson, a renowned American climber who met Fischer soon after his slip from Bridal Veil Falls. Peterson became something of a mentor to Fischer and climbed with him intermittently over the next two decades. "His will was astonishing. It didn't matter how much pain he was in—he would ignore it and keep going. He wasn't the kind of guy who would turn around because he had a sore foot.

"Scott had this burning ambition to be a great climber, to be one of the best in the world. I remember at the NOLS headquarters there was a crude sort of gym. Scott would go into that room and regularly work out so hard that he threw up. Regularly. One doesn't meet many people with that kind of drive."

People were drawn to Fischer's energy and generosity, his absence of guile, his almost childlike enthusiasm. Raw and emotional, disinclined toward introspection, he had the kind of gregarious, magnetic personality that instantly won him friends for life; hundreds of individuals—including some he'd met just once or twice—considered him a bosom buddy. He was also strikingly handsome with a bodybuilder's physique and the chiseled features of a movie star. Among those attracted to him were not a few members of the opposite sex, and he wasn't immune to the attention.

A man of rampant appetites, Fischer smoked a lot of cannabis (although not while working) and drank more than was healthy. A back room at the Mountain Madness office functioned as a sort of secret clubhouse for Scott: after putting his kids to bed he liked to retire there with his pals to pass around a pipe and look at slides of their brave deeds on the heights.

During the 1980s Fischer made a number of impressive ascents that earned him a modicum of local renown, but celebrity in the world climbing community eluded him. Despite his concerted efforts, he was unable to land a lucrative commercial sponsorship of the sort enjoyed by some of his more famous peers. He worried that some of these top climbers didn't respect him.

"Recognition was important to Scott," says Jane Bromet, his publicist, confidant, and frequent climbing partner, who accompanied the Mountain Madness expedition to Base Camp to file Internet reports for Outside Online. "He ached for it. He had a vulnerable side that most people didn't see; it really bothered him that he wasn't more widely respected as a butt-kicking climber. He felt slighted, and it hurt."

By the time Fischer left for Nepal in the spring of 1996, he'd begun to garner more of the recognition that he thought was his due. Much of it came in the wake of his 1994 ascent of Everest, accomplished without supplemental oxygen. Christened the Sagarmatha Environmental Expedition, Fischer's team removed 5,000 pounds of trash from the mountain—which was very good for the landscape and turned out to be even better public relations. In January 1996, Fischer led a high-profile fund-raising ascent of Kilimanjaro, the highest mountain in Africa, that netted half a million dollars for the charity CARE. Thanks largely to the 1994 Everest clean-up expedition and this latter charity climb, by the time Fischer left for Everest in 1996 he had been featured prominently and often in the Seattle news media, and his climbing career was soaring.

Journalists inevitably asked Fischer about the risks associated with the kind of climbing he did and wondered how he reconciled it with being a husband and father. Fischer answered that he now took far fewer chances than he had during his reckless youth—that he had become a much more careful, more conservative climber. Shortly before leaving for Everest in 1996, he told Seattle writer Bruce Barcott, "I believe 100 percent I'm coming back. . . . My wife believes 100 percent I'm coming back. She isn't concerned about me at all when I'm guiding because I'm gonna make all the right choices. When accidents happen, I think it's always human error. So that's what I want to eliminate. I've had lots of climbing accidents in my youth. You come up with lots of reasons, but ultimately it's human error."

Fischer's assurances notwithstanding, his peripatetic alpine career was rough on his family. He was crazy about his kids, and when he was in Seattle he was an unusually attentive father, but climbing regularly took him away from home for months at a time. He'd been absent for seven of his son's nine birthdays. In fact, say his friends, by the time he departed for Everest in 1996, Fischer's marriage had been seriously strained, a situation that was exacerbated by his financial dependence on his wife.

Like most of its rivals, Mountain Madness was a fiscally marginal enterprise and had been since its inception: in 1995 Fischer took home only about $12,000. But things were finally starting to look more promising, thanks to Fischer's growing celebrity and to the efforts of his business partner–cum–office manager, Karen Dickinson, whose organizational skills and levelheadedness compensated for Fischer's seat-of-the-pants, what-me-worry modus operandi. Taking note of Rob Hall's success in guiding Everest—and the large fees he was able to command as a consequence—Fischer decided it was time for him to enter the Everest market. If he could emulate Hall, it would quickly catapult Mountain Madness to profitability.

The money itself didn't seem terribly important to Fischer. He cared little for material things, but he hungered for respect—from his family, from his peers, from society at large—and he knew that in our culture money is the principal gauge of success.

A few weeks after Fischer returned victorious from Everest in 1994, I encountered him in Seattle. I didn't know him well, but we had some friends in common and often ran into each other at the crags or at climbers' parties. On this occasion he buttonholed me to talk about the guided Everest expedition he was planning: I should come along, he cajoled, and write an article about the climb for *Outside.* When I replied that it would be crazy for someone with my limited high-altitude experience to attempt Everest, he said, "Hey, experience is overrated. It's not the altitude that's important, it's your attitude, bro. You'll do fine. You've done some pretty sick climbs—stuff that's way harder than Everest. We've got the big E figured out, we've got it totally wired. These days, I'm telling you, we've built a yellow brick road to the summit."

Scott had piqued my interest—more, even, than he probably realized—and he was relentless. He talked up Everest every time he saw me and repeatedly harangued Brad Wetzler, an editor at *Outside,* about the idea. By January 1996, thanks in no small part to Fischer's concerted lobbying, the magazine made a firm commitment to send me to Everest—probably, Wetzler indicated, as a member of Fischer's expedition. In Scott's mind it was a done deal.

A month before my scheduled departure, however, I got a call from Wetzler saying there'd been a change in plans: Rob Hall had offered the magazine a significantly better deal, so Wetzler proposed that I join the Adventure Consultants expedition instead of Fischer's. I knew and liked Fischer, and I didn't know much about Hall at that point, so I was initially reluctant. But after a trusted climbing buddy confirmed Hall's sterling reputation, I enthusiastically agreed to go to Everest with Adventure Consultants.

One afternoon in Base Camp I asked Hall why he'd been so eager to have me along. He candidly explained that it wasn't me he was actually interested in, or even the publicity he hoped my article would generate, particularly. What was so enticing was the bounty of valuable advertising he would reap from the deal he struck with *Outside.*

Hall told me that according to the terms of this arrangement, he'd agreed to accept only $10,000 of his usual fee in cash; the balance would be bartered for expensive ad space in the magazine, which targeted an upscale, adventurous, physically active audience—the core of his client base. And most important, Hall said, "It's an American audience. Probably eighty or ninety percent of the potential market for guided expeditions to Everest and the other Seven Summits is in the United States. After this season, when my mate Scott has established himself as an Everest guide, he'll have a great advantage over Adventure Consultants simply because he's based in America. To compete with him we'll have to step up our advertising there significantly."

In January, when Fischer found out that Hall had won me away from his team, he was apoplectic. He called me from Colorado, as upset as I'd ever heard him, to insist that he wasn't about to concede victory to Hall. (Like Hall, Fischer didn't bother trying to hide the fact that it wasn't me he was interested in, but rather the collateral publicity and advertising.) In the end, however, he was unwilling to match Hall's offer to the magazine.

When I arrived in Base Camp as a member of the Adventure Consultants group, not Fischer's Mountain Madness expedition, Scott didn't appear to hold a grudge. When I went down to his camp to visit he poured me a mug of coffee, put an arm around my shoulder, and seemed genuinely happy to see me.

| | |

Despite the many trappings of civilization at Base Camp, there was no forgetting that we were more than three miles above sea level. Walking to the mess tent at mealtime left me wheezing for several minutes. If I sat up too quickly, my head reeled and vertigo set in. The deep, rasping cough I'd developed in Lobuje worsened day by day. Sleep became elusive, a common symptom of minor altitude illness. Most nights I'd wake up three or four times gasping for breath, feeling like I was suffocating. Cuts and scrapes refused to heal. My appetite vanished and my digestive system, which required abundant oxygen to metabolize food, failed to make use of much of what I forced myself to eat; instead my body began consuming itself for sustenance. My arms and legs gradually began to wither to sticklike proportions.

Some of my teammates fared even worse than I in the meager air and unhygenic environment. Andy, Mike, Caroline, Lou, Stuart, and John suffered attacks of gastrointestinal distress that kept them racing to the latrine. Helen and Doug were plagued by severe headaches. As Doug described it to me, "It feels like somebody's driven a nail between my eyes."

This was Doug's second shot at Everest with Hall. The year before, Rob had forced him and three other clients to turn back just 330 feet below the top because the hour was late and the summit ridge was buried beneath a mantle of deep, unstable snow. "The summit looked *sooooo* close," Doug recalled with a painful laugh. "Believe me, there hasn't been a day since that I haven't thought about it." He'd been talked into returning this year by Hall, who felt sorry that Hansen had been denied the summit and had significantly discounted Hansen's fee to entice him to give it another try.

Among my fellow clients, Doug was the only one who'd climbed extensively without relying on a professional guide; although he wasn't an elite mountaineer, his fifteen years of experience made him fully capable of looking after himself on the heights. If anyone was going to reach the summit from our expedition, I assumed it would be Doug: he was strong, he was driven, and he had already been very high on Everest.

Less than two months shy of his forty-seventh birthday, divorced for seventeen years, Doug confided to me that he'd been involved with a succession of women, each of whom eventually left him after growing tired of competing with the mountains for his attention. A few weeks before leaving for Everest in 1996, Doug had met another woman while visiting a friend in Tucson, and they'd fallen in love. For a while they'd sent a flurry of faxes to each other, then several days passed without Doug hearing from her. "Guess she got smart and blew me off," he sighed, looking despondent. "And she was really nice, too. I really thought this one might be a keeper."

Later that afternoon he approached my tent waving a fresh fax in his hand. "Karen Marie says she's moving to the Seattle area!" he blurted ecstatically. "Whoa! This could be serious. I better make the summit and get Everest out of my system before she changes her mind."

In addition to corresponding with the new woman in his life, Doug filled his hours at Base Camp by writing countless postcards to the students of Sunrise Elementary School, a public institution in Kent, Washington, that had sold T-shirts to help fund his climb. He showed me many of the cards: "Some people have big dreams, some people have small dreams," he penned to a girl named Vanessa. "Whatever you have, the important thing is that you never stop dreaming."

Doug spent even more time writing faxes to his two grown kids—Angie, nineteen, and, Jaime, twenty-seven—whom he'd raised as a single father. He bunked in the tent next to mine, and every time a fax would arrive from Angie he'd read it to me, beaming. "Jeez," he would announce, "how do you suppose a screwup like me could have raised such a great kid?"

For my part, I wrote few postcards or faxes to anybody. Instead, I spent most of my time in Base Camp brooding about how I'd perform higher on the mountain, especially in the so-called Death Zone above 25,000 feet. I'd logged considerably more time on technical rock and ice than most of the other clients and many of the guides. But technical expertise counted for next to nothing on Everest, and I'd spent less time at high altitude than virtually every other climber present. Indeed, here at Base Camp—the mere toe of Everest—I was already higher than I'd ever been in my life.

This didn't seem to worry Hall. After seven Everest expeditions, he explained, he'd fine-tuned a remarkably effective acclimatization plan that would enable us to adapt to the paucity of oxygen in the atmosphere. (At Base Camp there was approximately half as much oxygen as at sea level; at the summit only a third as much.) When confronted with an increase in altitude, the human body adjusts in manifold ways, from increasing respiration, to changing the pH of the blood, to radically boosting the number of oxygen-carrying red blood cells—a conversion that takes weeks to complete.

Hall insisted, however, that after just three trips above Base Camp, climbing 2,000 feet higher on the mountain each time, our bodies would adapt sufficiently to permit safe passage to the 29,028-foot summit. "It's worked thirty-nine times so far, pal," Hall assured me with a crooked grin when I confessed my doubts. "And a few of the blokes who've summitted with me were nearly as pathetic as you."

Chapter Six

EVEREST BASE CAMP APRIL 12, 1996 17,600 FEET

The more improbable the situation and the greater the demands made on [the climber], the more sweetly the blood flows later in release from all that tension. The possibility of danger serves merely to sharpen his awareness and control. And perhaps this is the rationale of all risky sports: You deliberately raise the ante of effort and concentration in order, as it were, to clear your mind of trivialities. It's a small scale model for living, but with a difference: Unlike your routine life, where mistakes can usually be recouped and some kind of compromise patched up, your actions, for however brief a period, are deadly serious.

A. Alvarez
The Savage God: A Study of Suicide

Ascending Everest is a long, tedious process, more like a mammoth construction project than climbing as I'd previously known it. Counting our Sherpa staff, there were twenty-six people on Hall's team, and keeping everyone fed, sheltered, and in good health at 17,600 feet, a hundred miles by foot from the nearest road head, was no mean feat. Hall, however, was a quartermaster nonpareil, and he relished the challenge. At Base Camp he pored over reams of computer printouts detailing logistical minutiae: menus, spare parts, tools, medicines, communications hardware, load-hauling schedules, yak availability. A natural-born engineer, Rob loved infrastructure, electronics, and gadgets of all kinds; he spent his spare time endlessly tinkering with the solar electrical system or reading back issues of *Popular Science.*

In the tradition of George Leigh Mallory and most other Everesters, Hall's strategy was to lay siege to the mountain. Sherpas would progressively establish a series of four camps above Base Camp—each approximately 2,000 feet higher than the last—by shuttling cumbersome loads of food, cooking fuel, and oxygen from encampment to encampment until the requisite matériel had been fully stocked at

26,000 feet on the South Col. If all went according to Hall's grand plan, our summit assault would be launched from this highest camp—Camp Four—a month hence.

Even though we clients wouldn't be asked to share in the load hauling,* we would need to make repeated forays above Base Camp before the summit push in order to acclimatize. Rob announced that the first of these acclimatization sorties would occur on April 13—a one-day round-trip to Camp One, perched on the uppermost brow of the Khumbu Icefall, a vertical half mile above.

We spent the afternoon of April 12, my forty-second birthday, preparing our climbing equipment. The camp resembled an expensive yard sale as we spread our gear among the boulders to sort clothing, adjust harnesses, rig safety tethers, and fit crampons to our boots (a crampon is a grid of two-inch steel spikes that is clamped to the sole of each boot for purchase on ice). I was surprised and concerned to see Beck, Stuart, and Lou unpacking brand-new mountaineering boots that, by their own admission, had scarcely been worn. I wondered if they knew the chance they were taking by coming to Everest with untried footwear: two decades earlier I'd gone on an expedition with new boots and had learned the hard way that heavy, rigid mountaineering boots can cause debilitating foot injuries before they've been broken in.

Stuart, the young Canadian cardiologist, discovered that his crampons didn't even fit his new boots. Fortunately, after applying his extensive tool kit and considerable ingenuity to the problem, Rob managed to rivet together a special strap that made the crampons work.

As I loaded my backpack for the morrow, I learned that between the demands of their families and their high-powered careers, few of my fellow clients had had the opportunity to go climbing more than

* Ever since the first Everest attempts, most expeditions—commercial and noncommercial alike—have relied on Sherpas to carry the majority of the loads on the mountain. But as clients on a guided trip, we carried no loads at all beyond a small amount of personal gear, and in this regard we differed significantly from noncommercial expeditions of yore.

once or twice in the previous year. Although everyone appeared to be in superb physical shape, circumstances had forced them to do the bulk of their training on StairMasters and treadmills rather than on actual peaks. This gave me pause. Physical conditioning is a crucial component of mountaineering, but there are many other equally important elements, none of which can be practiced in a gym.

But maybe I'm just being a snob, I scolded myself. In any case, it was obvious that all of my teammates were as excited as I was about the prospect of kicking their crampons into a genuine mountain come the morning.

Our route to the summit would follow the Khumbu Glacier up the lower half of the mountain. From the *bergschrund** at 23,000 feet that marked its upper end, this great river of ice flowed two and a half miles down a relatively gentle valley called the Western Cwm. As the glacier inched over humps and dips in the Cwm's underlying strata, it fractured into countless vertical fissures—crevasses. Some of these crevasses were narrow enough to step across; others were eighty feet wide, several hundred feet deep, and ran half a mile from end to end. The big ones were apt to be vexing obstacles to our ascent, and when hidden beneath a crust of snow they would pose a serious hazard, but the challenges presented by the crevasses in the Cwm had proven over the years to be predictable and manageable.

The Icefall was a different story. No part of the South Col route was feared more by climbers. At around 20,000 feet, where the glacier emerged from the lower end of the Cwm, it pitched abruptly over a precipitous drop. This was the infamous Khumbu Icefall, the most technically demanding section on the entire route.

The movement of the glacier in the Icefall has been measured at between three and four feet a day. As it skids down the steep, irregular terrain in fits and starts, the mass of ice splinters into a jumble of huge, tottering blocks called *seracs,* some as large as office buildings.

* A *bergschrund* is a deep slit that delineates a glacier's upper terminus; it forms as the body of ice slides away from the steeper wall immediately above, leaving a gap between glacier and rock.

Because the climbing route wove under, around, and between hundreds of these unstable towers, each trip through the Icefall was a little like playing a round of Russian roulette: sooner or later any given serac was going to fall over without warning, and you could only hope you weren't beneath it when it toppled. Since 1963, when a teammate of Hornbein and Unsoeld's named Jake Breitenbach was crushed by an avalanching serac to become the Icefall's first victim, eighteen other climbers had died here.

The previous winter, as he had done in winters past, Hall had consulted with the leaders of all the expeditions planning to climb Everest in the spring, and together they'd agreed on one team among them who would be responsible for establishing and maintaining a route through the Icefall. For its trouble, the designated team was to be paid $2,200 from each of the other expeditions on the mountain. In recent years this cooperative approach had been met with wide, if not universal, acceptance, but it wasn't always so.

The first time one expedition thought to charge another to travel through the ice was in 1988, when a lavishly funded American team announced that any expedition that intended to follow the route they'd engineered up the Icefall would have to fork over $2,000. Some of the other teams on the mountain that year, failing to understand that Everest was no longer merely a mountain but a commodity as well, were incensed. And the greatest hue and cry came from Rob Hall, who was leading a small, impecunious New Zealand team.

Hall carped that the Americans were "violating the spirit of the hills" and practicing a shameful form of alpine extortion, but Jim Frush, the unsentimental attorney who was the leader of the American group, remained unmoved. Hall eventually agreed through clenched teeth to send Frush a check and was granted passage through the Icefall. (Frush later reported that Hall never made good on his IOU.)

Within two years, however, Hall did an about-face and came to see the logic of treating the Icefall as a toll road. Indeed, from 1993 through '95 he volunteered to put in the route and collect the toll himself. In the spring of 1996 he elected not to assume responsibility for the Icefall, but he was happy to pay the leader of a rival commercial* expedition—a Scottish Everest veteran named Mal Duff—to take over the job. Long before we'd even arrived at Base Camp, a team of Sherpas employed by Duff had blazed a zigzag path through the seracs, stringing out more than a mile of rope and installing some sixty aluminum ladders over the broken surface of the glacier. The ladders belonged to an enterprising Sherpa from the village of Gorak Shep who turned a nice profit by renting them out each season.

So it came to pass that at 4:45 A.M. on Saturday, April 13, I found myself at the foot of the fabled Icefall, strapping on my crampons in the frigid predawn gloom.

Crusty old alpinists who've survived a lifetime of close scrapes like to counsel young protégés that staying alive hinges on listening carefully to one's "inner voice." Tales abound of one or another climber who decided to remain in his or her sleeping bag after detecting some inauspicious vibe in the ether and thereby survived a catastrophe that wiped out others who failed to heed the portents.

I didn't doubt the potential value of paying attention to subconscious cues. As I waited for Rob to lead the way, the ice underfoot emitted a series of loud cracking noises, like small trees being snapped in two, and I felt myself wince with each pop and rumble from the glacier's shifting depths. Problem was, my inner voice resembled Chicken Little: it was screaming that I was about to die, but it did that almost every time I laced up my climbing boots. I therefore did my damnedest to ignore my histrionic imagination and grimly followed Rob into the eerie blue labyrinth.

Although I'd never been in an icefall as frightening as the Khumbu, I'd climbed many other icefalls. They typically have vertical or even overhanging passages that demand considerable expertise with ice ax and crampons. There was certainly no lack of steep ice in

* Although I use "commercial" to denote any expedition organized as a money-making venture, not all commercial expeditions are guided. For instance, Mal Duff—who charged his clients considerably less than the $65,000 fee requested by Hall and Fischer—provided leadership and the essential infrastructure necessary to climb Everest (food, tents, bottled oxygen, fixed ropes, Sherpa support staff, and so on) but did not purport to act as a guide; the climbers on his team were assumed to be sufficiently skilled to get themselves safely up Everest and back down again.

the Khumbu Icefall, but all of it had been rigged with ladders or ropes or both, rendering the conventional tools and techniques of ice climbing largely superfluous.

I soon learned that on Everest not even the rope—the quintessential climber's accoutrement—was to be utilized in the time-honored manner. Ordinarily, one climber is tied to one or two partners with a 150-foot length of rope, making each person directly responsible for the life of the others; roping up in this fashion is a serious and very intimate act. In the Icefall, though, expediency dictated that each of us climb independently, without being physically connected to one another in any way.

Mal Duff's Sherpas had anchored a static line of rope that extended from the bottom of the Icefall to its top. Attached to my waist was a three-foot-long safety tether with a carabiner, or snap-link, at the distal end. Security was achieved not by roping myself to a teammate but rather by clipping my safety tether to the fixed line and sliding it up the rope as I ascended. Climbing in this fashion, we would be able to move as quickly as possible through the most dangerous parts of the Icefall, and we wouldn't have to entrust our lives to teammates whose skill and experience were unknown. As it turned out, not once during the entire expedition would I ever have reason to rope myself to another climber.

If the Icefall required few orthodox climbing techniques, it demanded a whole new repertoire of skills in their stead—for instance, the ability to tiptoe in mountaineering boots and crampons across three wobbly ladders lashed end to end, bridging a sphincter-clenching chasm. There were many such crossings, and I never got used to them.

At one point I was balanced on an unsteady ladder in the predawn gloaming, stepping tenuously from one bent rung to the next, when the ice supporting the ladder on either end began to quiver as if an earthquake had struck. A moment later came an explosive roar as a large serac somewhere close above came crashing down. I froze, my heart in my throat, but the avalanching ice passed fifty yards to the left, out of sight, without doing any damage. After waiting a few minutes to regain my composure I resumed my herky-jerky passage to the far side of the ladder.

The glacier's continual and often violent state of flux added an element of uncertainty to every ladder crossing. As the glacier moved, crevasses would sometimes compress, buckling ladders like toothpicks; other times a crevasse might expand, leaving a ladder dangling in the air, only tenuously supported, with neither end mounted on solid ice. Anchors* securing the ladders and lines routinely melted out when the afternoon sun warmed the surrounding ice and snow. Despite daily maintenance, there was a very real danger that any given rope might pull loose under body weight.

But if the Icefall was strenuous and terrifying, it had a surprising allure as well. As dawn washed the darkness from the sky, the shattered glacier was revealed to be a three-dimensional landscape of phantasmal beauty. The temperature was six degrees Fahrenheit. My crampons crunched reassuringly into the glacier's rind. Following the fixed line, I meandered through a vertical maze of crystalline blue stalagmites. Sheer rock buttresses seamed with ice pressed in from both edges of the glacier, rising like the shoulders of a malevolent god. Absorbed by my surroundings and the gravity of the labor, I lost myself in the unfettered pleasures of ascent, and for an hour or two actually forgot to be afraid.

Three-quarters of the way to Camp One, Hall remarked at a rest stop that the Icefall was in better shape than he'd ever seen it: "The route's a bloody freeway this season." But only slightly higher, at 19,000 feet, the ropes brought us to the base of a gargantuan, perilously balanced serac. As massive as a twelve-story building, it loomed over our heads, leaning 30 degrees past vertical. The route followed a natural catwalk that angled sharply up the overhanging face: we would have to climb up and over the entire off-kilter tower to escape its threatening tonnage.

Safety, I understood, hinged on speed. I huffed toward the relative security of the serac's crest with all the haste I could muster, but

* Three-foot long aluminum stakes called pickets were used to anchor ropes and ladders to snow slopes; when the terrain was hard glacial ice, "ice screws" were employed: hollow, threaded tubes about ten inches long that were twisted into the frozen glacier.

since I wasn't acclimatized my fastest pace was no better than a crawl. Every four or five steps I'd have to stop, lean against the rope, and suck desperately at the thin, bitter air, searing my lungs in the process.

I reached the top of the serac without it collapsing and flopped breathless onto its flat summit, my heart pounding like a jackhammer. A little later, around 8:30 A.M., I arrived at the top of the Icefall itself, just beyond the last of the seracs. The safety of Camp One didn't supply much peace of mind, however: I couldn't stop thinking about the ominously tilted slab a short distance below, and the fact that I would have to pass beneath its faltering bulk at least seven more times if I was going to make it to the summit of Everest. Climbers who snidely denigrate this as the Yak Route, I decided, had obviously never been through the Khumbu Icefall.

Before leaving the tents Rob had explained that we would turn around at 10:00 A.M. sharp, even if some of us hadn't reached Camp One, in order to return to Base Camp before the midday sun made the Icefall even more unstable. At the appointed hour only Rob, Frank Fischbeck, John Taske, Doug Hansen, and I had arrived at Camp One; Yasuko Namba, Stuart Hutchison, Beck Weathers, and Lou Kasischke, escorted by guides Mike Groom and Andy Harris, were within 200 vertical feet of the camp when Rob got on the radio and turned everybody around.

For the first time we had seen one another actually climbing and could better assess the strengths and weaknesses of the people on whom we would each depend over the coming weeks. Doug and John—at fifty-six, the oldest person on the team—had both looked solid. But Frank, the gentlemanly, soft-spoken publisher from Hong Kong, was the most impressive: demonstrating the savvy he'd acquired over three previous Everest expeditions, he'd started out slowly but kept moving at the same steady pace; by the top of the Icefall he'd quietly passed almost everyone, and he never even seemed to be breathing hard.

In marked contrast, Stuart—the youngest and seemingly strongest client on the whole team—had dashed out of camp at the front of the group, soon exhausted himself, and by the top of the Icefall was in visible agony at the back of the line. Lou, hampered by a leg muscle he'd injured on the first morning of the trek to Base Camp, was slow but competent. Beck, and especially Yasuko, on the other hand, had looked sketchy.

Several times both Beck and Yasuko had appeared to be in danger of falling off a ladder and plummeting into a crevasse, and Yasuko seemed to know next to nothing about how to use crampons.* Andy, who revealed himself to be a gifted, extremely patient teacher—and who, as the junior guide, had been assigned to climb with the slowest clients, at the rear—spent the whole morning coaching her on basic ice-climbing techniques.

Whatever our group's various shortcomings, at the top of the Icefall Rob announced that he was quite pleased with everyone's performance. "For your first time above Base Camp you've all done remarkably well," he proclaimed like a proud father. "I think we've got a good strong bunch this year."

It took little more than an hour to descend back to Base Camp. By the time I removed my crampons to walk the last hundred yards to the tents, the sun felt like it was boring a hole through the crown of my skull. The full force of the headache struck a few minutes later, as I was chatting with Helen and Chhongba in the mess tent. I'd never experienced anything like it: crushing pain between my temples—pain so severe that it was accompanied by shuddering waves of nausea and made it impossible for me to speak in coherent sentences. Fearing that I'd suffered some sort of stroke, I staggered away in midconversation, retreated to my sleeping bag, and pulled my hat over my eyes.

The headache had the blinding intensity of a migraine, and I had no idea what had caused it. I doubted that it was due to the altitude, because it didn't strike until I'd returned to Base Camp. More likely it was a reaction to the fierce ultraviolet radiation that had burned my retinas and baked my brain. Whatever had brought it on, the agony was intense and unrelenting. For the next five hours I lay in my tent

* Although Yasuko had used crampons previously during her climbs of Aconcagua, McKinley, Elbrus, and Vinson, none of these ascents involved much, if any, true ice climbing: the terrain in each case consisted primarily of relatively gentle slopes of snow and/or gravel-like scree.

trying to avoid sensory stimuli of any kind. If I opened my eyes, or even just moved them from side to side behind closed eyelids, I received a withering jolt of pain. At sunset, unable to bear it any longer, I stumbled over to the medical tent to seek advice from Caroline, the expedition doctor.

She gave me a strong analgesic and told me to drink some water, but after a few swallows I regurgitated the pills, the liquid, and the remnants of lunch. "Hmmm," mused Caro, observing the vomitus splashed across my boots. "I guess we'll have to try something else." I was instructed to dissolve a tiny pill under my tongue, which would keep me from vomiting, and then swallow two codeine pills. An hour later the pain began to fade; nearly weeping with gratitude I drifted into unconsciousness.

| | |

I was dozing in my sleeping bag, watching the morning sun cast shadows across the walls of my tent, when Helen yelled, "Jon! Telephone! It's Linda!" I yanked on a pair of sandals, sprinted the fifty yards to the communications tent, and grabbed the handset as I fought to catch my breath.

The entire satellite phone-and-fax apparatus wasn't much larger than a laptop computer. Calls were expensive—about five dollars a minute—and they didn't always go through, but the fact that my wife could dial a thirteen-digit number in Seattle and speak to me on Mount Everest astounded me. Although the call was a great comfort, the resignation in Linda's voice was unmistakable even from the far side of the globe. "I'm doing fine," she assured me, "but I wish you were here."

Eighteen days earlier she'd broken into tears when she'd taken me to the plane to Nepal. "Driving home from the airport," she confessed, "I couldn't stop crying. Saying good-bye to you was one of the saddest things I've ever done. I guess I knew on some level that you might not be coming back, and it seemed like such a waste. It seemed so fucking stupid and pointless."

We'd been married for fifteen and a half years. Within a week of first talking about taking the plunge, we'd visited a justice of the peace and done the deed. I was twenty-six at the time and had recently decided to quit climbing and get serious about life.

When I first met Linda she had been a climber herself—and an exceptionally gifted one—but she'd given it up after breaking an arm, injuring her back, and subsequently making a cold appraisal of the inherent risks. Linda would never have considered asking me to abandon the sport, but the announcement that I intended to quit had reinforced her decision to marry me. I'd failed to appreciate the grip climbing had on my soul, however, or the purpose it lent to my otherwise rudderless life. I didn't anticipate the void that would loom in its absence. Within a year I sneaked my rope out of storage and was back on the rock. By 1984, when I went to Switzerland to climb a notoriously dangerous alpine wall called the Eiger Nordwand, Linda and I had advanced to within millimeters of splitting up, and my climbing lay at the core of our troubles.

Our relationship remained rocky for two or three years after my failed attempt on the Eiger, but the marriage somehow survived that rough patch. Linda came to accept my climbing: she saw that it was a crucial (if perplexing) part of who I was. Mountaineering, she understood, was an essential expression of some odd, immutable aspect of my personality that I could no sooner alter than change the color of my eyes. Then, in the midst of this delicate rapprochement, *Outside* magazine confirmed it was sending me to Everest.

At first I pretended that I'd be going as a journalist more than a climber—that I'd accepted the assignment because the commercialization of Everest was an interesting subject and the money was pretty good. I explained to Linda and anyone else who expressed skepticism about my Himalayan qualifications that I didn't expect to ascend very high on the mountain. "I'll probably climb only a little way above Base Camp," I insisted. "Just to get a taste of what high altitude is about."

This was bullshit, of course. Given the length of the trip and the time I'd have to spend training for it, I stood to make a lot more money staying home and taking other writing jobs. I accepted the assignment because I was in the grip of the Everest mystique. In truth, I wanted to climb the mountain as badly as I'd ever wanted anything in my life. From the moment I agreed to go to Nepal my intention was to ascend every bit as high as my unexceptional legs and lungs would carry me.

By the time Linda drove me to the airport she had long since seen through my prevarications. She sensed the true dimensions of my desire, and it scared her. "If you get killed," she argued with a mix of despair and anger, "it's not just you who'll pay the price. I'll have to pay, too, you know, for the rest of my life. Doesn't that matter to you?"

"I'm not going to get killed," I answered. "Don't be melodramatic."

Chapter Seven

CAMP ONE   APRIL 13, 1996   19,500 FEET

But there are men for whom the unattainable has a special attraction. Usually they are not experts: their ambitions and fantasies are strong enough to brush aside the doubts which more cautious men might have. Determination and faith are their strongest weapons. At best such men are regarded as eccentric; at worst, mad. . . .

Everest has attracted its share of men like these. Their mountaineering experience varied from none at all to very slight—certainly none of them had the kind of experience which would make an ascent of Everest a reasonable goal. Three things they all had in common: faith in themselves, great determination, and endurance.

Walt Unsworth
Everest

I grew up with an ambition and determination without which I would have been a good deal happier. I thought a lot and developed the far-away look of a dreamer, for it was always the distant heights which fascinated me and drew me to them in spirit. I was not sure what could be accomplished by means of tenacity and little else, but the target was set high and each rebuff only saw me more determined to see at least one major dream through to its fulfillment.

Earl Denman
Alone to Everest

The slopes of Everest did not lack for dreamers in the spring of 1996; the credentials of many who'd come to climb the mountain were as thin as mine, or thinner. When it came time for each of us to assess our own abilities and weigh them against the formidable challenges of the world's highest mountain, it sometimes seemed as though half the population at Base Camp was clinically delusional. But perhaps this shouldn't have come as a surprise. Everest has always been a magnet for kooks, publicity seekers, hopeless romantics, and others with a shaky hold on reality.

In March 1947, a poverty-stricken Canadian engineer named Earl Denman arrived in Darjeeling and announced his intention to climb Everest, despite the fact that he had little mountaineering experience and lacked official permission to enter Tibet. Somehow he managed to convince two Sherpas to accompany him, Ang Dawa and Tenzing Norgay.

Tenzing—the same man who would later make the first ascent of Everest with Hillary—had immigrated to Darjeeling from Nepal in 1933 as a seventeen-year-old, hoping to be hired by an expedition departing for the peak that spring under the leadership of an eminent British mountaineer named Eric Shipton. The eager young Sherpa wasn't chosen that year, but he remained in India and was hired by Shipton for the 1935 British Everest expedition. By the time he agreed to go with Denman in 1947, Tenzing had already been on the great mountain three times. He later conceded that he knew all along Denman's plans were foolhardy, but Tenzing, too, was powerless to resist the pull of Everest:

> [N]othing made sense about it. First, we would probably not even get into Tibet. Second, if we did get in we would probably be caught, and, as his guides, we, as well as Denman, would be in serious trouble. Third, I did not for a moment believe that, even if we reached the mountain, a party such as this would be able to climb it. Fourth, the attempt would be highly dangerous. Fifth, Denman had the money neither to pay us well nor to guarantee a decent sum to our dependents in case something happened to us. And so on and so on. Any man in his right mind would have said no. But I couldn't say no. For in my heart I needed to go, and the pull of Everest was

> stronger for me than any force on earth. Ang Dawa and I talked for a few minutes, and then we made our decision. "Well," I told Denman, "we will try."

As the small expedition marched across Tibet toward Everest, the two Sherpas increasingly came to like and respect the Canadian. Despite his inexperience, they admired his courage and physical strength. And Denman, to his credit, was ultimately willing to acknowledge his shortcomings when they arrived on the slopes of the mountain and reality stared him in the face. Pounded hard by a storm at 22,000 feet, Denman admitted defeat, and the three men turned around, returning safely to Darjeeling just five weeks after they'd departed.

An idealistic, melancholic Englishman named Maurice Wilson had not been so fortunate when he'd attempted a similarly reckless ascent thirteen years before Denman. Motivated by a misguided desire to help his fellow man, Wilson had concluded that climbing Everest would be the perfect way to publicize his belief that the myriad ills of humankind could be cured through a combination of fasting and faith in the powers of God. He hatched a scheme to fly a small airplane to Tibet, crash-land it on the flanks of Everest, and proceed to the summit from there. The fact that he knew absolutely nothing about either mountaineering or flying didn't strike him as a major impediment.

Wilson bought a fabric-winged Gypsy Moth, christened it *Ever Wrest,* and learned the rudiments of flying. He next spent five weeks tramping about the modest hills of Snowdonia and the English Lake District to learn what he thought he needed to know about climbing. And then, in May 1933, he took off in his tiny airplane and set a course for Everest by way of Cairo, Tehran, and India.

By this time Wilson had already received considerable coverage in the press. He flew to Purtabpore, India, but having not received permission from the Nepalese government to fly over Nepal, he sold the airplane for five hundred pounds and traveled overland to Darjeeling, where he learned that he had been denied permission to enter Tibet. This didn't faze him, either: in March 1934 he hired three Sherpas, disguised himself as a Buddhist monk, and, defying the authorities of the Raj, surreptitiously trekked 300 miles through the forests of Sikkim and the sere Tibetan plateau. By April 14 he was at the foot of Everest.

Hiking up the rock-strewn ice of the East Rongbuk Glacier, he initially made fair progress, but as his ignorance of glacier travel caught up to him, he repeatedly lost his way and became frustrated and exhausted. Yet he refused to give up.

By mid-May he had reached the head of the East Rongbuk Glacier at 21,000 feet, where he plundered a supply of food and equipment cached by Eric Shipton's unsuccessful 1933 expedition. From there Wilson started ascending the slopes leading up to the North Col, getting as high as 22,700 feet before a vertical ice cliff proved too much for him and he was forced to retreat back to the site of Shipton's cache. And still he wouldn't quit. On May 28 he wrote in his diary, "This will be a last effort, and I feel successful," and then headed up the mountain one more time.

One year later, when Shipton returned to Everest, his expedition came across Wilson's frozen body lying in the snow at the foot of the North Col. "After some discussion we decided to bury him in a crevasse," wrote Charles Warren, one of the climbers who'd found the corpse. "We all raised our hats at the time and I think that everyone was rather upset at the business. I thought I had grown immune to the sight of the dead; but somehow or other, in the circumstances, and because of the fact that he was, after all, doing much the same as ourselves, his tragedy seemed to have been brought a little too near home for us."

| | |

The recent proliferation on the slopes of Everest of latter-day Wilsons and Denmans—marginally qualified dreamers like some of my cohorts—is a phenomenon that has provoked strong criticism. But the question of who belongs on Everest and who doesn't is more complicated than it might first appear. The fact that a climber has paid a large sum of money to join a guided expedition does not, by itself, mean that he or she is unfit to be on the mountain. Indeed, at least two of the commercial expeditions on Everest in the spring of 1996 included Himalayan veterans who would be considered qualified by the most rigorous standards.

As I waited at Camp One on April 13 for my teammates to join me atop the Icefall, a pair of climbers from Scott Fischer's Mountain Madness team strode past at an impressive clip. One was Klev Schoening, a thirty-eight-year-old Seattle construction contractor and a former member of the U.S. Ski Team who, although exceptionally strong, had little previous high-altitude experience. However, with him was his uncle, Pete Schoening, a living Himalayan legend.

Dressed in faded, threadbare GoreTex, a couple of months shy of his sixty-ninth birthday, Pete was a gangly, slightly stooped man who had returned to the high reaches of the Himalaya after a long absence. In 1958 he'd made history as the driving force behind the first ascent of Hidden Peak, a 26,470-foot mountain in the Karakoram Range of Pakistan—the highest first ascent ever achieved by American climbers. Pete was even more famous, however, for playing a heroic role in an unsuccessful expedition to K2 in 1953, the same year Hillary and Tenzing reached the peak of Everest.

The eight-man expedition was pinned down in a ferocious blizzard high on K2, waiting to make an assault on the summit, when a team member named Art Gilkey developed thrombophlebitis, a life-threatening altitude-induced blood clot. Realizing that they would have to get Gilkey down immediately to have any hope of saving him, Schoening and the others started lowering him down the mountain's steep Abruzzi Ridge as the storm raged. At 25,000 feet, a climber named George Bell slipped and pulled four others off with him. Reflexively wrapping the rope around his shoulders and ice ax, Schoening somehow managed to single-handedly hold on to Gilkey and simultaneously arrest the slide of the five falling climbers without being pulled off the mountain himself. One of the more incredible feats in the annals of mountaineering, it was known forever after simply as The Belay.*

* *Belay* is a climbing term that denotes the act of securing a rope to safeguard one's companions as they climb.

And now Pete Schoening was being led up Everest by Fischer and his two guides, Neal Beidleman and Anatoli Boukreev. When I asked Beidleman, a powerful climber from Colorado, how it felt to be guiding a client of Schoening's stature, he quickly corrected me with a self-deprecating laugh: "Somebody like me doesn't 'guide' Pete Schoening anywhere. I just consider it a great honor to be on the same team as him." Schoening had signed on with Fischer's Mountain Madness group not because he needed a guide to lead him up the peak but to avoid the mammoth hassle of arranging for a permit, oxygen, tentage, provisions, Sherpa support, and other logistical details.

A few minutes after Pete and Klev Schoening climbed past en route to their own Camp One, their teammate Charlotte Fox appeared. Dynamic and statuesque, thirty-eight years old, Fox was a ski patroller from Aspen, Colorado, who'd previously summitted two 8,000-meter peaks: Gasherbrum II in Pakistan, at 26,361 feet, and Everest's 26,748-foot neighbor, Cho Oyu. Later still, I encountered a member of Mal Duff's commercial expedition, a twenty-eight-year-old Finn named Veikka Gustafsson whose record of previous Himalayan ascents included Everest, Dhaulagiri, Makalu, and Lhotse.

No client on Hall's team, by comparison, had ever reached the summit of any 8,000-meter peak. If someone like Pete Schoening was the equivalent of a major-league baseball star, my fellow clients and I were like a ragtag collection of pretty decent small-town softball players who'd bribed their way into the World Series. Yes, at the top of the Icefall Hall had called us "a good strong bunch." And we actually were strong, perhaps, relative to groups of clients Hall had ushered up the mountain in past years. It was clear to me, nevertheless, that none of us in Hall's group had a prayer of climbing Everest without considerable assistance from Hall, his guides, and his Sherpas.

On the other hand, our group was far more competent than a number of the other teams on the mountain. There were some climbers of very dubious ability on a commercial expedition led by an Englishman with undistinguished Himalayan credentials. But the least qualified people on Everest were not in fact guided clients at all; rather, they were members of traditionally structured, noncommercial expeditions.

As I was heading back to Base Camp through the lower Icefall, I overtook a pair of slower climbers outfitted with very strange looking clothing and equipment. It was apparent almost immediately that they weren't very familiar with the standard tools and techniques of glacier travel. The climber in back repeatedly snagged his crampons and stumbled. Waiting for them to cross a yawning crevasse bridged by two rickety ladders spliced end to end, I was shocked to see them go across together, almost in lockstep—a needlessly dangerous act. An awkward attempt at conversation on the far side of the crevasse revealed that they were members of a Taiwanese expedition.

The reputations of the Taiwanese preceded them to Everest. In the spring of 1995, the same team had traveled to Alaska to climb Mount McKinley as a shakedown for the attempt on Everest in 1996. Nine climbers reached the summit, but seven of them were caught by a storm on the descent, became disoriented, and spent a night in the open at 19,400 feet, initiating a costly, hazardous rescue by the National Park Service.

Responding to a request by park rangers, Alex Lowe and Conrad Anker, two of the most skilled alpinists in the United States, interrupted their own ascent and rushed up from 14,400 feet to aid the Taiwanese climbers, who were by then barely alive. With great difficulty and considerable risk to their own lives, Lowe and Anker each dragged a helpless Taiwanese from 19,400 feet down to 17,200 feet, at which point a helicopter was able to evacuate them from the mountain. All told, five members of the Taiwanese team—two with severe frostbite and one already dead—were plucked from McKinley by chopper. "Only one guy died," says Anker. "But if Alex and I hadn't arrived right when we did, two others would have died, too. Earlier, we'd noticed the Taiwanese group because they looked so incompetent. It wasn't any big surprise when they got into trouble."

The leader of the expedition, Gau Ming-Ho—a jovial freelance photographer who calls himself "Makalu," after the striking Himalayan peak of that name—was exhausted and frostbitten and had to be assisted down the upper mountain by a pair of Alaskan guides. "As the Alaskans brought him down," Anker reports, "Makalu was yelling 'Victory! Victory! We made summit!' to everyone they passed, as if the disaster hadn't even happened. Yeah, that Makalu dude struck me as pretty weird." When the survivors of the McKinley debacle showed up on the south side of Everest in 1996, Makalu Gau was again their leader.

The presence of the Taiwanese on Everest was a matter of grave concern to most of the other expeditions on the mountain. There was a very real fear that the Taiwanese would suffer a calamity that would compel other expeditions to come to their aid, risking further lives, to say nothing of jeopardizing the opportunity for other climbers to reach the summit. But the Taiwanese were by no means the only group that seemed egregiously unqualified. Camped beside us at Base Camp was a twenty-five-year-old Norwegian climber named Petter Neby, who announced his intention to make a solo ascent of the Southwest Face,* one of the peak's most dangerous and technically demanding routes—despite the fact that his Himalayan experience was limited to two ascents of neighboring Island Peak, a 20,274-foot bump on a subsidiary ridge of Lhotse involving nothing more technical than vigorous walking.

And then there were the South Africans. Sponsored by a major newspaper, the Johannesburg *Sunday Times,* their team had inspired effusive national pride and had received a personal blessing from President Nelson Mandela prior to their departure. They were the first South African expedition ever to be granted a permit to climb Everest, a mixed-race group that aspired to put the first black person on the summit. Their leader was Ian Woodall, thirty-nine, a loquacious, mouselike man who relished telling anecdotes about his brave exploits as a military commando behind enemy lines during South Africa's long, brutal conflict with Angola in the 1980s.

Woodall had recruited three of South Africa's strongest climbers to form the nucleus of his team: Andy de Klerk, Andy Hackland, and

* Although Neby's expedition was billed as a "solo" endeavor, he had employed eighteen Sherpas to carry his loads, fix ropes for him, establish his camps, and guide him up the mountain.

Edmund February. The biracial makeup of the team was of special significance to February, forty, a soft-spoken black paleoecologist and a climber of international renown. "My parents named me after Sir Edmund Hillary," he explains. "Climbing Everest had been a personal dream of mine ever since I was very young. But even more significantly, I saw the expedition as a powerful symbol of a young nation trying to unify itself and move toward democracy, trying to recover from its past. I grew up with the yoke of apartheid around my neck in many ways, and I am extremely bitter about that. But we are a new nation now. I firmly believe in the direction my country's taking. To show that we in South Africa could climb Everest together, black and white on the top—that would be a great thing."

The entire nation rallied behind the expedition. "Woodall proposed the project at a really fortuitous time," says de Klerk. "With the end of apartheid, South Africans were finally allowed to travel wherever they wanted, and our sports teams could compete around the world. South Africa had just won the Rugby World Cup. There was this national euphoria, a great upwelling of pride, yeah? So when Woodall came along and proposed a South African Everest expedition, everybody was in favor of it, and he was able to raise a lot of money—the equivalent of several hundred thousand dollars in U.S. currency—without anybody asking a lot of questions."

In addition to himself, the three male climbers, and a British climber and photographer named Bruce Herrod, Woodall wanted to include a woman on the expedition, so prior to leaving South Africa he invited six female candidates on a physically grueling but technically undemanding ascent of 19,340-foot Kilimanjaro. At the conclusion of the two-week trial, Woodall announced that he'd narrowed the field down to two finalists: Cathy O'Dowd, twenty-six, a white journalism instructor with limited mountaineering experience whose father is the director of Anglo American, the largest company in South Africa; and Deshun Deysel, twenty-five, a black physical-education teacher with no previous climbing experience whatsoever who'd grown up in a segregated township. Both women, said Woodall, would accompany the team to Base Camp, and he would choose one of them to continue up Everest after evaluating their performance during the trek.

On April 1, during the second day of my journey to Base Camp, I was surprised to run into February, Hackland, and de Klerk on the trail below Namche Bazaar, walking *out* of the mountains, bound for Kathmandu. De Klerk, a friend of mine, informed me that the three South African climbers and Charlotte Noble, their team's doctor, had resigned from the expedition before even getting to the base of the mountain. "Woodall, the leader, turned out to be a complete asshole," explained de Klerk. "A total control freak. And you couldn't trust him—we never knew if he was talking bullshit or telling the truth. We didn't want to put our lives in the hands of a guy like that. So we left."

Woodall had made claims to de Klerk and others that he'd climbed extensively in the Himalaya, including ascents above 26,000 feet. In fact, the whole of Woodall's Himalayan mountaineering experience consisted of reaching 21,300 feet as a paying client on a commercial expedition to Annapurna led by Mal Duff in 1990.

Additionally, before leaving for Everest Woodall had boasted on the expedition's Internet website of a distinguished military career in which he'd risen through the ranks of the British army "to command the elite Long Range Mountain Reconnaissance Unit that did much of its training in the Himalayas." He'd told the *Sunday Times* that he had been an instructor at the Royal Military Academy at Sandhurst, England, as well. As it happens, there is no such thing as a Long Range Mountain Reconnaissance Unit in the British army, and Woodall never served as an instructor at Sandhurst. Nor did he ever fight behind enemy lines in Angola. According to a spokesman for the British army, Woodall served as a pay clerk.

Woodall also lied about whom he'd listed on the Everest climbing permit* issued by the Nepalese Ministry of Tourism. From the beginning he'd said that both Cathy O'Dowd and Deshun Deysel were on

* Only climbers listed on the official permit—at a cost of $10,000 a head—are allowed to ascend above Base Camp. This rule is strictly enforced, and violators face prohibitive fines and expulsion from Nepal.

the permit and that the final decision about which woman would be invited to join the climbing team would be made at Base Camp. After leaving the expedition de Klerk discovered that O'Dowd was listed on the permit, as well as Woodall's sixty-nine-year-old father and a Frenchman named Tierry Renard (who'd paid Woodall $35,000 to join the South African team), but Deshun Deysel—the only black member after the resignation of Ed February—was not. This suggested to de Klerk that Woodall had never had any intention of letting Deysel climb the mountain.

Adding insult to injury, before leaving South Africa Woodall had cautioned de Klerk—who is married to an American woman and has dual citizenship—that he would not be allowed on the expedition unless he agreed to use his South African passport to enter Nepal. "He made a big fuss about it," recalls de Klerk, "because we were the first South African Everest expedition and all that. But it turns out that Woodall doesn't hold a South African passport himself. He's not even a South African citizen—the guy's a Brit, and he entered Nepal on his British passport."

Woodall's numerous deceits became an international scandal, reported on the front pages of newspapers throughout the British Commonwealth. As the negative press filtered back to him, the megalomaniacal leader turned a cold shoulder to the criticism and insulated his team as much as possible from the other expeditions. He also banished *Sunday Times* reporter Ken Vernon and photographer Richard Shorey from the expedition, even though Woodall had signed a contract stipulating that in return for receiving financial backing from the newspaper, the two journalists would be "allowed to accompany the expedition at all times," and that failure to honor this stipulation "would be cause for breach of contract."

The editor of the *Sunday Times,* Ken Owen, was en route to Base Camp with his wife at the time, midway through a trekking vacation that had been arranged to coincide with the South African Everest expedition, and was being led by Woodall's girlfriend, a young Frenchwoman named Alexandrine Gaudin. In Pheriche, Owen learned that Woodall had given the boot to his reporter and photographer. Flabbergasted, he sent a note to the expedition leader explaining that the newspaper had no intention of pulling Vernon and Shorey from the story and that the journalists had been ordered to rejoin the expedition. When Woodall received this message, he flew into a rage and rushed down to Pheriche from Base Camp to have it out with Owen.

According to Owen, during the ensuing confrontation he asked Woodall point-blank if Deysel's name was on the permit. Woodall replied, "That's none of your business."

When Owen suggested that Deysel had been reduced to "serving as a token black woman to give the team a spurious South Africanism," Woodall threatened to kill both Owen and his wife. At one point the overwrought expedition leader declared, "I'm going to rip your fucking head off and ram it up your arse."

Shortly thereafter, journalist Ken Vernon arrived at the South African Base Camp—an incident he first reported from Rob Hall's satellite fax machine—only to be informed "by a grim-faced Ms. O'Dowd that I was 'not welcome' at the camp." As Vernon later wrote in the *Sunday Times:*

> I told her she had no right to bar me from a camp my newspaper had paid for. When pressed further she said she was acting on "instructions" from Mr. Woodall. She said Shorey had already been thrown out of the camp and I should follow as I would not be given food or shelter there. My legs were still shaky from the walk and, before deciding whether to fight the edict or leave, I asked for a cup of tea. "No way," came the reply. Ms. O'Dowd walked to the team's Sherpa leader, Ang Dorje, and said audibly: "This is Ken Vernon, one of the ones we told you about. He is to be given no assistance whatsoever." Ang Dorje is a tough, nuggety rock of a man and we had already shared several glasses of Chang, the fiery local brew. I looked at him and said, "Not even a cup of tea?" To his credit, and in the best tra-

> dition of Sherpa hospitality, he looked at Ms. O'Dowd and said: "Bullshit." He grabbed me by the arm, dragged me into the mess tent and served up a mug of steaming tea and a plate of biscuits.

Following what Owen described as his "blood-chilling exchange" with Woodall in Pheriche, the editor was "persuaded . . . that the atmosphere of the expedition was deranged and that the *Sunday Times* staffers, Ken Vernon and Richard Shorey, might be in danger of their lives." Owen therefore instructed Vernon and Shorey to return to South Africa, and the newspaper published a statement declaring that it had rescinded its sponsorship of the expedition.

Because Woodall had already received the newspaper's money, however, this act was purely symbolic and had almost no impact on his actions on the mountain. Indeed, Woodall refused to relinquish leadership of the expedition or make any kind of compromise, even after he received a letter from President Mandela appealing for reconciliation as a matter of national interest. Woodall stubbornly insisted that the Everest climb would proceed as planned, with him firmly at the helm.

Back in Cape Town after the expedition fell apart, February described his disappointment. "Maybe I was naive," he said in a halting voice freighted with emotion. "But I hated growing up under apartheid. Climbing Everest with Andrew and the others would have been a great symbol to show the old ways had broken down. Woodall had no interest in the birth of a new South Africa. He took the dreams of the entire nation and utilized them for his own selfish purposes. Deciding to leave the expedition was the hardest decision of my life."

With the departure of February, Hackland, and de Klerk, none of the climbers remaining on the team (aside from the Frenchman Renard, who had joined the expedition merely to be listed on the permit and who climbed independently from the others, with his own Sherpas) had more than minimal alpine experience; at least two of them, says de Klerk, "didn't even know how to put their crampons on."

The solo Norwegian, the Taiwanese, and especially the South Africans were frequent topics of discussion in Hall's mess tent. "With so many incompetent people on the mountain," Rob said with a frown one evening in late April, "I think it's pretty unlikely that we'll get through this season without something bad happening up high."

Chapter Eight

CAMP ONE APRIL 16, 1996 19,500 FEET

I doubt if anyone would claim to enjoy life at high altitudes—enjoy, that is, in the ordinary sense of the word. There is a certain grim satisfaction to be derived from struggling upwards, however slowly; but the bulk of one's time is necessarily spent in the extreme squalor of a high camp, when even this solace is lacking. Smoking is impossible; eating tends to make one vomit; the necessity of reducing weight to a bare minimum forbids the importation of literature beyond that supplied by the labels on tins of food; sardine oil, condensed milk and treacle spill themselves all over the place; except for the briefest moments, during which one is not usually in a mood for aesthetic enjoyment, there is nothing to look at but the bleak confusion inside the tent and the scaly, bearded countenance of one's companion—fortunately the noise of the wind usually drowns out his stuffy breathing; worst of all is the feeling of complete helplessness and inability to deal with any emergency that might arise. I used to try to console myself with the thought that a year ago I would have been thrilled by the very idea of taking part in our present adventure, a prospect that had then seemed like an impossible dream; but altitude has the same effect on the mind as upon the body, one's intellect becomes dull and unresponsive, and my only desire was to finish the wretched job and to get down to a more reasonable clime.

Eric Shipton
Upon That Mountain

Just before dawn on Tuesday, April 16, after resting for two days at Base Camp, we headed up into the Icefall to begin our second acclimatization excursion. As I nervously threaded my way through the frozen, groaning disorder, I noticed that my breathing wasn't quite as labored as it had been during our first trip up the glacier; already my body was starting to adapt to the altitude. My dread of getting crushed by a falling serac, however, was at least as great as before.

I'd hoped that the giant, overhanging tower at 19,000 feet—christened the Mousetrap by some wag on Fischer's team—had toppled by now, but it was still precariously upright, leaning even farther over. Again I redlined my cardiovascular output rushing to ascend from its threatening shadow, and again dropped to my knees when I arrived on the serac's summit, gasping for air and trembling from the excess of adrenaline fizzing through my veins.

Unlike our first acclimatization sally, during which we stayed at Camp One for less than an hour before returning to Base Camp, Rob intended for us to spend Tuesday and Wednesday nights at Camp One and then continue up to Camp Two for three additional nights before heading down.

At 9:00 A.M., when I reached the Camp One site, Ang Dorje,* our climbing sirdar,† was excavating platforms for our tents in the hard-frozen snow slope. Twenty-nine years old, he is a slender man with delicate features, a shy, moody temperament, and astounding physical strength. While waiting for my teammates to arrive, I picked up a spare shovel and started helping him dig. Within minutes I was exhausted from the effort and had to sit down to rest, prompting a belly laugh from the Sherpa. "Are you not feeling good, Jon?" he mocked. "This is only Camp One, six thousand meters. The air here is still very thick."

Ang Dorje hailed from Pangboche, an aggregation of stone-walled houses and terraced potato fields clinging to a rugged hillside at 13,000 feet. His father is a respected climbing Sherpa who taught

* He should not be confused with the Sherpa on the South African team who has the same name. Ang Dorje—like Pemba, Lhakpa, Ang Tshering, Ngawang, Dawa, Nima, and Pasang—is a very common Sherpa appellation; the fact that each of these names was shared by two or more Sherpas on Everest in 1996 was a source of occasional confusion.

† The sirdar is the head Sherpa. Hall's team had a Base Camp sirdar, named Ang Tshering, who was in charge of all the Sherpas employed by the expedition; Ang Dorje, the climbing sirdar, answered to Ang Tshering but supervised the climbing Sherpas while they were on the mountain above Base Camp.

him the basics of mountaineering at an early age so that the boy would have marketable skills. By the time Ang Dorje was in his teens, his father had gone blind from cataracts, and Ang Dorje was pulled from school to earn money for the family.

In 1984 he was working as a cook boy for a group of Western trekkers when he caught the attention of a Canadian couple, Marion Boyd and Graem Nelson. According to Boyd, "I was missing my kids, and as I grew to know Ang Dorje he reminded me of my eldest son. Ang Dorje was bright, interested, keen to learn, and conscientious almost to a fault. He was carrying a huge load and he had nose bleeds every day at high altitude. I was intrigued."

After seeking the approval of Ang Dorje's mother, Boyd and Nelson started supporting the young Sherpa financially so that he could return to school. "I will never forget his entry exam [to gain admission to the regional primary school in Khumjung, built by Sir Edmund Hillary]. He was very small in stature and prepubescent. We were crammed into a small room with the headmaster and four teachers. Ang Dorje stood in the middle with his knees quaking as he tried to resurrect the bit of formal learning he had for this oral exam. We all sweated blood . . . but he was accepted with the proviso that he would have to sit with the little kids in the first grades."

Ang Dorje became an able student and achieved the equivalent of an eighth-grade education before quitting to go back to work in the mountaineering and trekking industry. Boyd and Nelson, who returned to the Khumbu several times, witnessed his maturation. "With access for the first time to a good diet, he began to grow tall and strong," recalls Boyd. "He told us with great excitement when he learned to swim in a pool in Kathmandu. At age twenty-five or so he learned to ride a bicycle and took a brief fancy to the music of Madonna. We knew he was really grown up when he presented us with his first gift, a carefully selected Tibetan carpet. He wanted to be a giver, not a taker."

As Ang Dorje's reputation for being a strong and resourceful climber spread among Western climbers, he was promoted to the role of sirdar, and in 1992 he went to work for Rob Hall on Everest; by the launch of Hall's 1996 expedition, Ang Dorje had climbed the peak three times. With respect and obvious affection, Hall referred to him as "my main man" and mentioned several times that he considered Ang Dorje's role crucial to the success of our expedition.

The sun was bright when the last of my teammates pulled into Camp One, but by noon a scum of high cirrus had blown in from the south; by three o'clock dense clouds swirled above the glacier and snow pelted the tents with a furious clamor. It stormed through the night; in the morning when I crawled out of the shelter I shared with Doug, more than a foot of fresh snow blanketed the glacier. Dozens of avalanches rumbled down the steep walls above, but our camp was safely beyond their reach.

At first light on Thursday, April 18, by which time the sky had cleared, we gathered our belongings and embarked for Camp Two, four miles and 1,700 vertical feet above. The route took us up the gently sloping floor of the Western Cwm, the highest box canyon on earth, a horseshoe-shaped defile gouged from the heart of the Everest massif by the Khumbu Glacier. The 25,790-foot ramparts of Nuptse defined the right wall of the Cwm, Everest's massive Southwest Face formed the left wall, and the broad frozen thrust of the Lhotse Face loomed above its head.

The temperature had been brutally cold when we set out from Camp One, turning my hands into stiff, aching claws, but as the first of the sun's rays struck the glacier, the ice-spackled walls of the Cwm collected and amplified the radiant heat like a huge solar oven. Suddenly I was sweltering, and I feared the onset of another migraine-intensity headache like the one that had hammered me at Base Camp, so I stripped down to my long underwear and stuffed a fistful of snow beneath my baseball cap. For the next three hours I slogged steadily up the glacier, pausing only to drink from my water bottle and replenish the snow supply in my hat as it melted into my matted hair.

At 21,000 feet, dizzy from the heat, I came upon a large object wrapped in blue plastic sheeting beside the trail. It took my altitude-impaired gray matter a minute or two to comprehend that the object was a human body. Shocked and disturbed, I stared at it for several minutes. That night when I asked Rob about it he said he wasn't certain, but he thought the victim was a Sherpa who'd died three years earlier.

At 21,300 feet, Camp Two consisted of some 120 tents scattered across the bare rocks of the lateral moraine along the glacier's edge. The altitude here manifested itself as a malicious force, making me feel as though I were afflicted with a raging red-wine hangover. Too miserable to eat or even read, for the next two days I mostly lay in my tent with my head in my hands, trying to exert myself as little as possible. Feeling slightly better on Saturday, I climbed a thousand feet above camp to get some exercise and accelerate my acclimatization, and there, at the head of the Cwm, fifty yards off the main track, I came upon another body in the snow, or more accurately the lower half of a body. The style of the clothing and the vintage leather boots suggested that the victim was European and that the corpse had lain on the mountain at least ten or fifteen years.

The first body had left me badly shaken for several hours; the shock of encountering the second wore off almost immediately. Few of the climbers trudging by had given either corpse more than a passing glance. It was as if there were an unspoken agreement on the mountain to pretend that these desiccated remains weren't real—as if none of us dared to acknowledge what was at stake here.

| | |

On Monday, April 22, a day after returning from Camp Two to Base Camp, Andy Harris and I hiked over to the South African compound to meet their team and try to gain some insight into why they had become such pariahs. Fifteen minutes down the glacier from our tents, their camp was clustered atop a hump of glacial debris. The national flags of Nepal and South Africa, along with banners from Kodak, Apple Computer, and other sponsors, flew from a pair of tall aluminum flagpoles. Andy stuck his head inside the door of their mess tent, flashed his most winning smile, and inquired, "Hi, there. Is anybody home?"

It turned out that Ian Woodall, Cathy O'Dowd, and Bruce Herrod were in the Icefall, making their way down from Camp Two, but

Woodall's girlfriend, Alexandrine Gaudin, was present, as was his brother, Philip. Also in the mess tent was an effervescent young woman who introduced herself as Deshun Deysel and immediately invited Andy and me in for tea. The three teammates seemed unconcerned by the reports of Ian's reprehensible behavior and rumors predicting their expedition's imminent disintegration.

"I went ice climbing for the first time the other day," Deysel offered enthusiastically, gesturing toward a nearby serac where climbers from several expeditions had been practicing their ice craft. "I thought it was quite exciting. I hope to go up the Icefall in a few days." I'd intended to ask her about Ian's dishonesty and how she felt when she learned she'd been left off the Everest permit, but she was so cheerful and ingenuous that I didn't have the stomach for it. After chatting for twenty minutes Andy extended an invitation to their whole team, including Ian, "to come 'round our camp for a wee snort" later that evening.

I arrived back at our own camp to find Rob, Dr. Caroline Mackenzie, and Scott Fischer's doctor, Ingrid Hunt, engaged in a tense radio conversation with someone higher on the mountain. Earlier in the day, Fischer was descending from Camp Two to Base Camp when he encountered one of his Sherpas, Ngawang Topche, sitting on the glacier at 21,000 feet. A veteran thirty-eight-year-old climber from the Rolwaling Valley, gap-toothed and sweet-natured, Ngawang had been hauling loads and performing other duties above Base Camp for three days, but his Sherpa cohorts complained that he had been sitting around a lot and not doing his share of the work.

When Fischer questioned Ngawang, he admitted that he'd been feeling weak, groggy, and short of breath for more than two days, so Fischer directed him to descend to Base Camp immediately. But there is an element of machismo in the Sherpa culture that makes many men extremely reluctant to acknowledge physical infirmities. Sherpas aren't supposed to get altitude illness, especially those from Rolwaling, a region famous for its powerful climbers. Those who do become sick and openly acknowledge it, moreover, will often be blacklisted from future employment on expeditions. Thus it came to pass that

Ngawang ignored Scott's instructions and, instead of going down, went up to Camp Two to spend the night.

By the time he arrived at the tents late that afternoon Ngawang was delirious, stumbling like a drunk, and coughing up pink, blood-laced froth: symptoms indicating an advanced case of High Altitude Pulmonary Edema, or HAPE—a mysterious, potentially lethal illness typically brought on by climbing too high, too fast in which the lungs fill with fluid.* The only real cure for HAPE is rapid descent; if the victim remains at high altitude very long, death is the most likely outcome.

Unlike Hall, who insisted that our group stay together while climbing above Base Camp, under the close watch of the guides, Fischer believed in giving his clients free rein to go up and down the mountain independently during the acclimatization period. As a consequence, when it was recognized that Ngawang was seriously ill at Camp Two, four of Fischer's clients were present—Dale Kruse, Pete Schoening, Klev Schoening, and Tim Madsen—but no guides. Responsibility for initiating Ngawang's rescue thus fell to Klev Schoening and Madsen—the latter a thirty-three-year-old ski patrolman from Aspen, Colorado, who'd never been higher than 14,000 feet before this expedition, which he had been persuaded to join by his girlfriend, Himalayan veteran Charlotte Fox.

When I walked into Hall's mess tent, Dr. Mackenzie was on the radio telling somebody at Camp Two, "give Ngawang acetazolamide, dexamethasone, and ten milligrams of sublingual nifedipine. . . . Yes, I know the risk. Give it to him anyway. . . . I'm telling you, the danger that he will die from HAPE before we can get him down is much, much greater than the danger that the nifedipine will reduce his blood pressure to a dangerous level. Please, trust me on this! Just give him the medication! Quickly!"

None of the drugs seemed to help, however, nor did giving Ngawang supplemental oxygen or placing him inside a Gamow Bag—

* The root of the problem is believed to be a paucity of oxygen, compounded by high pressure in the pulmonary arteries, causing the arteries to leak fluid into the lungs.

an inflatable plastic chamber about the size of a coffin in which the atmospheric pressure is increased to simulate a lower altitude. With daylight waning, Schoening and Madsen therefore began dragging Ngawang laboriously down the mountain, using the deflated Gamow Bag as a makeshift toboggan, while guide Neal Beidleman and a team of Sherpas climbed as quickly as they could from Base Camp to meet them.

Beidleman reached Ngawang at sunset near the top of the Icefall and took over the rescue, allowing Schoening and Madsen to return to Camp Two to continue their acclimatization. The sick Sherpa had so much fluid in his lungs, Beidleman recalled, "that when he breathed it sounded like a straw slurping a milkshake from the bottom of a glass. Halfway down the Icefall, Ngawang took off his oxygen mask and reached inside to clear some snot from the intake valve. When he pulled his hand out I shined my headlamp on his glove and it was totally red, soaked with blood he'd been coughing up into the mask. Then I shined the light on his face and it was covered with blood, too.

"Ngawang's eyes met mine and I could see how frightened he was," Beidleman continued. "Thinking fast, I lied and told him not to worry, that the blood was from a cut on his lip. That calmed him a little, and we continued down." To keep Ngawang from having to exert himself, which would have exacerbated his edema, at several points during the descent, Beidleman picked up the ailing Sherpa and carried him on his back. It was after midnight by the time they arrived in Base Camp.

The next morning, Tuesday, Fischer considered calling for a helicopter to evacuate Ngawang from Base Camp to Kathmandu at an estimated cost of five to ten thousand dollars. But both Fischer and Dr. Hunt were confident that the Sherpa's condition would improve rapidly now that he was 3,700 feet lower than Camp Two—descending as little as 3,000 feet is typically enough to bring about complete recovery from HAPE. The upshot was that instead of being evacuated by air, Ngawang was escorted down the valley on foot. Immediately below Base Camp, however, he collapsed and had to be brought back up to the Mountain Madness encampment for treatment, where his condition continued to worsen throughout the day. When Hunt attempted to put him back in the Gamow Bag, Ngawang refused, arguing that he didn't have HAPE or any other form of altitude sickness. A radio call went out to the American doctor Jim Litch—an eminence in the specialized field of high-altitude medicine who was staffing the Himalayan Rescue Association clinic in Pheriche that spring—requesting that he hurry to Base Camp to assist in Ngawang's treatment.

Fischer, by this time, had embarked for Camp Two to bring down Tim Madsen, who had exhausted himself while hauling Ngawang down the Western Cwm and had subsequently come down with a mild case of HAPE himself. In Fischer's absence, Hunt consulted with the other doctors at Base Camp, but she was forced to make some critical decisions on her own, and, as one of her fellow physicians observed, "Ingrid was in way over her head."

A nonclimber in her midtwenties who'd just completed a residency in family practice, Hunt had done extensive volunteer medical-relief work in the foothills of eastern Nepal, but she had no previous experience in high-altitude medicine. She'd met Fischer by chance some months earlier in Kathmandu when he was finalizing his Everest permit, and he subsequently invited her to accompany his upcoming Everest expedition in the dual roles of team physician and Base Camp manager.

Although she expressed some ambivalence about the invitation in a letter to Fischer in January, Hunt ultimately accepted the unpaid job and arrived in Nepal at the end of March, eager to contribute to the expedition's success. The demands of simultaneously running Base Camp and meeting the medical needs of some twenty-five people proved to be more than she'd bargained for, however. (By comparison, Rob Hall paid two highly experienced, full-time staff members—team physician Caroline Mackenzie and Base Camp manager Helen Wilton—to do what Hunt did alone, without pay.) Compounding her difficulties, moreover, Hunt had trouble acclimatizing and suffered severe headaches and shortness of breath during most of her stay at Base Camp.

After Ngawang collapsed trying to walk down the valley Tuesday morning and was brought back up to Base Camp, he was not put back on oxygen, even though his condition continued to deteriorate, in part because he stubbornly kept insisting that he wasn't sick. At seven o'clock that evening, Dr. Litch arrived after running up from Pheriche and suggested rather emphatically that Hunt immediately start Ngawang on oxygen at maximal flow and then call for a helicopter.

By this time Ngawang was slipping in and out of consciousness and was having extreme difficulty breathing. A helicopter evacuation was requested for Wednesday morning, April 24, but clouds and snow squalls made a flight impossible, so Ngawang was loaded into a basket and, under Hunt's care, carried down the glacier to Pheriche on the backs of Sherpas.

That afternoon Hall's furrowed brow betrayed his concern. "Ngawang is in a bad way," he said. "He has one of the worst cases of pulmonary edema I've ever seen. They should have flown him out yesterday when they had a chance. If it had been one of Scott's clients who was this sick, instead of a Sherpa, I don't think he would have been treated so haphazardly. By the time they get Ngawang down to Pheriche it may be too late to save him."

When the sick Sherpa arrived at the HRA clinic on Wednesday evening after a twelve-hour journey from Base Camp to Pheriche, his condition continued to worsen, despite the fact that he was now at 14,000 feet (an elevation not substantially higher than the village where he'd spent most of his life), compelling Hunt to put him inside the pressurized Gamow Bag against his wishes. Unable to grasp the benefits of the inflatable chamber and terrified of it, Ngawang asked that a Buddhist lama be summoned, and before consenting to being zipped into its claustrophobic interior, he requested that prayer books be placed in the bag with him.

For the Gamow Bag to function properly an attendant has to continuously inject fresh air into the chamber with a foot pump. By Wednesday night, Hunt was exhausted from caring for Ngawang virtually nonstop for the previous forty-eight hours, so she turned over responsibility for pumping the chamber to several of Ngawang's Sherpa friends. While she was dozing, one of these Sherpas noticed through the bag's plastic window that Ngawang was frothing at the mouth and had apparently stopped breathing.

Awakened with this news, Hunt immediately tore open the bag, commenced cardiopulmonary resuscitation, and summoned Dr. Larry Silver, one of the volunteers working at the HRA clinic. After Silver inserted a tube down Ngawang's trachea and began forcing air into his lungs with a rubber "ambu bag"—a manual pump—Ngawang began breathing again, but only after a period of at least four or five minutes when no oxygen was reaching his brain.

Two days later, on Friday, April 26, the weather finally improved enough to permit a helicopter evacuation, and Ngawang was flown to a hospital in Kathmandu, but doctors there announced that he'd suffered grave damage to his brain. Ngawang was now little more than a vegetable. Over the weeks that followed he languished in the hospital, staring blankly at the ceiling, arms curled tightly at his sides, muscles atrophying, his weight dropping below eighty pounds. By mid-June he would be dead, leaving behind a wife and four daughters in Rolwaling.

| | |

Oddly, most climbers on Everest knew less about Ngawang's plight than tens of thousands of people who were nowhere near the mountain. The information warp was due to the Internet, and to those of us at Base Camp it was nothing less than surreal. A teammate might call home on a satellite phone, for instance, and learn what the South Africans were doing at Camp Two from a spouse in New Zealand or Michigan who'd been surfing the World Wide Web.

At least five Internet sites were posting dispatches* from correspondents at Everest Base Camp. The South African team maintained a website, as did Mal Duff's International Commercial

* Despite considerable hoopla about "direct, interactive links between the slopes of Mount Everest and the World Wide Web," technological limitations prevented direct hookups from Base Camp to the Internet. Instead, correspondents filed their reports by voice or fax via satellite phone, and those reports were typed into computers for dissemination on the Web by editors in New York, Boston, and Seattle. E-mail was received in Kathmandu, printed out, and the hard copy was transported by yak to Base Camp. Likewise, all photos that ran on the Web had first been sent by yak and then air courier to New York for transmission. Internet chat sessions were done via satellite phone and a typist in New York.

Expedition. *Nova,* the PBS television show, produced an elaborate and very informative website featuring daily updates from Liesl Clark and the eminent Everest historian Audrey Salkeld, who were members of the MacGillivray Freeman IMAX expedition. (Headed by the award-winning filmmaker and expert climber David Breashears, who'd guided Dick Bass up Everest in 1985, the IMAX team was shooting a $5.5 million giant-screen movie about climbing the mountain.) Scott Fischer's expedition had no less than two correspondents filing online dispatches for a pair of competing websites.

Jane Bromet, who phoned in daily reports for Outside Online,* was one of the correspondents on Fischer's team, but she wasn't a client and didn't have permission to climb higher than Base Camp. The other Internet correspondent on Fischer's expedition, however, was a client who intended to go all the way to the summit and file daily dispatches for NBC Interactive Media en route. Her name was Sandy Hill Pittman, and nobody on the mountain cut a higher profile or generated as much gossip.

Pittman, a millionaire socialite-cum-climber, was back for her third attempt on Everest. This year she was more determined than ever to reach the top and thereby complete her much publicized crusade to climb the Seven Summits.

In 1993 Pittman joined a guided expedition attempting the South Col and Southeast Ridge route, and she caused a minor stir by showing up at Base Camp with her nine-year-old son, Bo, along with a nanny to look after him. Pittman experienced a number of problems, however, and reached only 24,000 feet before turning around.

She was back on Everest in 1994 after raising more than a quarter of a million dollars from corporate sponsors to secure the talents of

* Several magazines and newspapers have erroneously reported that I was a correspondent for Outside Online. The confusion stemmed from the fact that Jane Bromet interviewed me at Base Camp and posted a transcript of the interview on the Outside Online website. I was not, however, affiliated with Outside Online in any capacity. I had gone to Everest on assignment for *Outside* magazine, an independent entity (based in Santa Fe, New Mexico) that works in loose partnership with Outside Online (based in the Seattle area) to publish a version of the magazine on the Internet. But *Outside* magazine and Outside Online are autonomous to such a degree that I didn't even know Outside Online had sent a correspondent to Everest until I arrived at Base Camp.

four of the finest alpinists in North America: Breashears (who was under contract to film the expedition for NBC television), Steve Swenson, Barry Blanchard, and Alex Lowe. Lowe—arguably the world's pre-eminent all-around climber—was hired to be Sandy's personal guide, a job for which he was paid a substantial sum. In advance of Pittman, the four men strung ropes partway up the Kangshung Face, an extremely difficult and hazardous wall on the Tibetan side of the mountain. With a great deal of assistance from Lowe, Pittman ascended the fixed ropes to 22,000 feet, but once again she was forced to surrender her attempt before the summit; this time the problem was dangerously unstable snow conditions that forced the whole team to abandon the mountain.

Until I bumped into her at Gorak Shep during the trek to Base Camp, I'd never met Pittman face-to-face, although I'd been hearing about her for years. In 1992, *Men's Journal* assigned me to write an article about riding a Harley-Davidson motorcycle from New York to San Francisco in the company of Jann Wenner—the legendary, exceedingly rich publisher of *Rolling Stone, Men's Journal,* and *Us*—and several of his wealthy friends, including Rocky Hill, Pittman's brother and her husband, Bob Pittman, the co-founder of MTV.

The ear-splitting, chrome-encrusted Hog that Jann loaned me was a thrilling ride, and my high-rolling companions were friendly enough. But I had precious little in common with any of them, and there was no forgetting that I had been brought along as Jann's hired help. Over dinner Bob and Jann and Rocky compared the various aircraft they owned (Jann recommended a Gulfstream IV the next time I was in the market for a personal jet), discussed their country estates, and talked about Sandy—who happened to be climbing Mount McKinley at the time. "Hey," Bob suggested when he learned that I, too, was a climber, "you and Sandy ought to get together and go climb a mountain." Now, four years later, we were.

At five foot eleven, Sandy Pittman stood two inches taller than me. Her tomboyishly short hair looked expertly coiffed, even here at 17,000 feet. Ebullient and direct, she'd grown up in northern California, where her father had introduced her to camping, hiking, and skiing as a young girl. Delighting in the freedoms and pleasures of the hills, she continued to dabble in outdoor pursuits through her college years and beyond, although the frequency of her visits to the mountains diminished sharply after she moved to New York in the mid-1970s in the aftermath of a failed first marriage.

In Manhattan Pittman worked variously as a buyer at Bonwit Teller, a merchandising editor at *Mademoiselle,* and a beauty editor at a magazine called *Bride's,* then in 1979 married Bob Pittman. An indefatigable seeker of public attention, Sandy made her name and picture regular fare in New York society columns. She hobnobbed with Blaine Trump, Tom and Meredith Brokaw, Isaac Mizrahi, Martha Stewart. In order to commute more efficiently between their opulent Connecticut manor and an art-filled apartment on Central Park West staffed with uniformed servants, she and her husband bought a helicopter and learned to fly it. In 1990 Sandy and Bob Pittman were featured on the cover of *New York* magazine as "The Couple of the Minute."

Soon thereafter Sandy began her expensive, widely trumpeted campaign to become the first American woman to climb the Seven Summits. The last—Everest—proved elusive, however, and in March 1994 Pittman lost the race to a forty-seven-year-old Alaskan mountaineer and midwife named Dolly Lefever. She continued her dogged pursuit of Everest just the same.

As Beck Weathers observed one night at Base Camp, "when Sandy goes to climb a mountain, she doesn't do it exactly like you and me." In 1993 Beck had been in Antarctica making a guided ascent of Vinson Massif at the same time Pittman was climbing the mountain with a different guided group, and he recalled with a chuckle that "she brought this humongous duffel bag full of gourmet food that took about four people to even lift. She also brought a portable television and video player so she could watch movies in her tent. I mean, hey, you've got to hand it to Sandy: there aren't too many people who climb mountains in that kind of high style." Beck reported that Pittman had generously shared the swag she'd brought with the other climbers and that "she was pleasant and interesting to be around."

For her assault on Everest in 1996, Pittman once again assembled the sort of kit not commonly seen in climbers' encampments. The day before departing for Nepal, in one of her first Web postings for NBC Interactive Media, she gushed,

> All my personal stuff is packed. . . . It looks like I'll have as much computer and electronic equipment as I will have climbing gear. . . . Two IBM laptops, a video camera, three 35mm cameras, one Kodak digital camera, two tape recorders, a CD-ROM player, a printer, and enough (I hope) solar panels and batteries to power the whole project. . . . I wouldn't dream of leaving town without an ample supply of Dean & DeLuca's Near East blend and my espresso maker. Since we'll be on Everest on Easter, I brought four wrapped chocolate eggs. An Easter egg hunt at 18,000 feet? We'll see!

That night, the society columnist Billy Norwich hosted a farewell party for Pittman at Nell's in downtown Manhattan. The guest list included Bianca Jagger and Calvin Klein. Fond of costumes, Sandy appeared wearing a high-altitude climbing suit over her evening dress, complemented by mountaineering boots, crampons, ice ax, and a bandolier of carabiners.

Upon arrival in the Himalaya, Pittman appeared to adhere as closely as possible to the proprieties of high society. During the trek to Base Camp, a young Sherpa named Pemba rolled up her sleeping bag every morning and packed her rucksack for her. When she reached the foot of Everest with the rest of Fischer's group in early April, her pile of luggage included stacks of press clippings about herself to hand out to the other denizens of Base Camp. Within a few days Sherpa runners began to arrive on a regular basis with packages for Pittman, shipped to Base Camp via DHL Worldwide Express; they included the latest issues of *Vogue, Vanity Fair, People, Allure.* The Sherpas were fascinated by the lingerie ads and thought the perfume scent-strips were a hoot.

Scott Fischer's team was a congenial and cohesive group; most of Pittman's teammates took her idiosyncrasies in stride and seemed to have little trouble accepting her into their midst. "Sandy could be exhausting to be around, because she needed to be the center of attention and was always yapping away about herself," remembers Jane Bromet. "But she wasn't a negative person. She didn't bring down the mood of the group. She was energetic and upbeat almost every day."

Nevertheless, several accomplished alpinists not on her team regarded Pittman as a grandstanding dilettante. Following her unsuccessful 1994 attempt on Everest's Kangshung Face, a television commercial for Vaseline Intensive Care (the expedition's primary sponsor) was loudly derided by knowledgeable mountaineers because it advertised Pittman as a "world-class climber." But Pittman never overtly made such a claim herself; indeed, she emphasized in an article for *Men's Journal* that she wanted Breashears, Lowe, Swenson, and Blanchard "to understand that I didn't confuse my avid-hobbyist abilities with their world-class skill."

Her eminent companions on the 1994 attempt said nothing disparaging about Pittman, at least not in public. After that expedition, in fact, Breashears became a close friend of hers, and Swenson repeatedly defended Pittman against her critics. "Look," Swenson had explained to me at a social gathering in Seattle shortly after they'd both returned from Everest, "maybe Sandy's not a great climber, but on the Kangshung Face she recognized her limitations. Yes, it's true that Alex and Barry and David and I did all the leading and fixed all the ropes, but she contributed to the effort in her own way by having a positive attitude, by raising money, and by dealing with the media."

Pittman did not lack for detractors, however. A great many people were offended by her ostentatious displays of wealth, and by the shameless way she chased the limelight. As Joanne Kaufman reported in the *Wall Street Journal,*

> Ms. Pittman was known in certain elevated circles more as a social climber than mountain climber. She and Mr. Pittman were habitués of all the correct soirees and benefits and staples of all the right gossip columns. "Many coattails were wrinkled by Sandy Pittman latching on to them," says a former business associate of Mr. Pittman who insisted on anonymity. "She's interested in publicity. If she had to do it anonymously I don't think she'd be climbing mountains."

Fairly or unfairly, to her derogators Pittman epitomized all that was reprehensible about Dick Bass's popularization of the Seven Summits and the ensuing debasement of the world's highest mountain. But insulated by her money, a staff of paid attendants, and unwavering self-absorption, Pittman was heedless of the resentment and scorn she inspired in others; she remained as oblivious as Jane Austen's Emma.

Chapter Nine

CAMP TWO APRIL 28, 1996 21,300 FEET

We tell ourselves stories in order to live. . . . We look for the sermon in the suicide, for the social or moral lesson in the murder of five. We interpret what we see, select the most workable of the multiple choices. We live entirely, especially if we are writers, by the imposition of a narrative line upon disparate images, by the "ideas" with which we have learned to freeze the shifting phantasmagoria which is our actual experience.

Joan Didion
The White Album

I was already awake at 4:00 A.M. when the alarm on my wristwatch began to beep; I'd been awake most of the night, struggling for breath in the meager air. And now it was time to commence the dreaded ritual of emerging from the warmth of my goose-down cocoon into the withering cold of 21,300 feet. Two days earlier—on Friday, April 26—we'd humped all the way from Base Camp to Camp Two in one long day to begin our third and final acclimatization sortie in preparation for the summit push. This morning, according to Rob's grand plan, we would climb from Camp Two to Camp Three and spend a night at 24,000 feet.

Rob had told us to be ready to leave at 4:45 sharp—forty-five minutes hence—which allowed barely enough time to dress, force down a candy bar and some tea, and strap on my crampons. Shining my headlamp on a dime-store thermometer clipped to the parka I'd been using as a pillow, I saw that the temperature inside the cramped, two-person tent was seven degrees below zero Fahrenheit. "Doug!" I yelled at the lump burrowed in the sleeping bag beside me. "Time to get rolling, Slick. You awake over there?"

"Awake?" he rasped in a weary voice. "What makes you think I ever went to sleep? I feel like shit. I think something's wrong with my throat. Man, I'm gettin' too old for this stuff."

During the night, our fetid exhalations had condensed on the tent fabric to form a fragile, interior sheath of hoarfrost; as I sat up and began rooting around in the dark for my clothing, it was impossible not to brush against the low nylon walls, and every time I did so it instigated a blizzard inside the tent, covering everything with ice crystals. Shivering hard, I zipped my body into three layers of fuzzy polypropylene pile underwear and an outer shell of windproof nylon, then pulled my clunky plastic boots on. Yanking the laces tight made me wince in pain; for the past two weeks the condition of my cracked, bleeding fingertips had been steadily deteriorating in the cold air.

I tramped out of camp by headlamp behind Rob and Frank, wending between ice towers and piles of rock rubble to reach the main body of the glacier. For the next two hours we ascended an incline pitched as gently as a beginner's ski slope, eventually arriving at the bergschrund that delineated the Khumbu Glacier's upper end. Immediately above rose the Lhotse Face, a vast, tilted sea of ice that gleamed like dirty chrome in the dawn's slanting light. Snaking down the frozen expanse as if suspended from heaven, a single strand of nine-millimeter rope beckoned like Jack's beanstalk. I picked up the bottom end of it, attached my jumar* to the slightly frayed line, and began to climb.

I'd been uncomfortably cold since leaving camp, having underdressed in anticipation of the solar-oven effect that had occurred every other morning when the sun hit the Western Cwm. But on this morning the temperature was held in check by a biting wind that gusted down from the upper mountain, creating a windchill that dipped to perhaps forty below zero. I had an extra pile sweater in my backpack, but to put it on I would first have to remove my gloves, pack, and wind jacket while dangling from the fixed rope. Worrying that I was likely to drop something, I decided to wait until I reached a part of the face that was less steep, where I could stand in balance

* A jumar (also known as a mechanical ascender) is a wallet-sized device that grips the rope by means of a metal cam. The cam allows the jumar to slide upward without hindrance, but it pinches the rope securely when the device is weighted. Essentially ratcheting himself upward, a climber thereby ascends the rope.

without hanging from the rope. So I continued climbing, and as I did so I grew colder and colder.

The wind kicked up huge swirling waves of powder snow that washed down the mountain like breaking surf, plastering my clothing with frost. A carapace of ice formed over my goggles, making it difficult to see. I began to lose feeling in my feet. My fingers turned to wood. It seemed increasingly unsafe to keep going up in these conditions. I was at the head of the line, at 23,000 feet, fifteen minutes in front of guide Mike Groom; I decided to wait for him and talk things over. But just before he reached me, Rob's voice barked over the radio Mike carried inside his jacket, and he stopped climbing to answer the call. "Rob wants everybody to go down!" he declared, shouting to make himself heard above the wind. "We're getting out of here!"

It was noon by the time we arrived back at Camp Two and took stock of the damage. I was tired but otherwise fine. John Taske, the Australian doctor, had some minor frostnip on the tips of his fingers. Doug, on the other hand, had suffered some serious harm. When he removed his boots he discovered incipient frostbite on several toes. On Everest in 1995 he'd frostbitten his feet badly enough to lose some tissue from a big toe and permanently impair his circulation, making him particularly susceptible to cold; now this additional frostbite would make him yet more vulnerable to the cruel conditions of the upper mountain.

Even worse, however, was the injury to Doug's respiratory tract. Less than two weeks before departing for Nepal he had undergone minor throat surgery, leaving his trachea in an extremely sensitive condition. This morning, gasping lungfuls of caustic, snow-filled air, he had apparently frozen his larynx. "I'm fucked," Doug croaked in a barely audible whisper, looking crushed. "I can't even talk. The climb is over for me."

"Don't write yourself off just yet, Douglas," Rob offered. "Wait and see how you feel in a couple of days. You're a tough bastard. I think you've still got a good shot at the top once you recover." Unconvinced, Doug retreated to our tent and pulled his sleeping bag over his head. It was rough seeing him so discouraged. He'd become a good friend, unstintingly sharing the wisdom he'd gained during his failed attempt on the peak in 1995. Around my neck I wore a Xi-stone—a sacred Buddhist amulet blessed by the lama from the Pangboche monastery—that Doug had given me early on in the expedition. I wanted him to reach the summit almost as badly as I wanted to reach it myself.

An air of shock and mild depression hovered over the camp for the remainder of the day. Even without unleashing the worst it could dish out, the mountain had sent us scurrying for safety. And it wasn't just our team that was chastened and doubtful. Morale seemed to be at a low ebb for several of the expeditions at Camp Two.

The bad humor was most apparent in the bickering that broke out between Hall and the leaders of the Taiwanese and South African teams over sharing responsibility for stringing more than a mile of rope that was needed to safeguard the route up the Lhotse Face. By late April, a line of ropes had already been fixed between the head of the Cwm and Camp Three, halfway up the face. To complete the job, Hall, Fischer, Ian Woodall, Makalu Gau, and Todd Burleson (the American leader of the Alpine Ascents guided expedition) had agreed that on April 26 one or two members from each team would join forces and put ropes up the remainder of the face, the passage between Camp Three and 26,000-foot Camp Four. But it hadn't happened as planned.

When Ang Dorje and Lhakpa Chhiri from Hall's team, guide Anatoli Boukreev from Fischer's team, and one Sherpa from Burleson's team departed Camp Two on the morning of April 26, the Sherpas who were supposed to join them from the South African and Taiwanese teams stayed in their sleeping bags and refused to cooperate. That afternoon, when Hall arrived at Camp Two and learned of this, he immediately made some radio calls to find out why the plan had broken down. Kami Dorje Sherpa, the sirdar for the Taiwanese team, apologized profusely and promised to make amends. But when Hall raised Woodall on the radio, the impenitent South African–expedition leader responded with a barrage of obscenities and insults.

"Let's keep it civil, mate," Hall implored. "I thought we had an agreement." Woodall replied that his Sherpas stayed in their tents only because nobody came around to wake them up and tell them their assistance was needed. Hall shot back that Ang Dorje had in fact tried repeatedly to rouse them but they had ignored his entreaties.

At that point Woodall declared, "Either you're a bloody liar or your Sherpa is." Then he threatened to send over a couple of Sherpas from his team to "sort out" Ang Dorje with their fists.

Two days after this unpleasant exchange, the ill will between our team and the South Africans remained high. And contributing to the sour mood at Camp Two were disturbing snippets of news we received about Ngawang Topche's worsening condition. As he continued to grow sicker and sicker even at low altitude, the doctors postulated that his illness was perhaps not simple HAPE but rather HAPE complicated by tuberculosis or some other pre-existing pulmonary condition. The Sherpas, however, had a different diagnosis: they believed that one of the climbers on Fischer's team had angered Everest—Sagarmatha, goddess of the sky—and the deity had taken her revenge on Ngawang.

The climber in question had struck up a relationship with a member of an expedition attempting Lhotse. Because privacy is nonexistent in the tenementlike confines of Base Camp, the amorous assignations that took place in this woman's tent were duly noted by other members of her team, especially the Sherpas, who sat outside pointing and snickering during the encounters. "[X] and [Y] are sauce-making, sauce-making," they would giggle, miming the sex act by pumping a finger into the open fist of the other hand.

But despite the Sherpas' laughter (to say nothing of their own notoriously libertine habits), they fundamentally disapproved of sex between unmarried couples on the divine flanks of Sagarmatha. Whenever the weather would turn nasty, one or another Sherpa was apt to point up at the clouds boiling heavenward and earnestly declare, "Somebody has been sauce-making. Make bad luck. Now storm is coming."

Sandy Pittman had noted this superstition in a diary entry from her 1994 expedition posted on the Internet in 1996:

April 29, 1994

Everest Base Camp (17,800 feet), The Kangshung Face, Tibet

. . . a mail runner had arrived that afternoon with letters from home for everyone *and* a girlie magazine which had been sent by a caring climber buddy back home as a joke. . . . Half of the Sherpa had taken it to a tent for closer inspection, while the others fretted over the disaster they were certain that any examination of it would bring. The goddess Chomolungma, they claimed, doesn't tolerate "jiggy jiggy"—*anything* unclean—on her sacred mountain.

Buddhism as it is practiced in the high reaches of the Khumbu has a distinctly animistic flavor: the Sherpas venerate a tangled mélange of deities and spirits who are said to inhabit the canyons, rivers, and peaks of the region. And paying proper homage to this ensemble of deities is considered crucially important to ensure safe passage through the treacherous landscape.

To appease Sagarmatha, this year—as every year—the Sherpas had built more than a dozen beautiful, meticulously constructed stone chortens at Base Camp, one for each expedition. A perfect cube five feet high, the altar in our camp was capped with a triumvirate of carefully selected pointed stones, above which rose a ten-foot wooden pole crowned with an elegant juniper bough. Five long chains of brightly colored prayer flags* were then strung radially from the pole above our tents to protect the camp from harm. Every morning before dawn our Base Camp sirdar—an avuncular, highly respected, forty-

* Prayer flags are printed with holy Buddhist invocations—most commonly *Om mani padme hum*—which are dispatched to God with each flap of the pennant. Often prayer flags bear the image of a winged horse in addition to written prayers; horses are sacred creatures in the Sherpa cosmology and are believed to carry the prayers heavenward with special speed. The Sherpa term for prayer flag is *lung ta,* which translates literally as "wind horse."

something Sherpa named Ang Tshering—would light sprigs of juniper incense and chant prayers at the chorten; before heading into the Icefall, Westerners and Sherpas alike would walk past the altar—keeping it always on the right—and through the sweet clouds of smoke to receive a blessing from Ang Tshering.

But for all the attention paid to such rituals, Buddhism as practiced by the Sherpas was a refreshingly supple and nondogmatic religion. To stay in Sagarmatha's good graces, for instance, no team was permitted to enter the Icefall for the first time without first undertaking an elaborate *puja,* or religious ceremony. But when the frail, wizened lama slated to preside over the puja had been unable to make the trip from his distant village on the appointed day, Ang Tshering declared that it would be O.K. for us to climb through the Icefall after all, because Sagarmatha understood that we intended to perform the puja very soon thereafter.

There seemed to be a similarly lax attitude concerning fornication on the slopes of Everest: even though they paid lip service to the prohibition, more than a few Sherpas made exceptions for their own behavior—in 1996, a romance even blossomed between a Sherpa and an American woman associated with the IMAX expedition. It therefore seemed strange that the Sherpas would blame Ngawang's illness on the extramarital encounters taking place in one of the Mountain Madness tents. But when I pointed out the inconsistency to Lopsang Jangbu Sherpa—Fischer's twenty-three-year-old climbing sirdar—he insisted that the real problem was not that one of Fischer's climbers had been "sauce-making" at Base Camp but rather that she continued to sleep with her paramour high on the mountain.

"Mount Everest is God—for me, for everybody," Lopsang solemnly mused ten weeks after the expedition. "Just husband and wife sleep together, is good. But when [X] and [Y] sleep together, is bad luck for my team. . . . So I tell to Scott: Please Scott, you are leader. Please tell to [X] not to sleep with boyfriend at Camp Two. Please. But Scott just laughs. The first day [X] and [Y] in tent, just after, Ngawang Topche is sick at Camp Two. So he is dead now."

Ngawang was Lopsang's uncle; the two men had been very close, and Lopsang had been in the rescue party that brought Ngawang down the Icefall on the night of April 22. Then, when Ngawang stopped breathing in Pheriche and had to be evacuated to Kathmandu, Lopsang rushed down from Base Camp (with Fischer's encouragement) in time to accompany his uncle on the helicopter flight. His brief trip to Kathmandu and speedy trek back to Base Camp left him quite fatigued and relatively poorly acclimatized—which didn't bode well for Fischer's team: Fischer relied on him at least as much as Hall relied on his climbing sirdar, Ang Dorje.

A number of very accomplished Himalayan mountaineers were in attendance on the Nepalese side of Everest in 1996—veterans such as Hall, Fischer, Breashears, Pete Schoening, Ang Dorje, Mike Groom, and Robert Schauer, an Austrian on the IMAX team. But four luminaries stood out even in this distinguished company—climbers who demonstrated such astonishing prowess above 26,000 feet that they were in a league of their own: Ed Viesturs, the American who was starring in the IMAX film; Anatoli Boukreev, a guide from Kazakhstan working for Fischer; Ang Babu Sherpa, who was employed by the South African expedition; and Lopsang.

Gregarious and good-looking, kind to a fault, Lopsang was extremely cocky yet hugely appealing. He was raised in the Rolwaling region, his parents' only child, and he neither smoked nor drank, which was unusual among Sherpas. He sported a gold incisor and had an easy laugh. Though he was small-boned and slight in stature, his flashy manner, appetite for hard work, and extraordinary athletic gifts earned him renown as the Deion Sanders of the Khumbu. Fischer told me that he thought Lopsang had the potential to be "the second coming of Reinhold Messner"—the famous Tyrolean alpinist who is far and away the greatest Himalayan climber of all time.

Lopsang first made a splash in 1993, at the age of twenty, when he was hired to carry loads for a joint Indian-Nepalese Everest team led by an Indian woman, Bachendri Pal, and largely composed of female climbers. Being the youngest member of the expedition, Lopsang was initially relegated to a supporting role, but his strength was so impressive that at the last minute he was assigned to a summit party, and on May 16 he reached the top without supplemental oxygen.

Five months after his Everest climb Lopsang summitted Cho Oyu with a Japanese team. In the spring of 1994 he worked for Fischer on the Sagarmatha Environmental Expedition and reached the top of Everest a second time, again without bottled oxygen. The following September he was attempting the West Ridge of Everest with a Norwegian team when he was hit by an avalanche; after tumbling 200 feet down the mountain he somehow managed to arrest his fall with an ice ax, thereby saving the lives of himself and two ropemates, but an uncle who wasn't tied to the others, Mingma Norbu Sherpa, was swept to his death. Although the loss rocked Lopsang hard, it didn't diminish his ardor for climbing.

In May 1995, he summitted Everest a third time without using gas, on this occasion as an employee of Hall's expedition, and three months later he climbed 26,400-foot Broad Peak, in Pakistan, while working for Fischer. By the time Lopsang went to Everest with Fischer in 1996, he'd only been climbing for three years, but in that span he'd participated in no fewer than ten Himalayan expeditions and had established a reputation as a high-altitude mountaineer of the highest caliber.

Climbing together on Everest in 1994, Fischer and Lopsang grew to admire each other immensely. Both men had boundless energy, irresistible charm, and a knack for making women swoon. Regarding Fischer as a mentor and a role model, Lopsang even started wearing his hair in a ponytail, as Fischer did. "Scott is very strong guy, I am very strong guy," Lopsang explained to me with characteristic immodesty. "We make good team. Scott does not pay me as well as Rob or Japanese, but I no need money; I am looking to future, and Scott is my future. He tell to me, 'Lopsang, my strong Sherpa! I making you famous!' . . . I think Scott has many big plans for me with Mountain Madness."

Chapter Ten

LHOTSE FACE APRIL 29, 1996 23,400 FEET

[T]he American public had no inherent national sympathy for mountain climbing, unlike the Alpine countries of Europe, or the British, who had invented the sport. In those countries there was something akin to understanding, and though the man in the street might on the whole consider it a reckless risk to life, he acknowledged that it was something that had to be done. There was no such acceptance in America.

Walt Unsworth
Everest

A day after our first attempt to reach Camp Three was thwarted by wind and barbarous cold, everybody on Hall's team except Doug (who stayed at Camp Two to let his injured larynx heal) made another try. A thousand feet up the immense slant of the Lhotse Face, I ascended a faded nylon rope that seemed to go on forever, and the higher I got, the more laggardly I moved. I slid my jumar up the fixed line with a gloved hand, rested my weight on the device to draw two burning, labored breaths; then I moved my left foot up and stamped the crampon into the ice, desperately sucked in another two lungfuls of air; planted my right foot next to my left, inhaled and exhaled from the bottom of my chest, inhaled and exhaled again; and slid the jumar up the rope one more time. I'd been exerting myself at full bore for the past three hours, and I expected to be at it for at least an hour more before taking a rest. In this agonizing fashion I climbed toward a cluster of tents reputed to be perched somewhere on the sheer face above, progressing in increments calibrated in inches.

People who don't climb mountains—the great majority of humankind, that is to say—tend to assume that the sport is a reckless, Dionysian pursuit of ever escalating thrills. But the notion that climbers are merely adrenaline junkies chasing a righteous fix is a fallacy, at least in the case of Everest. What I was doing up there had almost nothing in common with bungee jumping or skydiving or riding a motorcycle at 120 miles per hour.

Above the comforts of Base Camp, the expedition in fact became an almost Calvinistic undertaking. The ratio of misery to pleasure was greater by an order of magnitude than any other mountain I'd been on; I quickly came to understand that climbing Everest was primarily about enduring pain. And in subjecting ourselves to week after week of toil, tedium, and suffering, it struck me that most of us were probably seeking, above all else, something like a state of grace.

Of course for some Everesters myriad other, less virtuous, motives came into play, as well: minor celebrity, career advancement, ego massage, ordinary bragging rights, filthy lucre. But such ignoble enticements were less a factor than many critics might presume. Indeed, what I observed as the weeks went by forced me to substantially revise my presuppositions about some of my teammates.

Take Beck Weathers, for instance, who at that moment appeared as a tiny red speck on the ice 500 feet below, near the end of a long queue of climbers. My first impression of Beck had not been favorable: a back-slapping Dallas pathologist with less-than-mediocre mountaineering skills, at first blush he came across as a rich Republican blowhard looking to buy the summit of Everest for his trophy case. Yet the better I got to know him, the more he earned my respect. Even though his inflexible new boots had chewed his feet into hamburger, Beck kept hobbling upward, day in and day out, scarcely mentioning what must have been horrific pain. He was tough, driven, stoic. And what I initially took to be arrogance was looking more and more like exuberance. The man seemed to bear no ill will toward anybody in the world (Hillary Clinton notwithstanding). Beck's cheer and limitless optimism were so winning that, in spite of myself, I grew to like him a lot.

The son of a career Air Force officer, Beck had spent his childhood shuttling from one military base to another before landing in Wichita Falls to attend college. He graduated from medical school, got married and had two children, settled comfortably into a lucrative Dallas practice. Then, in 1986, pushing forty, he took a vacation in

Colorado, felt the siren song of the heights, and enrolled in a rudimentary mountaineering course in Rocky Mountain National Park.

It is not uncommon for doctors to be chronic overachievers; Beck wasn't the first physician to go overboard with a new hobby. But climbing was unlike golf or tennis or the various other pastimes that consumed his cronies. The demands of mountaineering—the physical and emotional struggles, the very real hazards—made it more than just a game. Climbing was like life itself, only it was cast in much sharper relief, and nothing had ever hooked Beck to such a degree. His wife, Peach, became increasingly concerned about his immersion and the way climbing robbed their family of his presence. She was less than pleased when, not long after taking up the sport, Beck announced that he'd decided to have a go at the Seven Summits.

Selfish and grandiose though Beck's obsession may have been, it wasn't frivolous. I began to recognize a similar seriousness of purpose in Lou Kasischke, the lawyer from Bloomfield Hills; in Yasuko Namba, the quiet Japanese woman who ate noodles every morning for breakfast; and in John Taske, the fifty-six-year-old anesthesiologist from Brisbane who took up climbing after retiring from the army.

"When I left the military, I sort of lost my way," Taske bemoaned in a thick Aussie accent. He'd been a big deal in the army—a full-bird colonel in the Special Air Service, Australia's equivalent of the Green Berets. Having served two tours in Vietnam at the height of the war, he found himself woefully unprepared for the flat pitch of life out of uniform. "I discovered that I couldn't really speak to civilians," he continued. "My marriage fell apart. All I could see was this long dark tunnel closing in, ending in infirmity, old age, and death. Then I started to climb, and the sport provided most of what had been missing for me in civvy street—the challenge, the camaraderie, the sense of mission."

As my sympathy for Taske, Weathers, and some of my other teammates mounted, I felt increasingly uncomfortable in my role as a journalist. I had no qualms when it came to writing frankly about Hall, Fischer, or Sandy Pittman, each of whom had been aggressively seeking media attention for years. But my fellow clients were a different matter. When they signed up with Hall's expedition, none of them had known that a reporter would be in their midst—scribbling constantly, quietly recording their words and deeds in order to share their foibles with a potentially unsympathetic public.

After the expedition was over, Weathers was interviewed for the television program *Turning Point.* In a segment of the interview that wasn't included in the version edited for broadcast, ABC News anchor Forrest Sawyer asked Beck, "How'd you feel about a reporter being along?" Beck replied,

> It added a lot of stress. I was always a little concerned with the idea—you know, this guy's going to come back and write a story that's going to be read by a couple of million people. And, I mean, it's bad enough to go up there and make a fool of yourself if it's just you and the climbing group. That somebody may have you written across the pages of some magazine as a buffoon and a clown has got to play upon your psyche as to how you perform, how hard you'll push. And I was concerned that it might drive people further than they wanted to go. And it might even for the guides. I mean, they want to get people on top of the mountain because, once again, they're going to be written about, and they're going to be judged.

A moment later Sawyer asked, "Did you sense that having a reporter along put extra pressure on Rob Hall?" Beck answered,

> I can't imagine it didn't. This is what [Rob] does for a living, and if one of his clients got injured, that's the worst thing that can happen to a guide. . . . He certainly had a great season two years before this in which they got everybody on top of the summit, which is extraor-

> dinary. And I actually think that he thought that our group was strong enough that we could repeat that. . . . So I think there is a push so that when you wind up again in the news, in the magazine, it's all reported favorably.

| | |

It was late morning by the time I finally humped into Camp Three: a trio of small yellow tents, halfway up the vertiginous sprawl of the Lhotse Face, jammed side by side onto a platform that had been hewn from the icy slope by our Sherpas. When I arrived, Lhakpa Chhiri and Arita were still hard at work on a platform for a fourth tent, so I took off my pack and helped them chop. At 24,000 feet, I could manage only seven or eight blows of my ice ax before having to pause for more than a minute to catch my breath. My contribution to the effort was negligible, needless to say, and it took nearly an hour to complete the job.

Our tiny camp, a hundred feet above the tents of the other expeditions, was a spectacularly exposed perch. For weeks we'd been toiling in what amounted to a canyon; now, for the first time on the expedition the vista was primarily sky rather than earth. Herds of puffy cumulus raced beneath the sun, imprinting the landscape with a shifting matrix of shadow and blinding light. Waiting for my teammates to arrive, I sat with my feet hanging over the abyss, staring across the clouds, looking down on the tops of 22,000-foot peaks that a month earlier had towered overhead. At long last, it seemed as though I was really nearing the roof of the world.

The summit, however, was still a vertical mile above, wreathed in a nimbus of gale-borne condensation. But even as the upper mountain was raked by winds in excess of a hundred miles per hour, the air at Camp Three barely stirred, and as the afternoon wore on I began to feel increasingly woozy from the fierce solar radiation—at least I hoped it was the heat that was making me stupid, and not the onset of cerebral edema.

High Altitude Cerebral Edema (HACE) is less common than High Altitude Pulmonary Edema (HAPE), but it tends to be even more deadly. A baffling ailment, HACE occurs when fluid leaks from oxygen-starved cerebral blood vessels, causing severe swelling of the brain, and it can strike with little or no warning. As pressure builds inside the skull, motor and mental skills deteriorate with alarming speed—typically within a few hours or less—and often without the victim even noticing the change. The next step is coma, and then, unless the afflicted party is quickly evacuated to lower altitude, death.

HACE happened to be on my mind that afternoon because just two days earlier a client of Fischer's named Dale Kruse, a forty-four-year-old dentist from Colorado, had come down with a serious case of it right here at Camp Three. A longtime friend of Fischer's, Kruse was a strong, very experienced climber. On April 26 he'd climbed from Camp Two to Camp Three, brewed some tea for himself and his teammates, and then lay down in his tent to take a nap. "I fell right asleep," Kruse recalls, "and ended up sleeping almost twenty-four hours, until about two P.M. the following day. When somebody finally woke me up it immediately became apparent to the others that my mind wasn't working, although it wasn't apparent to me. Scott told me, 'We gotta get you down right away.' "

Kruse was having an incredibly difficult time simply trying to dress himself. He put his climbing harness on inside out, threaded it through the fly of his wind suit, and failed to fasten the buckle; fortunately, Fischer and Neal Beidleman noticed the screwup before Kruse started to descend. "If he'd tried to rappel down the ropes like that," says Beidleman, "he would have immediately popped out of his harness and fallen to the bottom of the Lhotse Face."

"It was like I was very drunk," Kruse recollects. "I couldn't walk without stumbling, and completely lost the ability to think or speak. It was a really strange feeling. I'd have some word in my mind, but I couldn't figure out how to bring it to my lips. So Scott and Neal had to get me dressed and make sure my harness was on correctly, then Scott lowered me down the fixed ropes." By the time Kruse arrived in Base Camp, he says, "it was still another three or four days before I could walk from my tent to the mess tent without stumbling all over the place."

| | |

When the evening sun slid behind Pumori, the temperature at Camp Three plummeted more than fifty degrees, and as the air chilled my head cleared: my anxiety about coming down with HACE proved to be unfounded, at least for the time being. The next morning, after a miserable, sleepless night at 24,000 feet, we descended to Camp Two, and a day later, on May 1, continued down to Base Camp to recoup our strength for the summit push.

Our acclimatization was now officially complete—and to my pleasant surprise Hall's strategy appeared to be working: After three weeks on the mountain, I found that the air at Base Camp seemed thick and rich and voluptuously saturated with oxygen compared to the brutally thin atmosphere of the camps above.

All was not well with my body, however. I'd lost nearly twenty pounds of muscle mass, largely from my shoulders, back, and legs. I'd also burned up virtually all my subcutaneous fat, making me vastly more sensitive to the cold. My worst problem, though, was my chest: the dry hack I'd picked up weeks earlier in Lobuje had gotten so bad that I'd torn some thoracic cartilage during an especially robust bout of coughing at Camp Three. The coughing had continued unabated, and each hack felt like a stiff kick between the ribs.

Most of the other climbers in Base Camp were in similarly battered shape—it was simply a fact of life on Everest. In five days those of us on Hall's and Fischer's teams would be leaving Base Camp for the top. Hoping to stanch my decline, I resolved to rest, gobble ibuprofen, and force down as many calories as possible in that time.

From the beginning, Hall had planned that May 10 would be our summit day. "Of the four times I've summitted," he explained, "twice it was on the tenth of May. As the Sherpas would put it, the tenth is an 'auspicious' date for me." But there was also a more down-to-earth reason for selecting this date: the annual ebb and flow of the monsoon made it likely that the most favorable weather of the year would fall on or near May 10.

For all of April, the jet stream had been trained on Everest like a fire hose, blasting the summit pyramid with hurricane-force winds. Even on days when Base Camp was perfectly calm and flooded with sunshine, an immense banner of wind-driven snow flew from the summit. But in early May, we hoped, the approach of the monsoon from the Bay of Bengal would force the jet stream north into Tibet. If this year was like past years, between the departure of the wind and the arrival of the monsoon storms we would be presented with a brief window of clear, calm weather, during which a summit assault would be possible.

Unfortunately, the annual weather pattern was no secret, and every expedition had set their sights on the same window of fair weather. Hoping to avoid dangerous gridlock on the summit ridge, Hall held a big powwow with leaders of the other expeditions in Base Camp. It was determined that Göran Kropp, a young Swede who had ridden a bicycle from Stockholm to Nepal, would make the first attempt, alone, on May 3. Next would be a team from Montenegro. Then, on May 8 or 9, it would be the turn of the IMAX expedition.

Hall's team, it was decided, would share a summit date of May 10 with Fischer's expedition. After nearly getting killed by a falling rock low on the Southwest Face, Petter Neby, the solo Norwegian climber, was already gone: he'd quietly left Base Camp one morning and returned to Scandinavia. A guided group led by Americans Todd Burleson and Pete Athans, as well as Mal Duff's commercial team and another British commercial team, all promised to steer clear of May 10, as did the Taiwanese. Ian Woodall, however, declared that the South Africans would go to the top whenever they damn well pleased, probably on May 10, and anyone who didn't like it could bugger off.

Hall, ordinarily extremely slow to rile, flew into a rage when he learned of Woodall's refusal to cooperate. "I don't want to be anywhere near the upper mountain when those punters are up there," he seethed.

Chapter Eleven

BASE CAMP MAY 6, 1996 17,600 FEET

How much of the appeal of mountaineering lies in its simplification of interpersonal relationships, its reduction of friendship to smooth interaction (like war), its substitution of an Other (the mountain, the challenge) for the relationship itself? Behind a mystique of adventure, toughness, footloose vagabondage—all much needed antidotes to our culture's built-in comfort and convenience—may lie a kind of adolescent refusal to take seriously aging, the frailty of others, interpersonal responsibility, weakness of all kinds, the slow and unspectacular course of life itself. . . .

[T]op climbers . . . can be deeply moved, in fact maudlin; but only for worthy martyred ex-comrades. A certain coldness, strikingly similar in tone, emerges from the writings of Buhl, John Harlin, Bonatti, Bonington, and Haston: the coldness of competence. Perhaps this is what extreme climbing is about: to get to a point where, in Haston's words, "If anything goes wrong it will be a fight to the end. If your training is good enough, survival is there; if not nature claims its forfeit."

David Roberts
"Patey Agonistes"
Moments of Doubt

We left Base Camp at 4:30 A.M. on May 6 to commence our summit bid. The top of Everest, two vertical miles above, seemed so impossibly distant that I tried to limit my thoughts to Camp Two, our destination for the day. By the time the first sunlight struck the glacier I was at 20,000 feet, in the maw of the Western Cwm, grateful that the Icefall was below me and that I would have to go through it only one more time, on the final trip down.

I had been plagued by heat in the Cwm every time I'd traveled through it, and this trip was no exception. Climbing with Andy Harris at the front of the group, I continually stuffed snow under my hat and moved as fast as my legs and lungs would propel me, hoping to reach the shade of the tents before succumbing to the solar radiation. As the morning dragged on and the sun beat down, my head began to pound. My tongue swelled so much that it was difficult to breathe through my mouth, and I noticed that it was becoming harder and harder to think clearly.

Andy and I dragged into Camp Two at 10:30 A.M. After I guzzled two liters of Gatorade my equilibrium returned. "It feels good to at last be on our way to the summit, yeah?" Andy inquired. He'd been laid low with various intestinal ailments for most of the expedition and was finally getting his strength back. A gifted tutor blessed with astonishing patience, he'd usually been assigned to watch over the slower clients at the back of the herd and was thrilled when Rob had turned him loose this morning to go out on point. As the junior guide on Hall's team, and the only one who'd never been on Everest, Andy was eager to prove himself to his seasoned colleagues. "I think we're actually gonna knock this big bastard off," he confided in me with a huge smile, staring up at the summit.

Later that day, Göran Kropp, the twenty-nine-year-old Swedish soloist, passed Camp Two on his way down to Base Camp, looking utterly worked. On October 16, 1995, he had left Stockholm on a custom-built bicycle loaded with 240 pounds of gear, intending to travel round-trip from sea level in Sweden to the top of Everest entirely under his own power, without Sherpa support or bottled oxygen. It was an exceedingly ambitious goal, but Kropp had the credentials to pull it off: he'd been on six previous Himalayan expeditions and had made solo ascents of Broad Peak, Cho Oyu, and K2.

During the 8,000-mile bike ride to Kathmandu, he was robbed by Romanian schoolchildren and assaulted by a crowd in Pakistan. In Iran, an irate motorcyclist broke a baseball bat over Kropp's (fortunately) helmeted head. He'd nevertheless arrived intact at the foot of Everest in early April with a film crew in tow, and immediately began making acclimatization trips up the lower mountain. Then, on Wednesday, May 1, he'd departed Base Camp for the top.

Kropp reached his high camp at 26,000 feet on the South Col on Thursday afternoon and left for the top the following morning just after midnight. Everybody at Base Camp stayed close by their radios throughout the day, anxiously awaiting word of his progress. Helen Wilton hung a sign in our mess tent that read, "Go, Göran, Go!"

For the first time in months almost no wind blasted the summit, but the snow on the upper mountain was thigh deep, making for slow, exhausting progress. Kropp bulled his way relentlessly upward through the drifts, however, and by two o'clock Thursday afternoon he'd reached 28,700 feet, just below the South Summit. But even though the top was no more than sixty minutes above, he decided to turn around, believing that he would be too tired to descend safely if he climbed any higher.

"To turn around that close to the summit . . . ," Hall mused with a shake of his head on May 6 as Kropp plodded past Camp Two on his way down the mountain. "*That* showed incredibly good judgment on young Göran's part. I'm impressed—considerably more impressed, actually, than if he'd continued climbing and made the top." Over the previous month, Rob had lectured us repeatedly about the importance of having a predetermined turn-around time on our summit day—in our case it would probably be 1:00 P.M., or 2:00 at the very latest—and abiding by it no matter how close we were to the top. "With enough determination, any bloody idiot can get *up* this hill," Hall observed. "The trick is to get back down alive."

Hall's easygoing facade masked an intense desire to succeed—which he defined in the fairly simple terms of getting as many clients as possible to the summit. To ensure success, he paid meticulous attention to detail: the health of the Sherpas, the efficiency of the solar-powered electrical system, the sharpness of his clients' crampons. Hall loved being a guide, and it pained him that some celebrated climbers—including but not limited to Sir Edmund Hillary—didn't appreciate how difficult guiding was, or give the profession the respect he felt it deserved.

| | |

Rob decreed that Tuesday, May 7, would be a rest day, so we got up late and sat around Camp Two, buzzing with nervous anticipation over the imminent summit assault. I fiddled with my crampons and some other gear, then tried to read a Carl Hiaasen paperback but was so focused on the climb that I kept scanning the same sentences over and over without the words registering.

Eventually I put the book down, snapped a few photos of Doug posing with a flag the Kent schoolkids had asked him to carry up the peak, and pumped him for detailed information about the difficulties of the summit pyramid, which he remembered well from the year before. "By the time we get to the top," he frowned, "I guarantee that you're gonna be one hurtin' hombre." Doug was hell-bent on joining the summit push, even though his throat was still bothering him and his strength seemed to be at a low ebb. As he put it, "I've put too much of myself into this mountain to quit now, without giving it everything I've got."

Late that afternoon Fischer walked through our camp with a clenched jaw, moving uncharacteristically slowly toward his own tents. He usually managed to maintain a relentlessly upbeat attitude; one of his favorite utterances was, "If you're bumming out, you're not gonna get to the top, so as long as we're up here we might as well make a point of grooving." At the moment, however, Scott did not appear to be grooving in the slightest; instead he looked anxious and extremely tired.

Because he'd encouraged his clients to move up and down the mountain independently during the acclimatization period, he ended up having to make a number of hurried, unplanned excursions between Base Camp and the upper camps when several clients experienced problems and needed to be escorted down. He'd already made special trips to assist Tim Madsen, Pete Schoening, and Dale Kruse. And now, on what should have been a badly needed day and a half of rest, Fischer had just been forced to make a hasty round-trip from Camp Two to Base Camp and back to help his good friend Kruse after he came down with what appeared to be a relapse of HACE.

Fischer had arrived at Camp Two around noon the previous day, just after Andy and me, having climbed from Base Camp well ahead of his clients; he'd directed guide Anatoli Boukreev to bring up the rear, stay close to the group, and keep an eye on everybody. But Boukreev ignored Fischer's instructions: instead of climbing with the team, he slept late, took a shower, and departed Base Camp some five hours behind the last of the clients. Thus, when Kruse collapsed at 20,000 feet with a splitting headache, Boukreev was nowhere in the vicinity, compelling Fischer and Beidleman to rush down from Camp Two to handle the emergency as soon as word of Kruse's condition arrived via climbers coming up the Western Cwm.

Not long after Fischer reached Kruse and began the troublesome descent to Base Camp, they encountered Boukreev at the top of the Icefall, ascending alone, and Fischer harshly reprimanded the guide for shirking his responsibilities. "Yeah," Kruse remembers, "Scott laid into Toli pretty good. He wanted to know why he was so far behind everybody—why he wasn't climbing with the team."

According to Kruse and other clients of Fischer's, tension between Fischer and Boukreev had been building throughout the expedition. Fischer paid Boukreev $25,000—an unusually generous fee for guiding Everest (most other guides on the mountain were paid $10,000 to $15,000; skilled climbing Sherpas received only $1,400 to $2,500), and Boukreev's performance hadn't been meeting his expectations. "Toli was very strong and a very good technical climber," Kruse explains, "but he had poor social skills. He didn't watch out for other people. He just wasn't a team player. Earlier, I'd told Scott that I didn't want to have to climb with Toli high on the mountain, because I doubted that I'd be able to count on him when it really mattered."

The underlying problem was that Boukreev's notion of his responsibilities differed substantially from Fischer's. As a Russian, Boukreev came from a tough, proud, hardscrabble climbing culture that did not believe in coddling the weak. In Eastern Europe guides were trained to act more like Sherpas—hauling loads, fixing ropes, establishing the route—and less like caretakers. Tall and blond, with handsome Slavic features, Boukreev was one of the most accomplished high-altitude climbers in the world, with twenty years of experience in the Himalaya, including two ascents of Everest without supplemental oxygen. And in the course of his distinguished career he'd formulated a number of unorthodox, very strongly held opinions about how the mountain should be ascended. He was quite outspoken in his belief that it was a mistake for guides to pamper their clients. "If client cannot climb Everest without big help from guide," Boukreev told me, "this client should not be on Everest. Otherwise there can be big problems up high."

But Boukreev's refusal or inability to play the role of a conventional guide in the Western tradition exasperated Fischer. It also forced him and Beidleman to shoulder a disproportionate share of the caretaker duties for their group, and by the first week in May the effort had taken an unmistakable toll on Fischer's health. After arriving in Base Camp with the ailing Kruse on the evening of May 6, Fischer made two satellite phone calls to Seattle in which he complained bitterly to his business partner, Karen Dickinson, and to his publicist, Jane Bromet,* about Boukreev's intransigence. Neither woman imagined that these would be the last conversations they would ever have with Fischer.

| | |

On May 8 both Hall's team and Fischer's team departed Camp Two and commenced the grinding ascent of the ropes up the Lhotse Face. Two thousand feet above the floor of the Western Cwm, just below Camp Three, a boulder the size of a small television came rocketing down from the cliffs above and smashed into Andy Harris's chest. It knocked him off his feet, slammed the wind out of him, and left him dangling from the fixed line in a state of shock for several minutes. Had he not been clipped in with a jumar he would have certainly fallen to his death.

* Bromet had left Base Camp in mid-April and returned to Seattle, whence she continued to file Internet dispatches about Fischer's expedition for Outside Online; she relied on regular phone updates from Fischer as the primary source for her reports.

When he arrived at the tents, Andy looked badly rattled but claimed that he wasn't injured. "I might be a bit stiff in the morning," he insisted, "but I think the bloody thing didn't do much more than bruise me." Just before the rock nailed him he'd been hunched forward with his head down; he happened to look up a moment before it struck, so that it merely grazed his chin before hitting him in the sternum, but it had come sickeningly close to smashing into his cranium. "If that rock had hit me in the head . . . ," Andy speculated with a grimace as he shed his pack, leaving the rest of the sentence unsaid.

Because Camp Three was the only camp on the entire mountain that we didn't share with the Sherpas (the ledge was too small to accommodate tents for all of us), it meant that here we had to do our own cooking—which mostly amounted to melting prodigious quantities of ice for drinking water. Due to the pronounced dehydration that was an inevitable by-product of heavy breathing in such desiccated air, each of us consumed more than a gallon of liquid every day. We therefore needed to produce approximately a dozen gallons of water to meet the needs of eight clients and three guides.

As the first person to reach the tents on May 8, I inherited the job of ice chopper. For three hours, as my companions trickled into camp and settled into their sleeping bags, I remained outside hacking at the slope with the adze of my ice ax, filling plastic garbage bags with frozen shards and distributing the ice to the tents for melting. At 24,000 feet it was fatiguing work. Every time one of my teammates yelled, "Hey, Jon! You still out there? We could use some more ice over here!" it gave me a fresh perspective on how much the Sherpas ordinarily did for us, and how little we truly appreciated it.

By late afternoon, as the sun eased toward the corrugated horizon and the temperature began to plunge, everyone had pulled into camp except Lou Kasischke, Frank Fischbeck, and Rob, who had volunteered to do the "sweep" and come up last. Around 4:30 P.M., guide Mike Groom received a call from Rob on his walkie-talkie: Lou and Frank were still a couple of hundred feet below the tents and moving extremely slowly; would Mike please come down to assist them? Mike hurriedly put his crampons back on and disappeared down the fixed ropes without complaint.

Nearly an hour passed before he reappeared, just ahead of the others. Lou, who was so tired he'd let Rob carry his pack, staggered into camp looking pale and distraught, muttering, "I'm finished. I'm finished. Completely out of gas." Frank showed up a few minutes later appearing even more exhausted, although he'd refused to give his pack to Mike. It was a shock to see these guys—both of whom had been climbing well lately—in such a state. Frank's apparent deterioration came as a particular blow: I'd assumed from the beginning that if any members of our team reached the top, Frank—who'd been high on the mountain three times previously and seemed so savvy and strong—would be among them.

| | |

As darkness enveloped the camp, our guides handed out oxygen canisters, regulators, and masks to everyone: for the remainder of the climb we would be breathing compressed gas.

Relying on bottled oxygen as an aid to ascent is a practice that's sparked acrimonious debate ever since the British first took experimental oxygen rigs to Everest in 1921. (Skeptical Sherpas promptly dubbed the unwieldy canisters "English Air.") Initially, the foremost critic of bottled gas was George Leigh Mallory, who protested that using it was "unsporting, and therefore un-British." But it soon became apparent that in the so-called Death Zone above 25,000 feet, without supplemental oxygen the body is vastly more vulnerable to HAPE and HACE, hypothermia, frostbite, and a host of other mortal perils. By 1924, when he returned for his third expedition to the mountain, Mallory had become convinced that the summit would never be reached without gas, and he resigned himself to using it.

Experiments conducted in decompression chambers had by then demonstrated that a human plucked from sea level and dropped on the summit of Everest, where the air holds only a third as much oxygen, would lose consciousness within minutes and die soon thereafter. But a number of idealistic mountaineers continued to insist that a gifted athlete blessed with rare physiological attributes could, after a lengthy period of acclimatization, climb the peak without bottled oxygen. Taking this line of reasoning to its logical extreme, the purists argued that using gas was therefore cheating.

In the 1970s, the famed Tyrolean alpinist Reinhold Messner emerged as the leading proponent of gasless climbing, declaring that he would ascend Everest "by fair means" or not at all. Shortly thereafter he and his longtime partner, the Austrian Peter Habeler, astounded the world climbing community by making good on the boast: at 1:00 P.M. on May 8, 1978, they ascended to the summit via the South Col and Southeast Ridge route without using supplemental oxygen. It was hailed by climbers in some circles as the first true ascent of Everest.

Messner and Habeler's historic deed was not greeted with hosannas in all quarters, however, especially among the Sherpas. Most of them simply refused to believe that Westerners were capable of such an achievement, which had eluded even the strongest Sherpas. Speculation was rampant that Messner and Habeler had sucked oxygen from miniature cylinders hidden in their clothing. Tenzing Norgay and other eminent Sherpas signed a petition demanding that the government of Nepal conduct an official inquiry of the purported ascent.

But the evidence verifying the oxygenless climb was irrefutable. Two years later Messner silenced all doubters, moreover, by traveling to the Tibetan side of Everest and making another ascent sans gas—this time entirely alone, without the support of Sherpas or anybody else. When he reached the summit at 3:00 P.M. on August 20, 1980, climbing through thick clouds and falling snow, Messner said, "I was in continual agony; I have never in my whole life been so tired." In *The Crystal Horizon,* his book about the ascent, he describes struggling up the final meters to the top:

> When I rest I feel utterly lifeless except that my throat burns when I draw breath. . . . I can scarcely go on. No despair, no happiness, no anxiety. I have not lost the mastery of my feelings, there are actually no more feelings. I consist only of will. After each few metres this

> too fizzles out in unending tiredness. Then I think nothing. I let myself fall, just lie there. For an indefinite time I remain completely irresolute. Then I make a few steps again.

Upon Messner's return to civilization, his ascent was widely lauded as the greatest mountaineering feat of all time.

After Messner and Habeler proved that Everest could be climbed without gas, a cadre of ambitious mountaineers agreed that it *should* be climbed without gas. Henceforth, if one aspired to be considered a member of the Himalayan elite, eschewing bottled oxygen was mandatory. By 1996 some sixty men and women had reached the summit without it—five of whom didn't make it back down alive.

However grandiose some of our individual ambitions may have been, nobody on Hall's team ever really considered going for the summit without bottled oxygen. Even Mike Groom, who'd climbed Everest three years earlier without gas, explained to me that he intended to use it this time around because he was working as a guide, and he knew from experience that without bottled oxygen he would be so severely impaired—both mentally and physically—that he would be unable to fulfill his professional duties. Like most veteran Everest guides, Groom believed that although it was acceptable—and, indeed, aesthetically preferable—to do without bottled oxygen when climbing on one's own, it would be extremely irresponsible to guide the peak without using it.

The state-of-the-art Russian-built oxygen system used by Hall consisted of a stiff plastic oxygen mask of the sort worn by MiG fighter pilots during the Vietnam War, connected via a rubber hose and a crude regulator to an orange steel and Kevlar gas canister. (Smaller and much lighter than a scuba tank, each one weighed 6.6 pounds when full.) Although we hadn't slept with oxygen during our previous stay at Camp Three, now that we had begun the push to the summit Rob strongly urged us to breathe gas through the night. "Every minute you remain at this altitude and above," he cautioned, "your minds and bodies are deteriorating." Brain cells were dying. Our blood was growing dangerously thick and sludgelike. Capillaries in our retinas were spontaneously hemorrhaging. Even at rest, our hearts beat at a furious rate. Rob promised that "bottled oxygen will slow the decline and help you sleep."

I tried to heed Rob's advice, but my latent claustrophobia prevailed. When I clamped the mask over my nose and mouth I kept imagining that it was suffocating me, so after a miserable hour I took it off and spent the rest of the night without gas, breathlessly flopping and fidgeting, checking my watch every twenty minutes to see if it was time to get up yet.

Dug into the slope a hundred feet below our camp, in an equally precarious setting, were the tents of most of the other teams—including Scott Fischer's group, the South Africans, and the Taiwanese. Early the next morning—Thursday, May 9—as I was pulling on my boots for the ascent to Camp Four, Chen Yu-Nan, a thirty-six-year-old steelworker from Taipei, crawled out of his tent to evacuate his bowels shod only in the smooth-soled liners of his mountaineering boots—a serious lapse of judgment.

As he squatted, he lost his footing on the ice and went hurtling down the Lhotse Face. Incredibly, after falling only 70 feet he plunged headfirst in a crevasse, which arrested his tumble. Sherpas who had seen the incident lowered a rope, quickly pulled him out of the slot, and assisted him back to his tent. Although he was battered and badly frightened, he didn't seem seriously injured. At the time, nobody on Hall's team, including me, was even aware that the mishap had occurred.

Shortly thereafter, Makalu Gau and the rest of the Taiwanese team left Chen alone in a tent to recover and departed for the South Col. Even though Gau had assured Rob and Scott that he wouldn't attempt the summit on May 10, he'd apparently changed his mind and now intended to go for the top the same day we did.

That afternoon a Sherpa named Jangbu, descending to Camp Two after hauling a load to the South Col, stopped at Camp Three to monitor Chen's condition and found that the Taiwanese climber's symptoms had worsened significantly: he was now disoriented and in great pain. Deciding that he needed to be evacuated, Jangbu recruited two other Sherpas and began escorting Chen down the Lhotse Face. Three hundred feet from the bottom of the ice slope, Chen abruptly keeled over and lost consciousness. A moment later, down at Camp Two, David Breashears's radio crackled to life: it was Jangbu, reporting in a panicked voice that Chen had stopped breathing.

Breashears and his IMAX teammate Ed Viesturs rushed up to see if they could revive him, but when they reached Chen some forty minutes later they found no vital signs. That evening, after Gau arrived at the South Col, Breashears called him on the radio. "Makalu," Breashears told the Taiwanese leader, "Chen has died."

"O.K.," Gau replied. "Thank you for the information." Then he assured his team that Chen's death would in no way affect their plans to leave for the summit at midnight. Breashears was flabbergasted. "I had just closed his friend's eyes for him," he says with more than a touch of anger. "I had just dragged Chen's body down. And all Makalu could say was, 'O.K.' I don't know, I guess maybe it was a cultural thing. Maybe he thought the best way to honor Chen's death was to continue to the summit."

Over the preceding six weeks there had been several serious accidents: Tenzing's fall into the crevasse before we even arrived at Base Camp; Ngawang Topche's case of HAPE and subsequent deterioration; a young, apparently fit English climber on Mal Duff's team named Ginge Fullen who'd had a serious heart attack near the top of the Icefall; a Dane on Duff's team named Kim Sejberg who was struck by a falling serac in the Icefall and broke several ribs. Until that moment, however, nobody had died.

Chen's death cast a pall over the mountain as rumors of the accident spread from tent to tent, but thirty-three climbers would be departing for the summit in a few short hours, and the gloom was quickly banished by nervous anticipation of what lay ahead. Most of us were simply wrapped too tightly in the grip of summit fever to engage in thoughtful reflection about the death of someone in our midst. There would be plenty of time for reflection later, we assumed, after we all had summitted and got back down.

Chapter Twelve

CAMP THREE MAY 9, 1996 24,000 FEET

I looked down. Descent was totally unappetizing. . . . Too much labor, too many sleepless nights, and too many dreams had been invested to bring us this far. We couldn't come back for another try next weekend. To go down now, even if we could have, would be descending to a future marked by one huge question: what might have been?

Thomas F. Hornbein
Everest: The West Ridge

Arising lethargic and groggy after my sleepless night at Camp Three, I was slow to dress, melt water, and get out of the tent on Thursday morning, May 9. By the time I loaded my backpack and strapped on my crampons, most of the rest of Hall's group was already ascending the ropes toward Camp Four. Surprisingly, Lou Kasischke and Frank Fischbeck were among them. Because of their ravaged state when they arrived in camp the previous evening, I'd assumed that both men would decide to throw in the towel. "Good on ya, mates," I exclaimed, borrowing a phrase from the antipodal contingent, impressed that my cohorts had sucked it up and resolved to push on.

As I rushed to join my teammates, I looked down to see a queue of approximately fifty climbers from other expeditions moving up the ropes, too; the first of them were now immediately below me. Not wanting to become entangled in what was sure to be a massive traffic jam (which would prolong my exposure to the intermittent fusillade of stones whizzing down the face from above, among other hazards), I picked up my pace and resolved to move toward the head of the line. Because only a single rope snaked up the Lhotse Face, however, it wasn't easy to pass slower climbers.

Andy's encounter with the falling rock was very much on my mind every time I unclipped from the line to move around somebody—even a small projectile would be enough to send me to the bottom of the face if it struck while I was disengaged from the rope. Leapfrogging past others, moreover, was not only nerve-racking but exhausting. Like an underpowered Yugo trying to pass a line of other vehicles on a steep hill, I had to keep the accelerator jammed to the floor for a distressingly long time to get around anybody, leaving me gasping so hard that I worried I was going to puke into my oxygen mask.

Climbing with oxygen for the first time in my life, I took a while to get used to it. Although the benefits of using gas at this altitude—24,000 feet—were genuine, they were hard to discern immediately. As I fought to catch my breath after moving past three climbers, the mask actually gave the illusion of asphyxiating me, so I tore it from my face—only to discover breathing was even harder without it.

By the time I surmounted the cliff of brittle, ocher-hued limestone known as the Yellow Band, I had worked my way to the front of the queue and was able to settle into a more comfortable pace. Moving slowly but steadily, I made a rising leftward traverse across the top of the Lhotse Face, then ascended a prow of shattered black schist called the Geneva Spur. I'd finally gotten the hang of breathing through my oxygen rig and had moved more than an hour ahead of my nearest companion. Solitude was a rare commodity on Everest, and I was grateful to be granted a bit of it on this day, in such a remarkable setting.

At 25,900 feet, I paused on the crest of the Spur to drink some water and take in the view. The thin air had a shimmering, crystalline quality that made even distant peaks seem close enough to touch. Extravagantly illuminated by the midday sun, Everest's summit pyramid loomed through an intermittent gauze of clouds. Squinting through my camera's telephoto lens at the upper Southeast Ridge, I was surprised to see four antlike figures moving almost imperceptibly toward the South Summit. I deduced that they must be climbers from the Montenegrin expedition; if they succeeded they would be the first team to reach the top this year. It would also mean that the rumors we'd been hearing of impossibly deep snow were unfounded—if they made the summit, maybe we had a chance of making it, too. But the plume of snow now blowing from the summit ridge was a bad sign: the Montenegrins were struggling upward through ferocious wind.

I arrived on the South Col, our launching pad for the summit assault, at 1:00 P.M. A forlorn plateau of bulletproof ice and windswept boulders 26,000 feet above sea level, it occupies a broad notch between the upper ramparts of Lhotse and Everest. Roughly rectangular in shape, about four football fields long by two across, the Col's eastern margin drops 7,000 feet down the Kangshung Face into Tibet; the other side plunges 4,000 feet to the Western Cwm. Just back from the lip of this chasm, at the Col's westernmost edge, the tents of Camp Four squatted on a patch of barren ground surrounded by more than a thousand discarded oxygen canisters.* If there is a more desolate, inhospitable habitation anywhere on the planet, I hope never to see it.

As the jet stream encounters the Everest massif and is squeezed through the V-shaped contours of the South Col, the wind accelerates to unimaginable velocities; it's not unusual for the winds at the Col actually to be stronger than the winds that rip the summit. The nearly constant hurricane blowing through the Col in early spring explains why it remains as naked rock and ice even when deep snow blankets adjacent slopes: everything not frozen in place here has been blasted into Tibet.

When I walked into Camp Four, six Sherpas were struggling to erect Hall's tents in a 50-knot tempest. Helping them put up my shelter, I anchored it to some discarded oxygen canisters wedged beneath the largest rocks I could lift, then dove inside to wait for my teammates and warm my icy hands.

* The spent oxygen bottles blighting the South Col have been accumulating since the 1950s, but thanks to an ongoing litter-removal program instigated in 1994 by Scott Fischer's Sagarmatha Environmental Expedition, there are fewer of them up there now than there used to be. Much of the credit belongs to a member of that expedition named Brent Bishop (the son of the late Barry Bishop, the eminent *National Geographic* photographer who summitted Everest in 1963), who initiated a highly successful incentive policy, funded by Nike, Inc., whereby Sherpas are paid a cash bonus for each oxygen bottle they bring down from the Col. Among the companies guiding Everest, Rob Hall's Adventure Consultants, Scott Fischer's Mountain Madness, and Todd Burleson's Alpine Ascents International have enthusiastically embraced Bishop's program, resulting in the removal of more than eight hundred oxygen canisters from the upper mountain from 1994 through 1996.

The weather deteriorated as the afternoon wore on. Lopsang Jangbu, Fischer's sirdar, showed up bearing a back-wrenching eighty-pound load, some thirty pounds of which consisted of a satellite telephone and its peripheral hardware: Sandy Pittman was intending to file Internet dispatches from 26,000 feet. The last of my teammates didn't arrive until 4:30 P.M., and the final stragglers in Fischer's group came in even later, by which time a serious storm was in full flower. At dark, the Montenegrins returned to the Col to report that the summit had remained out of reach: they'd turned around below the Hillary Step.

Between the weather and the Montenegrins' defeat, it didn't augur well for our own summit assault, scheduled to get under way in less than six hours. Everyone retreated to their nylon shelters the moment they reached the Col and did their best to nap, but the machine-gun rattle of the flapping tents and anxiety over what was to come made sleep out the question for most of us.

Stuart Hutchison—the young Canadian cardiologist—and I were assigned to one tent; Rob, Frank, Mike Groom, John Taske, and Yasuko Namba were in another; Lou, Beck Weathers, Andy Harris, and Doug Hansen occupied a third. Lou and his tent-mates were dozing in their shelter when an unfamiliar voice called from out of the gale, "Let him in quickly or he's going to die out here!" Lou unzipped the door, and a moment later a bearded man fell supine into his lap. It was Bruce Herrod, the amiable thirty-seven-year-old deputy leader of the South African team, and the sole remaining member of that expedition with real mountaineering credentials.

"Bruce was in real trouble," Lou remembers, "shivering uncontrollably, acting very spacey and irrational, basically unable to do anything for himself. He was so hypothermic he could barely talk. The rest of his group was apparently somewhere on the Col, or on their way to the Col. But he didn't know where, and he had no idea how to find his own tent, so we gave him something to drink and tried to warm him up."

Doug was also not doing well. "Doug didn't look good," Beck recalls. "He was complaining that he hadn't slept in a couple of days, hadn't eaten. But he was determined to strap his gear on and climb when the time came. I was concerned, because I'd gotten to know

Doug well enough at that point to realize that he'd spent the entire previous year agonizing over the fact that he'd gotten to within three hundred feet of the summit and had to turn around. And I mean it had gnawed at him every single day. It was pretty clear that he was not going to be denied a second time. Doug was going to keep climbing toward the top as long as he was still able to breathe."

There were more than fifty people camped on the Col that night, huddled in shelters pitched side by side, yet an odd feeling of isolation hung in the air. The roar of the wind made it impossible to communicate from one tent to the next. In this godforsaken place, I felt disconnected from the climbers around me—emotionally, spiritually, physically—to a degree I hadn't experienced on any previous expedition. We were a team in name only, I'd sadly come to realize. Although in a few hours we would leave camp as a group, we would ascend as individuals, linked to one another by neither rope nor any deep sense of loyalty. Each client was in it for himself or herself, pretty much. And I was no different: I sincerely hoped Doug got to the top, for instance, yet I would do everything in my power to keep pushing on if he turned around.

In another context this insight would have been depressing, but I was too preoccupied with the weather to dwell on it. If the wind didn't abate—and soon—the summit would be out of the question for all of us. Over the preceding week, Hall's Sherpas had stocked the Col with 363 pounds of bottled oxygen—55 cylinders. Although that sounds like a lot, it was only enough to permit a single attempt for three guides, eight clients, and four Sherpas. And the meter was running: even as we reclined in our tents, we were using up precious gas. If need be we could turn off our oxygen and safely remain up here for perhaps twenty-four hours; after that, however, we would need to either go up or go down.

But *mirabile visu,* at 7:30 P.M. the gale abruptly ceased. Herrod crawled out of Lou's tent and stumbled off to locate his teammates. The temperature was well below zero, but there was almost no wind: excellent conditions for a summit climb. Hall's instincts were uncanny: it appeared that he had timed our attempt perfectly. "Jonno!

Stuart!" he yelled from the tent next door. "Looks like we're on, lads. Be ready to rock and roll at eleven-thirty!"

As we sipped tea and readied our gear for the climb, nobody said much. All of us had suffered greatly to get to this moment. Like Doug, I had eaten little and slept not at all since leaving Camp Two, two days earlier. Every time I coughed, the pain from my torn thoracic cartilage felt like someone was jabbing a knife beneath my ribs, and brought tears to my eyes. But if I wanted a crack at the summit, I knew that I had no choice but to ignore my infirmities and climb.

Twenty-five minutes before midnight, I strapped on my oxygen mask, switched on my headlamp, and ascended into the darkness. There were fifteen of us in Hall's group: three guides, a full complement of eight clients, and Sherpas Ang Dorje, Lhakpa Chhiri, Ngawang Norbu, and Kami. Hall directed two other Sherpas—Arita and Chuldum—to remain at the tents in support, ready to mobilize in the event of trouble.

The Mountain Madness team—composed of guides Fischer, Beidleman, and Boukreev; six Sherpas; and clients Charlotte Fox, Tim Madsen, Klev Schoening, Sandy Pittman, Lene Gammelgaard, and Martin Adams—left the South Col half an hour after us.* Lopsang had intended that only five Mountain Madness Sherpas accompany the summit team, leaving two at the Col in support, but, he says, "Scott opens his heart, tells to my Sherpas, 'All can go to summit.' "† In the end, Lopsang went behind Fischer's back and ordered one Sherpa, his cousin "Big" Pemba, to remain behind. "Pemba angry to me," Lopsang acknowledged, "but I tell to him, 'You must stay, or I will not give you job again.' So he stays at Camp Four."

* Missing from Fischer's summit party were clients Dale Kruse, who had remained at Base Camp in the wake of his most recent bout with HACE, and Pete Schoening, the fabled sixty-eight-year-old veteran, who'd elected to go no higher than Camp Three after a cardiogram administered by Drs. Hutchison, Taske, and Mackenzie had indicated a potentially serious anomaly in his heartbeat.

† Most of the climbing Sherpas on Everest in 1996 wanted an opportunity to reach the top. Their underlying motives were no less varied than the motives of Western climbers, but at least part of the incentive was job security: as Lopsang explained, "After Sherpa climbs Everest, easy to find work. Everybody want to hire this Sherpa."

Leaving camp just after Fischer's team, Makalu Gau started up with two Sherpas—blatantly ignoring his promise that no Taiwanese would make a summit attempt the same day we did. The South Africans had intended to go for the top, too, but the grueling climb from Camp Three to the Col had taken so much out of them that they didn't even emerge from their tents.

All told, thirty-three climbers departed for the summit in the middle of that night. Although we left the Col as members of three distinct expeditions, our fates were already starting to intertwine—and they would become more and more tightly bound with every meter we ascended.

| | |

The night had a cold, phantasmal beauty that intensified as we climbed. More stars than I had ever seen smeared the frozen sky. A gibbous moon rose above the shoulder of 27,824-foot Makalu, washing the slope beneath my boots in ghostly light, obviating the need for a headlamp. Far to the southeast, along the India-Nepal frontier, colossal thunderheads drifted over the malarial swamps of the Terai, illuminating the heavens with surreal bursts of orange and blue lightning.

Within three hours of leaving the Col, Frank decided that something about the day just didn't feel right. Stepping out of the queue, he turned around and descended to the tents. His fourth attempt to climb Everest was over.

Not long after that, Doug stepped aside as well. "He was a little ahead of me at the time," recalls Lou. "All of a sudden he stepped out of line and just stood there. When I moved up beside him, he told me he was cold and feeling bad and was heading down." Then Rob, who was bringing up the rear, caught up to Doug, and a brief conversation ensued. Nobody overheard the dialogue, so there is no way of knowing what was said, but the upshot was that Doug got back in line and continued his ascent.

| | |

The day before departing Base Camp, Rob had sat the team down in the mess tent and given us a lecture about the importance of obeying his orders on summit day. "I will tolerate no dissension up there," he admonished, staring pointedly at me. "My word will be absolute law, beyond appeal. If you don't like a particular decision I make, I'd be happy to discuss it with you afterward, but not while we're on the hill."

The most obvious source of potential conflict was the likelihood that Rob might decide to turn us around before the summit. But there was another matter he was particularly concerned about. During the latter stages of the acclimatization period, he'd given us slightly freer rein to climb at our own pace—for instance, Hall sometimes allowed me to travel two hours or more out in front of the main group. He now stressed, however, that for the first half of the summit day he wanted everybody to climb in close proximity. "Until we all reach the crest of the Southeast Ridge," he pronounced, referring to a distinctive promontory at 27,600 feet known as the Balcony, "everyone needs to stay within a hundred meters of each other. This is very important. We will be climbing in the dark, and I want the guides to be able to keep close track of you."

Ascending through the predawn hours of May 10, those of us at the head of the pack were thus compelled to repeatedly stop and wait in the bone-cracking cold for our slowest members to catch up. On one occasion Mike Groom, sirdar Ang Dorje, and I sat on a snow-covered ledge for more than forty-five minutes, shivering and pounding our hands and feet to ward off frostbite, waiting for the others to arrive. But the squandered time was even more excruciating to bear than the cold.

At 3:45 A.M., Mike announced that we'd gotten too far ahead and needed to stop and wait yet again. Pressing my body against a shale outcrop, trying to escape the subzero breeze now blowing from the west, I stared down the precipitous slope and attempted to identify the climbers inching toward us in the moonlight. As they advanced, I could see that some members of Fischer's group had caught up with our group: Hall's team, the Mountain Madness team, and the Taiwanese were now jumbled into one long, intermittent queue. And then something peculiar caught my eye.

Sixty-five feet below, a tall figure in a bright yellow down jacket and pants was hitched to the back of a much smaller Sherpa by a three-foot length of cord; the Sherpa, not wearing an oxygen mask, huffing loudly, was hauling his partner up the slope like a horse pulling a plow. The odd pair was passing other people and making good time, but the arrangement—a technique for assisting a weak or injured climber known as short-roping—appeared to be hazardous and extremely uncomfortable for both parties. By and by, I recognized the Sherpa as Fischer's flamboyant sirdar, Lopsang Jangbu, and the climber in yellow as Sandy Pittman.

Guide Neal Beidleman, who also observed Lopsang towing Pittman, recalls, "As I came up from below, Lopsang was leaning into the slope, clinging to the rock like a spider, supporting Sandy on a tight tether. It looked awkward and quite dangerous. I wasn't sure what to make of it."

Around 4:15 A.M., Mike gave us the go-ahead to resume our ascent, and Ang Dorje and I started climbing as fast as we could in order to warm ourselves. As the first hint of daybreak brightened the eastern horizon, the rocky, terraced terrain we'd been ascending gave way to a broad gully of unconsolidated snow. Taking turns breaking trail through the calf-deep powder, Ang Dorje and I reached the crest of the Southeast Ridge at 5:30, just as the sun edged into the sky. Three of the world's five highest peaks stood out in craggy relief against the pastel dawn. My altimeter read 27,600 feet.

Hall had made it very clear that I was to climb no higher until the whole group had gathered at this balconylike roost, so I sat down on my pack to wait. When Rob and Beck finally arrived at the back of the herd, I'd been sitting for more than ninety minutes. As I waited, both Fischer's group and the Taiwanese team caught and passed me. I felt frustrated about wasting so much time and peeved at falling behind everybody else. But I understood Hall's rationale, so I kept a tight lid on my anger.

During my thirty-four-year tenure as a climber, I'd found that the most rewarding aspects of mountaineering derive from the sport's emphasis on self-reliance, on making critical decisions and dealing with the consequences, on personal responsibility. When you sign on as a client, I discovered, you are forced to give up all of that, and more. For safety's sake, a responsible guide will always insist on calling the shots—he or she simply can't afford to let each client make important decisions independently.

Passivity on the part of the clients had thus been encouraged throughout our expedition. Sherpas put in the route, set up the camps, did the cooking, hauled all the loads. This conserved our energy and vastly increased our chances of getting up Everest, but I found it hugely unsatisfying. I felt at times as if I wasn't really climbing the mountain—that surrogates were doing it for me. Although I had willingly accepted this role in order to climb Everest with Hall, I never got used to it. So I was happy as hell when, at 7:10 A.M., he arrived atop the Balcony and gave me the O.K. to continue climbing.

One of the first people I passed when I started moving again was Lopsang, kneeling in the snow over a pile of vomit. Ordinarily, he was the strongest member of any group he climbed with, even though he never used supplemental oxygen. As he proudly told me after the expedition, "Every mountain I climb, I go first, I fix line. In ninety-five on Everest with Rob Hall I go first from Base Camp to summit, I fix all ropes." His position near the back of Fischer's group on the morning of May 10, retching his guts out, seemed to indicate that something was seriously amiss.

The previous afternoon, Lopsang had exhausted himself carrying a satellite phone for Pittman, in addition to the rest of his load, from Camp Three to Camp Four. When Beidleman had seen Lopsang shoulder his crippling eighty-pound burden at Camp Three, he'd told the Sherpa that it wasn't necessary to carry the phone to the South Col and suggested that he leave it behind. "I don't want to carry telephone," Lopsang later admitted, in part because it had worked only marginally at Camp Three and it seemed even less likely to work in the colder, harsher environment of Camp Four.* "But Scott told to me, 'If

* The phone didn't work at all at Camp Four.

you don't carry, I will carry.' So I take telephone, tie on outside of my rucksack, carry to Camp Four. . . . This makes me very tired."

And now Lopsang had just towed Pittman on a short-rope for five or six hours above the South Col, substantially compounding his fatigue and preventing him from assuming his customary role in the lead, establishing the route. Because his unexpected absence from the head of the line had a bearing on the day's outcome, his decision to short-rope Pittman provoked criticism and bafflement after the fact. "I have no idea why Lopsang was short-roping Sandy," says Beidleman. "He lost sight of what he was supposed to be doing up there, what the priorities were."

For her part, Pittman didn't ask to be short-roped. As she left Camp Four at the front of Fischer's group, Lopsang abruptly pulled her aside and girth-hitched a bight of rope to the front of her climbing harness. Then, without consulting her, he clipped the other end to his own harness and began to pull. She maintains that Lopsang hauled her up the slope very much against her wishes. Which begs a question: as a notoriously assertive New Yorker (she was so adamantine that some Kiwis at Base Camp nicknamed her "Sandy Pit Bull") why didn't she simply unfasten the three-foot tether connecting her to Lopsang, which would have required nothing more than reaching up and unclipping a single carabiner?

Pittman explains that she didn't unclip herself from the Sherpa out of respect for his authority—as she put it, "I didn't want to hurt Lopsang's feelings." She also said that although she didn't consult her watch, her recollection was that he short-roped her for only "one to one and a half hours,"* not five to six hours, as several other climbers observed, and Lopsang confirmed.

For his part, when asked why he short-roped Pittman, for whom he had openly expressed contempt on multiple occasions, Lopsang gave conflicting accounts. He told Seattle attorney Peter Goldman—

* Pittman and I discussed these and other events during a seventy-minute phone conversation six months after returning from Everest. Except to clarify certain points about the short-roping incident, she requested that I not quote any part of that dialogue in this book, and I have honored that request.

who had climbed Broad Peak with both Scott and Lopsang in 1995 and was one of Fischer's oldest, most trusted friends—that in the darkness he had confused Pittman with the Danish client Lene Gammelgaard and that he stopped towing her as soon as he realized his mistake at daybreak. But in an extended, tape-recorded interview with me, Lopsang insisted rather convincingly that he knew all along he was hauling Pittman and had decided to do it "because Scott wants all members to go to summit, and I am thinking Sandy will be weakest member, I am thinking she will be slow, so I will take her first."

A perceptive young man, Lopsang was extremely devoted to Fischer; the Sherpa understood how important it was to his friend and employer to get Pittman to the summit. Indeed, one of the last times Fischer communicated with Jane Bromet from Base Camp he mused, "If I can get Sandy to the summit, I'll bet she'll be on TV talk shows. Do you think she will include me in her fame and fanfare?"

As Goldman explained, "Lopsang was totally loyal to Scott. To me it's inconceivable that he would have short-roped anybody unless he believed very strongly that Scott wanted him to do it."

Whatever motivated him, Lopsang's decision to tow a client didn't seem like a particularly serious mistake at the time. But it would end up being one of many little things—a slow accrual, compounding steadily and imperceptibly toward critical mass.

Chapter Thirteen

SOUTHEAST RIDGE MAY 10, 1996 27,600 FEET

Suffice it to say that [Everest] has the most steep ridges and appalling precipices that I have ever seen, and that all the talk of an easy snow slope is a myth. . . .

My darling, this is a thrilling business altogether, I can't tell you how it possesses me, and what a prospect it is. And the beauty of it all!

George Leigh Mallory,
in a letter to his wife,
June 28, 1921

Above the South Col, up in the Death Zone, survival is to no small degree a race against the clock. Upon setting out from Camp Four on May 10, each client carried two 6.6-pound oxygen bottles and would pick up a third bottle on the South Summit from a cache to be stocked by Sherpas. At a conservative flow rate of two liters per minute, each bottle would last between five and six hours. By 4:00 or 5:00 P.M., everyone's gas would be gone. Depending on each person's acclimatization and physiological makeup, we would still be able to function above the South Col—but not well, and not for long. We would instantly become more vulnerable to HAPE, HACE, hypothermia, impaired judgment, and frostbite. The risk of dying would skyrocket.

Hall, who had climbed Everest four times previously, understood as well as anybody the need to get up and down quickly. Recognizing that the basic climbing skills of some of his clients were highly suspect, Hall intended to rely on fixed lines to safeguard and expedite both our group and Fischer's group over the most difficult ground. The fact that no expedition had been to the top yet this year concerned him, therefore, because it meant that ropes had not been installed over much of this terrain.

Göran Kropp, the Swedish soloist, had ascended to within 350 vertical feet of top on May 3, but he hadn't bothered to put in any ropes at all. The Montenegrins, who'd got even higher, had installed some fixed line, but in their inexperience they'd used all they had in the first 1,400 feet above the South Col, wasting it on relatively gentle slopes where it wasn't really needed. Thus on the morning of our summit bid, the only ropes strung along the precipitous serrations of the upper Southeast Ridge were a few ancient, tattered remnants from past expeditions that emerged sporadically from the ice.

Anticipating this possibility, before leaving Base Camp Hall and Fischer convened a meeting of guides from both teams, during which they agreed that each expedition would dispatch two Sherpas—including the climbing sirdars, Ang Dorje and Lopsang—from Camp Four ninety minutes ahead of the main groups. This would give the Sherpas time to install fixed lines on the most exposed sections of the upper mountain before the clients arrived. "Rob made it very clear how important it was to do this," recalls Beidleman. "He wanted to avoid a time-consuming bottleneck at all costs."

For some unknown reason, however, no Sherpas left the South Col ahead of us on the night of May 9. Perhaps the violent gale, which didn't stop blowing until 7:30 P.M., prevented them from mobilizing as early as they'd hoped. After the expedition Lopsang insisted that at the last minute Hall and Fischer had simply scrapped the plan to fix ropes in advance of their clients, because they'd received erroneous information that the Montenegrins had already completed the job as high as the South Summit.

But if Lopsang's assertion is correct, neither Beidleman, Groom, nor Boukreev—the three surviving guides—were ever told of the altered scheme. And if the plan to fix lines had been intentionally abandoned, there would have been no reason for Lopsang and Ang Dorje to depart with the 300 feet of rope that each Sherpa carried when they set out from Camp Four at the front of their respective teams.

In any case, above 27,400 feet, no ropes had been fixed ahead of time. When Ang Dorje and I first arrived on the Balcony at 5:30 A.M., we were more than an hour in front of the rest of Hall's group. At that point we could easily have gone ahead to install the ropes. But Rob had explicitly forbidden me to go ahead, and Lopsang was still far below, short-roping Pittman, so there was nobody to accompany Ang Dorje.

Quiet and moody by nature, Ang Dorje seemed especially somber as we sat together watching the sun come up. My attempts to engage him in conversation went nowhere. His ill humor, I figured, was perhaps due to the abscessed tooth that had been causing him pain for the previous two weeks. Or maybe he was brooding over the disturbing vision he'd had four days earlier: on their last evening at Base Camp, he and some other Sherpas had celebrated the coming summit attempt by drinking a large quantity of *chhang*—a thick, sweet beer brewed from rice and millet. The next morning, severely hungover, he was extremely agitated; before ascending the Icefall he confided to a friend that he'd seen ghosts in the night. An intensely spiritual young man, Ang Dorje was not one to take such portents lightly.

It was possible, though, that he was simply angry at Lopsang, whom he regarded as a showboat. In 1995, Hall had employed both Lopsang and Ang Dorje on his Everest expedition, and the two Sherpas had not worked well together.

On summit day that year, Hall's team had reached the South Summit late, around 1:30 P.M., to find deep, unstable snow blanketing the final stretch of the summit ridge. Hall sent a Kiwi guide named Guy Cotter ahead with Lopsang, rather than Ang Dorje, to determine the feasibility of climbing higher—and Ang Dorje, who was the sirdar on that climb, took it as an insult. A little later, when Lopsang had climbed to the base of the Hillary Step, Hall decided to abort the summit attempt and signaled Cotter and Lopsang to turn around. But Lopsang ignored the command, untied from Cotter, and continued ascending to the summit alone. Hall had been angry about Lopsang's insubordination, and Ang Dorje had shared his employer's displeasure.

This year, even though they were on different teams, Ang Dorje had again been asked to work with Lopsang on summit day—and again Lopsang appeared to be acting squirrelly. Ang Dorje had been working well beyond the call of duty for six long weeks. Now, apparently, he was tired of doing more than his share. Looking sullen, he sat beside me in the snow, awaiting the arrival of Lopsang, and the ropes were left unfixed.

As a consequence, I ran smack into the first bottleneck ninety minutes after moving beyond the Balcony, at 28,000 feet, where the intermingled teams encountered a series of massive rock steps that required ropes for safe passage. Clients huddled restlessly at the base of the rock for nearly an hour while Beidleman—taking over the duties of an absent Lopsang—laboriously ran the rope out.

Here, the impatience and technical inexperience of Hall's client Yasuko Namba nearly caused a disaster. An accomplished businesswoman employed by Federal Express in Tokyo, Yasuko didn't fit the meek, deferential stereotype of a middle-aged Japanese woman. At home, she'd told me with a laugh, her husband did all the cooking and cleaning. Her quest for Everest had turned into a minor cause célèbre in Japan. Previously on the expedition she'd been a slow, uncertain climber, but today, with the summit in her crosshairs, she was energized as never before. "From the time we arrived at the South Col," says John Taske, who'd shared a tent with her at Camp Four, "Yasuko was totally focused on the top—it was almost like she was in a trance." Ever since leaving the Col she'd been pushing extremely hard, jostling her way toward the front of the line.

Now, as Beidleman clung precariously to the rock 100 feet above the clients, the overly eager Yasuko clamped her jumar to the dangling rope before the guide had anchored his end of it. As she was about to put her full body weight on the rope—which would have pulled Beidleman off—Mike Groom intervened in the nick of time and gently scolded her for being so impatient.

The traffic jam at the ropes grew with each arriving climber, so those at the rear of the scrum fell farther and farther behind. By late morning, three of Hall's clients—Stuart Hutchison, John Taske, and Lou Kasischke, climbing near the back with Hall—were becoming quite worried about the lagging pace. Immediately in front of them was the Taiwanese team, moving especially sluggishly. "They were climbing in a peculiar style, really close together," says Hutchison, "almost like slices in a loaf of bread, one behind the other, which meant it was nearly impossible to pass them. We spent a lot of time waiting for them to move up the ropes."

At Base Camp before our summit bid, Hall had contemplated two possible turn-around times—either 1:00 P.M. or 2:00 P.M. He never declared which of these times we were to abide by, however—which was curious, considering how much he'd talked about the importance of designating a hard deadline and sticking to it no matter what. We were simply left with a vaguely articulated understanding that Hall would withhold making a final decision until summit day, after assessing the weather and other factors, and would then personally take responsibility for turning everyone around at the proper hour.

By mid-morning on May 10, Hall still hadn't announced what our turn-around time would actually be. Hutchison, conservative by nature, was operating on the assumption that it would be 1:00 P.M. Around 11:00, Hall told Hutchison and Taske that the top was still three hours away, and then he sprinted to try and get past the Taiwanese. "It seemed increasingly unlikely that we would have any chance of summitting before the one P.M. turn-around time," says Hutchison. A brief discussion ensued. Kasischke was initially reluctant to concede defeat, but Taske and Hutchison were persuasive. At 11:30, the three men turned their backs on the summit and headed down, and Hall sent Sherpas Kami and Lhakpa Chhiri down with them.

Electing to descend must have been supremely difficult for these three clients, as well as for Frank Fischbeck, who'd turned around hours earlier. Mountaineering tends to draw men and women not easily deflected from their goals. By this late stage in the expedition we had all been subjected to levels of misery and peril that would have sent more balanced individuals packing for home long ago. To get this far one had to have an uncommonly obdurate personality.

Unfortunately, the sort of individual who is programmed to ignore personal distress and keep pushing for the top is frequently programmed to disregard signs of grave and imminent danger as well. This forms the nub of a dilemma that every Everest climber eventually comes up against: in order to succeed you must be exceedingly driven, but if you're too driven you're likely to die. Above 26,000 feet, moreover, the line between appropriate zeal and reckless summit fever becomes grievously thin. Thus the slopes of Everest are littered with corpses.

Taske, Hutchison, Kasischke, and Fischbeck had each spent as much as $70,000 and endured weeks of agony to be granted this one shot at the summit. All were ambitious men, unaccustomed to losing and even less to quitting. And yet, faced with a tough decision, they were among the few who made the right choice that day.

Above the rock step where John, Stuart, and Lou turned around, the fixed ropes ended. From this point the route angled steeply upward along a graceful arête of wind-compacted snow that culminated in the South Summit—where I arrived at 11:00 to find a second, even worse bottleneck. A little higher, seemingly no more than a stone's throw away, was the vertical gash of the Hillary Step, and slightly beyond that the summit itself. Rendered dumb with awe and fatigue, I took some photos, then sat down with guides Andy Harris, Neal Beidleman, and Anatoli Boukreev to wait for the Sherpas to fix ropes along the spectacularly corniced summit ridge.

I noticed that Boukreev, like Lopsang, wasn't using supplemental oxygen. Although the Russian had summitted Everest twice before without gas, and Lopsang thrice, I was surprised Fischer had given them permission to guide the peak without it, which didn't seem to be in their clients' best interest. I was also surprised to see that Boukreev didn't have a backpack—customarily a guide would carry a pack containing rope, first-aid supplies, crevasse-rescue gear, extra clothing, and other items necessary to assist clients in the event of an emergency. Boukreev was the first guide I'd ever seen, on any mountain, ignore this convention.

It turned out that he had departed Camp Four carrying both a backpack and an oxygen bottle; he later told me that although he didn't intend to use the gas, he wanted to have a bottle handy in the event that "his power was low" and he needed it higher on the peak. Upon reaching the Balcony, however, he jettisoned the pack and gave his oxygen canister, mask, and regulator to Beidleman to carry for him. Because Boukreev wasn't breathing supplemental oxygen, he had apparently decided to strip his load down to the bare minimum to gain every possible advantage in the appallingly thin air.

A 20-knot breeze raked the ridge, blowing a plume of spindrift far over the Kangshung Face, but overhead the sky was an achingly brilliant blue. Lounging in the sun at 28,700 feet inside my thick down suit, gazing across the roof of the world in a hypoxic stupor, I completely lost track of time. None of us paid much attention to the fact that Ang Dorje and Ngawang Norbu, another Sherpa on Hall's team, were sitting beside us sharing a thermos of tea and seemed to be in no hurry to go higher. Around 11:40, Beidleman eventually asked, "Hey, Ang Dorje, are you going to fix the ropes, or what?" Ang Dorje's reply was a quick, unequivocal "No"—perhaps because none of Fischer's Sherpas were there to share the work.

Growing alarmed at the crowd stacking up at the South Summit, Beidleman roused Harris and Boukreev and strongly suggested that the three guides install the ropes themselves; hearing this, I quickly volunteered to help. Beidleman pulled a 150-foot coil of rope from his pack, I grabbed another coil from Ang Dorje, and with Boukreev and Harris we got under way at noon to fix lines up the summit ridge. But by then another hour had already trickled away.

| | |

Bottled oxygen does not make the top of Everest feel like sea level. Climbing above the South Summit with my regulator delivering just under two liters of oxygen per minute, I had to stop and draw three or four lungfuls of air after each ponderous step. Then I'd take one more step and have to pause for another four heaving breaths—and this was the fastest pace I could manage. Because the oxygen systems we were using delivered a lean mix of compressed gas and ambient air, 29,000 feet with gas felt like approximately 26,000 feet without gas. But the bottled oxygen conferred other benefits that weren't so easily quantified.

Climbing along the blade of the summit ridge, sucking gas into my ragged lungs, I enjoyed a strange, unwarranted sense of calm. The world beyond the rubber mask was stupendously vivid but seemed not quite real, as if a movie were being projected in slow motion across the front of my goggles. I felt drugged, disengaged, thoroughly insulated from external stimuli. I had to remind myself over and over that there was 7,000 feet of sky on either side, that everything was at stake here, that I would pay for a single bungled step with my life.

Half an hour above the South Summit I arrived at the foot of the Hillary Step. One of the most famous pitches in all of mountaineering, its forty feet of near-vertical rock and ice looked daunting, but—as any serious climber would—I'd wanted very badly to take the "sharp end" of the rope and lead the Step. It was clear, however, that Boukreev, Beidleman, and Harris all felt the same way, and it was hypoxic delusion on my part to think that any of them was going to let a client hog such a coveted lead.

In the end, Boukreev—as senior guide and the only one of us who had climbed Everest previously—claimed the honor; with Beidleman paying out the rope, he did a masterful job of leading the pitch. But it was a slow process, and as he painstakingly ascended toward the crest of the Step, I nervously studied my watch and wondered whether I might run out of oxygen. My first canister had expired at 7:00 A.M. on the Balcony, after lasting about seven hours. Using this as a benchmark, at the South Summit I'd calculated that my second canister would expire around 2:00 P.M., which I'd stupidly assumed would allow plenty of time to reach the summit and return to the South Summit to retrieve my third oxygen bottle. But now it was already after 1:00, and I was beginning to have serious doubts.

At the top of the Step I shared my concern with Beidleman and asked whether he minded if I hurried ahead to the summit instead of pausing to help him string the last coil of rope along the ridge. "Go for it," he graciously offered. "I'll take care of the rope."

Plodding slowly up the last few steps to the summit, I had the sensation of being underwater, of life moving at quarter speed. And then I found myself atop a slender wedge of ice, adorned with a discarded oxygen cylinder and a battered aluminum survey pole, with nowhere higher to climb. A string of Buddhist prayer flags snapped furiously in the wind. Far below, down a side of the mountain I had never laid eyes on, the dry Tibetan plateau stretched to the horizon as a boundless expanse of dun-colored earth.

Reaching the top of Everest is supposed to trigger a surge of intense elation; against long odds, after all, I had just attained a goal I'd coveted since childhood. But the summit was really only the halfway point. Any impulse I might have felt toward self-congratulation was extinguished by overwhelming apprehension about the long, dangerous descent that lay ahead.

Chapter Fourteen

SUMMIT 1:12 P.M., MAY 10, 1996 29,028 FEET

Not only during the ascent but also during the descent my will-power is dulled. The longer I climb the less important the goal seems to me, the more indifferent I become to myself. My attention has diminished, my memory is weakened. My mental fatigue is now greater than the bodily. It is so pleasant to sit doing nothing—and therefore so dangerous. Death through exhaustion is—like death through freezing—a pleasant one.

Reinhold Messner
The Crystal Horizon

In my backpack was a banner from *Outside* magazine, a small pennant emblazoned with a whimsical lizard that Linda, my wife, had sewn, and some other mementos with which I'd intended to pose for a series of triumphant photos. Cognizant of my dwindling oxygen reserves, however, I left everything in my pack and stayed on top of the world just long enough to fire off four quick shots of Andy Harris and Anatoli Boukreev posing in front of the summit survey marker. Then I turned to descend. About twenty yards below the summit I passed Neal Beidleman and a client of Fischer's named Martin Adams on their way up. After exchanging a high five with Neal, I grabbed a handful of small stones from a wind-scoured patch of exposed shale, zipped the souvenirs into the pocket of my down suit, and hastened down the ridge.

A moment earlier I'd noticed that wispy clouds now filled the valleys to the south, obscuring all but the highest peaks. Adams—a small, pugnacious Texan who'd gotten rich selling bonds during the booming 1980s—is an experienced airplane pilot who'd spent many hours gazing down on the tops of clouds; later he told me that he recognized these innocent-looking puffs of water vapor to be the crowns of robust thunderheads immediately after reaching the top. "When you see a thunderhead in an airplane," he explained, "your first reaction is to get the fuck out of there. So that's what I did."

But unlike Adams, I was unaccustomed to peering down at cumulonimbus cells from 29,000 feet, and I therefore remained ignorant of the storm that was even then bearing down. My concerns revolved instead around the diminishing supply of oxygen in my tank.

Fifteen minutes after leaving the summit I reached the top of the Hillary Step, where I encountered a clot of climbers chuffing up the single strand of rope, and my descent came to an enforced halt. As I waited for the crowd to pass, Andy arrived on his way down. "Jon," he asked, "I don't seem to be getting enough air. Can you tell if the intake valve to my mask is iced up?"

A quick check revealed a fist-sized chunk of frozen drool blocking the rubber valve that admitted ambient air into the mask from the atmosphere. I chipped it off with the pick of my ice ax, then asked Andy to return the favor by turning off my regulator in order to conserve my gas until the Step cleared. He mistakenly opened the valve instead of closing it, however, and ten minutes later all my oxygen was gone. My cognitive functions, which had been marginal before, instantly went into a nosedive. I felt like I'd been slipped an overdose of a powerful sedative.

I fuzzily remember Sandy Pittman climbing past as I waited, bound for the summit, followed an indeterminate time later by Charlotte Fox and then Lopsang Jangbu. Yasuko materialized next, just below my precarious stance, but was flummoxed by the last and steepest portion of the Step. I watched helplessly for fifteen minutes as she struggled to haul herself up the uppermost brow of rock, too exhausted to manage it. Finally Tim Madsen, who was waiting impatiently directly below her, put his hands beneath her buttocks and pushed her to the top.

Rob Hall appeared not long after that. Disguising my rising panic, I thanked him for getting me to the top of Everest. "Yeah, it's turned out to be a pretty good expedition," he replied, then mentioned that Frank Fischbeck, Beck Weathers, Lou Kasischke, Stuart Hutchison, and John Taske had all turned back. Even in my state of hypoxic imbecility, it was obvious Hall was profoundly disappointed that five of his eight clients had packed it in—a sentiment that I suspected was heightened by the fact that Fischer's entire crew appeared to be plugging toward the summit. "I only wish we could have gotten more clients to the top," Rob lamented before continuing on his way.

Soon thereafter, Adams and Boukreev arrived on their way down, stopping immediately above me to wait for the traffic to clear. A minute later the overcrowding atop the Step intensified further as Makalu Gau, Ang Dorje, and several other Sherpas came up the rope, followed by Doug Hansen and Scott Fischer. Then, finally, the Hillary Step was clear—but only after I'd spent more than an hour at 28,900 feet without supplemental oxygen.

By that point, entire sectors of my cerebral cortex seemed to have shut down altogether. Dizzy, fearing that I would black out, I was frantic to reach the South Summit, where my third bottle was waiting. I started tenuously down the fixed lines, stiff with dread. Just below the step, Anatoli and Martin scooted around me and hurried down. Exercising extreme caution, I continued descending the tightrope of the ridge, but fifty feet above the oxygen cache the rope ended, and I balked at going farther without gas.

Over at the South Summit, I could see Andy Harris sorting through a pile of orange oxygen bottles. "Yo, Harold!" I yelled, "Could you bring me a fresh bottle?"

"There's no oxygen here!" the guide shouted back. "These bottles are all empty!" This was disturbing news. My brain screamed for oxygen. I didn't know what to do. Just then, Mike Groom caught up to me on his way down from the summit. Mike had climbed Everest in 1993 without gas, and he wasn't overly concerned about going without. He gave me his oxygen bottle, and we quickly scrambled over to the South Summit.

When we got there, an examination of the oxygen cache immediately revealed that there were at least six full bottles. Andy, however, refused to believe it. He kept insisting that they were all empty, and nothing Mike or I said could convince him otherwise.

The only way to know how much gas is in a canister is to attach it to your regulator and read the gauge; presumably this is how Andy had checked the bottles at the South Summit. After the expedition, Neal Beidleman pointed out that if Andy's regulator had become fouled with ice, the gauge might have registered empty even though the canisters were full, which would explain his bizarre obstinacy. And if his regulator was perhaps on the fritz and not delivering oxygen to his mask, that would also explain Andy's apparent lack of lucidity.

This possibility—which now seems so self-evident—didn't occur to either Mike or me at the time, however. In hindsight, Andy was acting irrationally and had plainly slipped well beyond routine hypoxia, but I was so mentally impeded myself that it simply didn't register.

My inability to discern the obvious was exacerbated to some degree by the guide-client protocol. Andy and I were very similar in terms of physical ability and technical expertise; had we been climbing together in a nonguided situation as equal partners, it's inconceivable to me that I would have neglected to recognize his plight. But on this expedition he had been cast in the role of invincible guide, there to look after me and the other clients; we had been specifically indoctrinated not to question our guides' judgment. The thought never entered my crippled mind that Andy might in fact be in terrible straits—that a guide might urgently need help from me.

As Andy continued to assert that there were no full bottles at the South Summit, Mike looked at me quizzically. I looked back and shrugged. Turning to Andy, I said, "No big deal, Harold. Much ado about nothing." Then I grabbed a new oxygen canister, screwed it onto my regulator, and headed down the mountain. Given what unfolded over the hours that followed, the ease with which I abdicated responsibility—my utter failure to consider that Andy might have been in serious trouble—was a lapse that's likely to haunt me for the rest of my life.

Around 3:30 P.M. I left the South Summit ahead of Mike, Yasuko, and Andy, and almost immediately descended into a dense layer of clouds. Light snow started to fall. I could scarcely tell where the mountain ended and where the sky began in the flat, diminishing light; it would have been very easy to blunder off the edge of the ridge and never be heard from again. And the conditions only worsened as I moved down the peak.

At the bottom of the rock steps on the Southeast Ridge I stopped with Mike to wait for Yasuko, who has having difficulty negotiating the fixed ropes. He attempted to call Rob on the radio, but Mike's transmitter was working only intermittently and he couldn't raise anybody. With Mike looking after Yasuko, and both Rob and Andy accompanying Doug Hansen—the only other client still above us—I assumed the situation was under control. So as Yasuko caught up to us, I asked Mike's permission to continue down alone. "Fine," he replied. "Just don't walk off any cornices."

About 4:45 P.M., when I reached the Balcony—the promontory at 27,600 feet on the Southeast Ridge where I'd sat watching the sunrise with Ang Dorje—I was shocked to encounter Beck Weathers, standing alone in the snow, shivering violently. I'd assumed that he'd descended to Camp Four hours earlier. "Beck!" I exclaimed, "what the fuck are you still doing up here?"

Years earlier, Beck had undergone a radial keratotomy* to correct his vision. A side effect of the surgery, he discovered early in the Everest climb, was that the low barometric pressure that exists at high altitude caused his eyesight to fail. The higher he climbed, the lower the barometric pressure fell, and the worse his vision became.

The previous afternoon as he was ascending from Camp Three to Camp Four, Beck later confessed to me, "my vision had gotten so bad that I couldn't see more than a few feet. So I just tucked right behind John Taske and when he'd lift a foot I'd place my foot right in his bootprint."

Beck had spoken openly of his vision problem earlier, but with the summit in reach he neglected to mention its increasing severity to Rob or anyone else. His bad eyes notwithstanding, he was climbing well and feeling stronger than he had since the beginning of the expedition, and, he explained, "I didn't want to bail out prematurely."

* A radial keratotomy is a surgical procedure to correct myopia in which a series of spokelike incisions are made from the outer edge of the cornea toward its center, thereby flattening it.

Climbing above the South Col through the night, Beck managed to keep up with the group by employing the same strategy he'd used the previous afternoon—stepping in the footsteps of the person directly in front of him. But by the time he reached the Balcony and the sun came up, he realized his vision was worse than ever. In addition, he'd inadvertently rubbed some ice crystals into his eyes, lacerating both corneas.

"At that point," Beck revealed, "one eye was completely blurred over, I could barely see out of the other, and I'd lost all depth perception. I felt that I couldn't see well enough to climb higher without being a danger to myself or a burden to someone else, so I told Rob what was going on."

"Sorry pal," Rob immediately announced, "you're going down. I'll send one of the Sherpas down with you." But Beck wasn't quite ready to give up his summit hopes: "I explained to Rob that I thought there was a pretty good chance my vision would improve once the sun got higher and my pupils contracted. I said I wanted to wait a little while, and then boogie on up after everybody else if I started seeing more clearly."

Rob considered Beck's proposal, then decreed, "O.K., fair enough. I'll give you half an hour to find out. But I can't have you going down to Camp Four on your own. If your vision isn't better in thirty minutes I want you to stay here so I know exactly where you are until I come back from the summit, then we can go down together. I'm very serious about this: either you go down right now, or you promise me you'll sit right here until I return."

"So I crossed my heart and hoped to die," Beck told me good-naturedly as we stood in the blowing snow and waning light. "And I've kept my word. Which is why I'm still standing here."

Shortly after noon, Stuart Hutchison, John Taske, and Lou Kasischke had gone past on their way down with Lhakpa and Kami, but Weathers elected not to accompany them. "The weather was still good," he explains, "and I saw no reason to break my promise to Rob at that point."

Now, however, it was getting dark and conditions were turning grim. "Come down with me," I implored. "It will be at least another two or three hours before Rob shows up. I'll be your eyes. I'll get you down, no problem." Beck was nearly persuaded to descend with me when I made the mistake of mentioning that Mike Groom was on his way down with Yasuko, a few minutes behind me. In a day of many mistakes, this would turn out to be one of the larger ones.

"Thanks anyway," Beck said. "I think I'll just wait for Mike. He's got a rope; he'll be able to short-rope me down."

"O.K., Beck," I replied. "It's your call. I guess I'll see you in camp, then." Secretly, I was relieved that I wouldn't have to deal with getting Beck down the problematic slopes to come, most of which were not protected by fixed lines. Daylight was waning, the weather was worsening, my reserves of strength were nearly gone. Yet I still didn't have any sense that calamity was around the corner. Indeed, after talking with Beck I even took the time to find a spent oxygen canister that I'd stashed in the snow on the way up some ten hours earlier. Wanting to remove all my trash from the mountain, I stuffed it into my pack with my other two bottles (one empty, one partially full) and then hurried toward the South Col, 1,600 feet below.

| | |

From the Balcony I descended a few hundred feet down a broad, gentle snow gully without incident, but then things began to get sketchy. The route meandered through outcroppings of broken shale blanketed with six inches of fresh snow. Negotiating the puzzling, infirm terrain demanded unceasing concentration, an all-but-impossible feat in my punch-drunk state.

Because the wind had erased the tracks of the climbers who'd gone down before me, I had difficulty determining the correct route. In 1993, Mike Groom's partner—Lopsang Tshering Bhutia, a skilled Himalayan climber who was a nephew of Tenzing Norgay's—had taken a wrong turn in this area and fallen to his death. Fighting to maintain a grip on reality, I started talking to myself out loud. "Keep it together, keep it together, keep it together," I chanted over and over, mantra-like. "You can't afford to fuck things up here. This is way serious. Keep it together."

I sat down to rest on a broad, sloping ledge, but after a few minutes a deafening BOOM! frightened me back to my feet. Enough new snow had accumulated that I feared a massive slab avalanche had released on the slopes above, but when I spun around to look I saw nothing. Then there was another BOOM!, accompanied by a flash that momentarily lit up the sky, and I realized I was hearing the crash of thunder.

In the morning, on the way up, I'd made a point of continually studying the route on this part of the mountain, frequently looking down to pick out landmarks that would be helpful on the descent, compulsively memorizing the terrain: "Remember to turn left at the buttress that looks like a ship's prow. Then follow that skinny line of snow until it curves sharply to the right." This was something I'd trained myself to do many years earlier, a drill I forced myself to go through every time I climbed, and on Everest it may have saved my life. By 6:00 P.M., as the storm escalated into a full-scale blizzard with driving snow and winds gusting in excess of 60 knots, I came upon the rope that had been fixed by the Montenegrins on the snow slope 600 feet above the Col. Sobered by the force of the rising tempest, I realized that I'd gotten down the trickiest ground just in the nick of time.

Wrapping the fixed line around my arms to rappel, I continued down through the blizzard. Some minutes later I was overwhelmed by a disturbingly familiar feeling of suffocation, and I realized that my oxygen had once again run out. Three hours earlier when I'd attached my regulator to my third and last oxygen canister, I'd noticed that the gauge indicated that the bottle was only half full. I'd figured that would be enough to get me most of the way down, though, so I hadn't bothered exchanging it for a full one. And now the gas was gone.

I pulled the mask from my face, left it hanging around my neck, and pressed onward, surprisingly unconcerned. However, without supplemental oxygen, I moved more slowly, and I had to stop and rest more often.

The literature of Everest is rife with accounts of hallucinatory experiences attributable to hypoxia and fatigue. In 1933, the noted English climber Frank Smythe observed "two curious looking objects floating in the sky" directly above him at 27,000 feet: "[One] possessed what appeared to be squat underdeveloped wings, and the other a protuberance suggestive of a beak. They hovered motionless but seemed slowly to pulsate." In 1980, during his solo ascent, Reinhold Messner imagined that an invisible companion was climbing beside him. Gradually, I became aware that my mind had gone haywire in a similar fashion, and I observed my own slide from reality with a blend of fascination and horror.

I was so far beyond ordinary exhaustion that I experienced a queer detachment from my body, as if I were observing my descent from a few feet overhead. I imagined that I was dressed in a green cardigan and wingtips. And although the gale was generating a windchill in excess of seventy below zero Fahrenheit, I felt strangely, disturbingly warm.

At 6:30, as the last of the daylight seeped from the sky, I'd descended to within 200 vertical feet of Camp Four. Only one obstacle now stood between me and safety: a bulging incline of hard, glassy ice that I would have to descend without a rope. Snow pellets borne by 70-knot gusts stung my face; any exposed flesh was instantly frozen. The tents, no more than 650 horizontal feet away, were only intermittently visible through the whiteout. There was no margin for error. Worried about making a critical blunder, I sat down to marshal my energy before descending further.

Once I was off my feet, inertia took hold. It was so much easier to remain at rest than to summon the initiative to tackle the dangerous ice slope; so I just sat there as the storm roared around me, letting my mind drift, doing nothing for perhaps forty-five minutes.

I'd tightened the drawstrings on my hood until only a tiny opening remained around my eyes, and I was removing the useless, frozen oxygen mask from beneath my chin when Andy Harris suddenly appeared out of the gloom beside me. Shining my headlamp in his direction, I reflexively recoiled when I saw the appalling condition of his face. His cheeks were coated with an armor of frost, one eye was frozen shut, and he was slurring his words badly. He looked in serious trouble. "Which way to the tents?" Andy blurted, frantic to reach shelter.

I pointed in the direction of Camp Four, then warned him about the ice just below us. "It's steeper than it looks!" I yelled, straining to make myself heard over the tempest. "Maybe I should go down first and get a rope from camp—" As I was in midsentence, Andy abruptly turned away and moved over the lip of the ice slope, leaving me sitting there dumbfounded.

Scooting on his butt, he started down the steepest part of the incline. "Andy," I shouted after him, "it's crazy to try it like that! You're going to blow it for sure!" He yelled something back, but his words were carried off by the screaming wind. A second later he lost his purchase, flipped ass over teakettle, and was suddenly rocketing headfirst down the ice.

Two hundred feet below, I could just make out Andy's motionless form slumped at the foot of the incline. I was sure he'd broken at least a leg, maybe his neck. But then, incredibly, he stood up, waved that he was O.K., and started lurching toward Camp Four, which, at the moment was in plain sight, 500 feet beyond.

I could see the shadowy forms of three or four people standing outside the tents; their headlamps flickered through curtains of blowing snow. I watched Harris walk toward them across the flats, a distance he covered in less than ten minutes. When the clouds closed in a moment later, cutting off my view, he was within sixty feet of the tents, maybe closer. I didn't see him again after that, but I was certain that he'd reached the security of camp, where Chuldum and Arita would doubtless be waiting with hot tea. Sitting out in the storm, with the ice bulge still standing between me and the tents, I felt a pang of envy. I was angry that my guide hadn't waited for me.

My backpack held little more than three empty oxygen canisters and a pint of frozen lemonade; it probably weighed no more than sixteen or eighteen pounds. But I was tired, and worried about getting down the incline without breaking a leg, so I tossed the pack over the edge and hoped it would come to rest where I could retrieve it. Then I stood up and started down the ice, which was as smooth and hard as the surface of a bowling ball.

Fifteen minutes of dicey, fatiguing crampon work brought me safely to the bottom of the incline, where I easily located my pack, and another ten minutes after that I was in camp myself. I lunged into my tent with my crampons still on, zipped the door tight, and sprawled across the frost-covered floor too tired to even sit upright. For the first time I had a sense of how wasted I really was: I was more exhausted than I'd ever been in my life. But I was safe. Andy was safe. The others would be coming into camp soon. We'd fucking done it. We'd climbed Everest. It had been a little sketchy there for a while, but in the end everything had turned out great.

| | |

It would be many hours before I learned that everything had not in fact turned out great—that nineteen men and women were stranded up on the mountain by the storm, caught in a desperate struggle for their lives.

Chapter Fifteen

SUMMIT 1:25 P.M., MAY 10, 1996 29,028 FEET

There are many shades in the danger of adventures and gales, and it is only now and then that there appears on the face of facts a sinister violence of intention—that indefinable something which forces it upon the mind and the heart of a man, that this complication of accidents or these elemental furies are coming at him with a purpose of malice, with a strength beyond control, with an unbridled cruelty that means to tear out of him his hope and fear, the pain of his fatigue and the longing for rest: which means to smash, to destroy, to annihilate all he has seen, known, loved, enjoyed, or hated; all that is priceless and necessary—the sunshine, the memories, the future; which means to sweep the whole precious world utterly away from his sight by the simple and appalling act of taking his life.

Joseph Conrad
Lord Jim

Neal Beidleman reached the summit at 1:25 P.M. with client Martin Adams. When they got there, Andy Harris and Anatoli Boukreev were already on top; I had departed eight minutes earlier. Assuming that the rest of his team would be appearing shortly, Beidleman snapped some photos, bantered with Boukreev, and sat down to wait. At 1:45, client Klev Schoening ascended the final rise, pulled out a photo of his wife and children, and commenced a tearful celebration of his arrival on top of the world.

From the summit, a bump in the ridge blocks one's view of the rest of the route, and by 2:00—the designated turn-around time—there was still no sign of Fischer or any other clients. Beidleman began to grow concerned about the lateness of the hour.

Thirty-six years old, an aerospace engineer by training, he was a quiet, thoughtful, extremely conscientious guide who was well liked by most members of his team and Hall's. Beidleman was also one of the strongest climbers on the mountain. Two years earlier he and Boukreev—whom he considered a good friend—had climbed 27,824-foot Makalu together in near-record time, without supplemental oxygen or Sherpa support. He first met Fischer and Hall on the slopes of K2 in 1992, where his competence and easygoing demeanor left a favorable impression on both men. But because Beidleman's high-altitude experience was relatively limited (Makalu was his only major Himalayan summit), his station in the Mountain Madness chain of command was below Fischer and Boukreev. And his pay reflected his junior status: he'd agreed to guide Everest for $10,000, compared to the $25,000 Fischer paid Boukreev.

Beidleman, sensitive by nature, was quite conscious of his place in the expedition pecking order. "I was definitely considered the third guide," he acknowledged after the expedition, "so I tried not to be too pushy. As a consequence, I didn't always speak up when maybe I should have, and now I kick myself for it."

Beidleman said that according to Fischer's loosely formulated plan for the summit day, Lopsang Jangbu was supposed to be at the front of the line, carrying a radio and two coils of rope to install ahead of the clients; Boukreev and Beidleman—neither of whom was given a radio—were to be "in the middle or near the front, depending on how the clients were moving; and Scott, carrying a second radio, was going to be 'sweep.' At Rob's suggestion, we'd decided to enforce a two o'clock turn-around time: anybody who wasn't within spitting distance of the summit by two P.M. had to turn around and go down.

"It was supposed to be Scott's job to turn clients around," Beidleman explained. "We'd talked about it. I'd told him that as the third guide, I didn't feel comfortable telling clients who'd paid sixty-five thousand dollars that they had to go down. So Scott agreed that would be his responsibility. But for whatever reason, it didn't happen." In fact, the only people to reach the summit before 2:00 P.M. were Boukreev, Harris, Beidleman, Adams, Schoening, and me; if Fischer and Hall had been true to their pre-arranged rules, everyone else would have turned back before the top.

Despite Beidleman's growing anxiety about the advancing clock, he didn't have a radio, so there was no way to discuss the situation with Fischer. Lopsang—who did have a radio—was still somewhere out of sight below. Early that morning, when Beidleman had encountered Lopsang on the Balcony, vomiting between his knees into the snow, he'd taken the Sherpa's two coils of rope to fix on the steep rock steps above. As he now laments, however, "It didn't even occur to me to grab his radio, too."

The upshot, Beidleman recalled, is that "I ended up sitting on the summit for a very long time, looking at my watch and waiting for Scott to show, thinking about heading down—but every time I stood up to leave, another one of our clients would roll over the crest of the ridge, and I'd sit back down to wait for them."

Sandy Pittman appeared over the final rise about 2:10, slightly ahead of Charlotte Fox, Lopsang Jangbu, Tim Madsen, and Lene Gammelgaard. But Pittman was moving very slowly, and shortly below the summit she abruptly dropped to her knees in the snow. When Lopsang came to her assistance he discovered that her third oxygen canister had run out. Early in the morning, when he'd started short-roping Pittman, he'd also cranked her oxygen flow as high as it would go—four liters per minute—and consequently she'd used up all her gas relatively quickly. Fortunately, Lopsang—who wasn't using oxygen himself—was carrying a spare oxygen canister in his pack. He attached Pittman's mask and regulator to the fresh bottle, and then they ascended the last few meters to the top and joined the celebration in progress.

Rob Hall, Mike Groom, and Yasuko Namba reached the summit around this time, too, and Hall radioed Helen Wilton at Base Camp to give her the good news. "Rob said it was cold and windy up there," Wilton recalled, "but he sounded good. He said, 'Doug is just coming up over the horizon; right after that I'll be heading down. . . . If you don't hear from me again, it means everything's fine.' " Wilton notified the Adventure Consultants office in New Zealand, and a flurry of faxes went out to friends and families around the world, announcing the expedition's triumphant culmination.

But Doug Hansen wasn't just below the summit at that point, as Hall believed, nor was Fischer. It would in fact be 3:40 before Fischer reached the top, and Hansen wouldn't get there until after 4:00 P.M.

| | |

The previous afternoon—Thursday, May 9—when all of us had climbed from Camp Three to Camp Four, Fischer hadn't reached the tents on the South Col until after 5:00 P.M., and he was visibly tired when he'd finally gotten there, although he did his best to disguise his fatigue from his clients. "That evening," recalled his tent-mate Charlotte Fox, "I couldn't tell that Scott might have been sick. He was acting like Mr. Gung Ho, getting everyone psyched up like a football coach before the big game."

In truth Fischer was exhausted from the physical and mental strain of the preceding weeks. Although he possessed extraordinary reserves of energy, he'd been profligate with those reserves, and by the time he got to Camp Four they were nearly depleted. "Scott strong person," Boukreev acknowledged after the expedition, "but before summit attempt is tired, has many problems, spend lots of power. Worry, worry, worry, worry. Scott nervous, but he keep inside."

Fischer hid the fact from everyone, as well, that he may have been clinically ill during the summit attempt. In 1984, during an expedition to Nepal's Annapurna massif, he'd been stricken with a mysterious disease that had degenerated into a chronic liver condition. Over the years he'd consulted numerous doctors and undergone batteries of medical tests, but a definitive diagnosis was never forthcoming. Fischer simply referred to his affliction as a "liver cyst," told few people about it, and tried to pretend that it was nothing to worry about.

"Whatever it was," says Jane Bromet, one of the handful of intimates who knew about the ailment, "it produced malaria-like symptoms, even though it wasn't malaria. He would break into these intense sweating spells and get the shakes. The spells would lay him low, but they would only last for ten or fifteen minutes and then pass.

In Seattle he'd get the attacks maybe once a week or so, but when he was stressed they'd occur more frequently. At Base Camp he was getting them more often—every other day, sometimes every day."

If Fischer suffered such attacks at Camp Four or above, he never mentioned it. Fox reported that soon after he crawled into their tent Thursday evening, "Scott conked out and slept really hard for about two hours." When he woke up at 10:00 P.M. he was slow getting ready and he remained in camp long after the last of his clients, guides, and Sherpas departed for the summit.

It's unclear when Fischer actually left Camp Four; perhaps as late as 1:00 A.M. on Friday, May 10. He dragged far behind everyone else through most of the summit day, and he didn't arrive at the South Summit until around 1:00 P.M. I first saw him at about 2:45, on my way down from the top, while I waited on the Hillary Step with Andy Harris for the crowd to clear out. Fischer was the last climber up the rope, and he looked extremely wasted.

After we exchanged pleasantries, he spoke briefly with Martin Adams and Anatoli Boukreev, who were standing just above Harris and me, waiting to descend the Step. "Hey, Martin," Fischer bantered through his oxygen mask, trying to affect a jocular tone. "Do you think you can summit Mount Everest?"

"Hey, Scott," Adams replied, sounding annoyed that Fischer hadn't offered any congratulations, "I just did."

Next Fischer had a few words with Boukreev. As Adams remembered the conversation, Boukreev told Fischer, "I am going down with Martin." Then Fischer plodded slowly on toward the summit, while Harris, Boukreev, Adams, and I turned to rappel down the Step. Nobody discussed Fischer's exhausted appearance. It didn't occur to any of us that he might be in trouble.

| | |

At 3:10 Friday afternoon Fischer still hadn't arrived on top, says Beidleman, adding, "I decided it was time to get the hell out of there, even though Scott hadn't showed up yet." He gathered up Pittman, Gammelgaard, Fox, and Madsen and started leading them down the

summit ridge. Twenty minutes later, just above the Hillary Step, they ran into Fischer. "I didn't really say anything to him," Beidleman recalls. "He just sort of raised his hand. He looked like he was having a hard time, but he was Scott, so I wasn't particularly worried. I figured he'd tag the summit and catch up to us pretty quick to help bring the clients down."

Beidleman's primary concern at the time was Pittman: "Everybody was pretty messed up by that point, but Sandy looked especially shaky. I thought that if I didn't keep real close tabs on her, there was a good chance she'd peel right off the ridge. So I made sure she was clipped into the fixed line, and in the places where there was no rope I grabbed her harness from behind and kept a tight hold on her until she could clip into the next section of rope. She was so out of it that I'm not sure she even knew I was there."

A short distance below the South Summit, as the climbers descended into thick clouds and falling snow, Pittman collapsed again and asked Fox to give her an injection of a powerful steroid called dexamethasone. "Dex," as it is known, can temporarily negate the deleterious effects of altitude; each member of Fischer's team carried a preprepared syringe of the drug in a plastic toothbrush case inside his or her down suit, where it wouldn't freeze, for emergencies. "I pulled aside Sandy's pants a little," Fox recalls, "and jammed the needle into her hip, right through her long underwear and everything."

Beidleman, who had lingered at the South Summit to inventory oxygen, arrived on the scene to see Fox plunging the syringe into Pittman, stretched out face down on the snow. "When I came over the rise and saw Sandy lying there, with Charlotte standing over her waving a hypodermic needle, I thought, 'Oh fuck, this looks bad.' So I asked Sandy what was going on, and when she tried to answer all that came out of her mouth was a bunch of garbled babble." Extremely concerned, Beidleman ordered Gammelgaard to exchange her full oxygen canister with Pittman's nearly empty one, made sure her regulator was turned to full flow, then grabbed the semicomatose Pittman by her harness and started dragging her down the steep snow of the Southeast Ridge. "Once I got her sliding," he explains, "I'd let go and glissade down in front of her. Every fifty meters I'd stop, wrap my hands around the fixed rope, and brace myself to arrest her slide with a body block. The first time Sandy came barreling into me, the points of her crampons sliced through my down suit. Feathers went flying everywhere." To everyone's relief, after about twenty minutes the injection and extra oxygen revived Pittman and she was able to resume the descent under her own power.

Around 5:00 P.M., as Beidleman accompanied his clients down the ridge, Mike Groom and Yasuko Namba were arriving at the Balcony some 500 feet below them. From this promontory at 27,600 feet, the route veers sharply off the ridge to the south toward Camp Four. When Groom looked in the other direction, however—down the north side of the ridge—through the billowing snow and faltering light he noticed a lone climber badly off route: it was Martin Adams, who'd become disoriented in the storm and mistakenly started to descend the Kangshung Face into Tibet.

As soon as Adams saw Groom and Namba above him, he realized his mistake and climbed slowly back toward the Balcony. "Martin was out of it by the time he got back up to Yasuko and me," Groom recalls. "His oxygen mask was off and his face was encrusted in snow. He asked, 'Which way to the tents?' " Groom pointed, and Adams immediately started down the correct side of the ridge, following the trail I'd blazed perhaps ten minutes earlier.

While Groom was waiting for Adams to climb back up to the ridge, he sent Namba down ahead and busied himself trying to find a camera case he'd left on the way up. As he was looking around, for the first time he noticed another person on the Balcony with him. "Because he was sort of camouflaged in the snow, I took him to be one of Fischer's group, and I ignored him. Then this person was standing in front of me saying, 'Hi, Mike,' and I realized it was Beck."

Groom, just as surprised to see Beck as I had been, got out his rope and began short-roping the Texan down toward the South Col. "Beck was so hopelessly blind," Groom reports, "that every ten meters he'd take a step into thin air and I'd have to catch him with the rope. I was worried he was going to pull me off many times. It was bloody nerve-racking. I had to make sure I had a good ice-ax belay and that all my points were clean and sticking into something solid at all times."

One by one, following the tracks I'd made fifteen or twenty minutes earlier, Beidleman and the remainder of Fischer's clients filed down through the worsening blizzard. Adams was behind me, ahead of the others; then came Namba, Groom and Weathers, Schoening and Gammelgaard, Beidleman, and finally Pittman, Fox, and Madsen.

Five hundred feet above the South Col, where the steep shale gave way to a gentler slope of snow, Namba's oxygen ran out, and the diminutive Japanese woman sat down, refusing to move. "When I tried to take her oxygen mask off so she could breathe more easily," says Groom, "she'd insist on putting it right back on. No amount of persuasion could convince her that she was out of oxygen, that the mask was actually suffocating her. By now, Beck had weakened to the point where he wasn't able to walk on his own, and I had to support him on my shoulder. Fortunately, right about then Neal caught up to us." Beidleman, seeing that Groom had his hands full with Weathers, started dragging Namba down toward Camp Four, even though she wasn't on Fischer's team.

It was now about 6:45 P.M. and almost completely dark. Beidleman, Groom, their clients, and two Sherpas from Fischer's team who had belatedly materialized out of the mist—Tashi Tshering and Ngawang Dorje—had coalesced into a single group. Although they were moving slowly, they had descended to within 200 vertical feet of Camp Four. At that moment I was just arriving at the tents—probably no more than fifteen minutes in front of the first members of Beidleman's group. But in that brief span the storm abruptly metastasized into a full-blown hurricane, and the visibility dropped to less than twenty feet.

Wanting to avoid the dangerous ice pitch, Beidleman led his group on an indirect route that looped far to the east, where the slope was much less steep, and around 7:30 they safely reached the broad, gently rolling expanse of the South Col. By then, however, only three or four people had headlamps with batteries that hadn't run down, and everyone was on the brink of physical collapse. Fox was increasingly relying on Madsen for assistance. Weathers and Namba were unable to walk without being supported by Groom and Beidleman, respectively.

Beidleman knew they were on the eastern, Tibetan side of the Col and that the tents lay somewhere to the west. But to move in that direction it was necessary to walk directly upwind into the teeth of the storm. Wind-whipped granules of ice and snow struck the climbers' faces with violent force, lacerating their eyes and making it impossible to see where they were going. "It was so difficult and painful," Schoening explains, "that there was an inevitable tendency to bear off the wind, to keep angling away from it to the left, and that's how we went wrong.

"At times you couldn't even see your own feet, it was blowing so hard," he continues. "I was worried somebody would sit down or get separated from the group and we'd never see them again. But once we got to the flats of the Col we started following the Sherpas, and I figured they knew where camp was. Then they suddenly stopped and doubled back, and it quickly became obvious they didn't have any idea where we were. At that point I got a sick feeling in the pit of my stomach. That's when I first knew we were in trouble."

For the next two hours, Beidleman, Groom, the two Sherpas, and the seven clients staggered blindly around in the storm, growing ever more exhausted and hypothermic, hoping to blunder across the camp. Once they came across a couple of discarded oxygen bottles, suggesting that the tents were near, but the climbers couldn't locate them. "It was total chaos," says Beidleman. "People are wandering all over the place; I'm yelling at everyone, trying to get them to follow a single leader. Finally, probably around ten o'clock, I walked over this little rise, and it felt like I was standing on the edge of the earth. I could sense a huge void just beyond."

The group had unwittingly strayed to the easternmost edge of the Col, at the lip of a 7,000-foot drop down the Kangshung Face. They were at the same elevation as Camp Four, just 1,000 horizontal feet from safety,* but, says Beidleman, "I knew that if we kept wandering in the storm, pretty soon we were going to lose somebody. I was exhausted from dragging Yasuko. Charlotte and Sandy were barely able to stand. So I screamed at everyone to huddle up right there and wait for a break in the storm."

Beidleman and Schoening searched for a protected place to escape the wind, but there was nowhere to hide. Everyone's oxygen had long since run out, making the group more vulnerable to the windchill, which exceeded a hundred below zero. In the lee of a boulder no larger than a dishwasher, the climbers hunkered in a pathetic row on a patch of gale-scoured ice. "By then the cold had about finished me off," says Charlotte Fox. "My eyes were frozen. I didn't see how we were going to get out of it alive. The cold was so painful, I didn't think I could endure it anymore. I just curled up in a ball and hoped death would come quickly."

"We tried to keep warm by pummeling each other," Weathers remembers. "Someone yelled at us to keep moving our arms and legs. Sandy was hysterical; she kept yelling over and over, 'I don't want to die! I don't want to die!' But nobody else was saying a whole lot."

| | |

Three hundred yards to the west I was shivering uncontrollably in my tent—even though I was zipped into my sleeping bag, and wearing my down suit and every other stitch of clothing I had. The gale threatened to blow the tent apart. Every time the door was opened, the shelter would fill with blowing spindrift, so everything inside was covered with an inch-thick layer of snow. Oblivious to the tragedy unfolding outside in the storm, I drifted in and out of consciousness, delirious from exhaustion, dehydration, and the cumulative effects of oxygen depletion.

* Although a strong climber might require three hours to ascend 1,000 *vertical* feet, in this case the distance was over more or less flat terrain, which the group would have been able to cover in perhaps fifteen minutes had they known where the tents were.

At some point early in the evening, Stuart Hutchison, my tentmate, came in, shook me hard, and asked if I would go outside with him to bang on pots and shine lights into the sky in the hope of guiding the lost climbers in, but I was too weak and incoherent to respond. Hutchison—who had gotten back to camp at 2:00 P.M. and was thus considerably less debilitated than me—then tried to rouse clients and Sherpas from the other tents. Everybody was too cold or too exhausted. So Hutchison went out into the storm alone.

He left our tent six times that night to look for the missing climbers, but the blizzard was so fierce that he never dared to venture more than a few yards beyond the margin of camp. "The winds were ballistically strong," he emphasizes. "The blowing spindrift felt like a sandblaster or something. I could only go out for fifteen minutes at a time before I became too cold and had to return to the tent."

Out among the climbers hunkered on the eastern edge of the Col, Beidelman willed himself to say alert for a sign that the storm might be blowing itself out. Just before midnight, his vigilance was rewarded when he suddenly noticed a few stars overhead and shouted to the others to look. The wind was still whipping up a furious ground-blizzard at the surface, but far above, the sky had begun to clear, revealing the hulking silhouettes of Everest and Lhotse. From these reference points, Klev Schoening thought he'd figured out where the group was in relation to Camp Four. After a shouting match with Beidleman, he convinced the guide that he knew the way to the tents.

Beidleman tried to coax everyone to their feet and get them moving in the direction indicated by Schoening, but Pittman, Fox, Weathers, and Namba were too feeble to walk. By then it was obvious to the guide that if somebody from the group didn't make it to the tents and summon a rescue party, they were all going to die. So Beidleman assembled those who were ambulatory, and then he, Schoening, Gammelgaard, Groom, and the two Sherpas stumbled off into the storm to get help, leaving behind the four incapacitated clients with Tim Madsen. Reluctant to abandon his girlfriend, Fox, Madsen selflessly volunteered to stay and look after everybody until help arrived.

Twenty minutes later, Beidleman's contingent limped into camp, where they had an emotional reunion with a very worried Anatoli Boukreev. Schoening and Beidleman, barely able to speak, told the Russian where to find the five clients who'd remained behind out in the elements and then collapsed in their respective tents, utterly spent.

Boukreev had come down to the South Col hours in front of anyone else in Fischer's team. Indeed, by 5:00 P.M., while his teammates were still struggling down through the clouds at 28,000 feet, Boukreev was already in his tent resting and drinking tea. Experienced guides would later question his decision to descend so far ahead of his clients—extremely unorthodox behavior for a guide. One of the clients from that group has nothing but contempt for Boukreev, insisting that when it mattered most, the guide "cut and ran."

Anatoli had left the summit around 2:00 P.M. and quickly became entangled in the traffic jam at the Hillary Step. As soon as the mob dispersed he moved very rapidly down the Southeast Ridge without waiting for any clients—despite telling Fischer atop the Step that he would be going down with Martin Adams. Boukreev thereby arrived at Camp Four well before the brunt of the storm.

After the expedition, when I asked Anatoli why he had hurried down ahead of his group, he handed me the transcript of an interview he'd given a few days previously to *Men's Journal* through a Russian interpreter. Boukreev told me that he'd read the transcript and confirmed its accuracy. Reading it on the spot, I quickly came to a series of questions about the descent, to which he had replied:

> I stayed [on the summit] for about an hour. . . . It is very cold, naturally, it takes your strength. . . . My position was that I would not be good if I stood around freezing, waiting. I would be more useful if I returned to Camp Four in order to be able to take oxygen up to the returning climbers or to go up to help them if some became weak

> during the descent. . . . If you are immobile at that altitude you lose strength in the cold, and then you are unable to do anything.

Boukreev's susceptibility to the cold was doubtless greatly exacerbated by the fact that he wasn't using supplemental oxygen; in the absence of gas he simply couldn't stop to wait for slow clients on the summit ridge without courting frostbite and hypothermia. For whatever reason, he raced down ahead of the group—which in fact had been his pattern throughout the entire expedition, as Fischer's final letters and phone calls from Base Camp to Seattle made clear.

When I questioned him about the wisdom of leaving his clients on the summit ridge, Anatoli insisted that it was for the good of the team: "It is much better for me to warm myself at South Col, be ready to carry up oxygen if clients run out." Indeed, shortly after dark, after Beidleman's group failed to return and the storm had risen to hurricane intensity, Boukreev realized they must be in trouble and made a courageous attempt to bring oxygen to them. But his stratagem had a serious flaw: because neither he nor Beidleman had a radio, Anatoli had no way of knowing the true nature of the missing climbers' predicament, or even where on the huge expanse of the upper mountain they might be.

Around 7:30 P.M., Boukreev left Camp Four to search for the group, regardless. By then, he recalled,

> Visibility was maybe a meter. It disappeared altogether. I had a lamp, and I began to use oxygen to speed up my ascent. I was carrying three bottles. I tried to go faster, but visibility was gone. . . . It is like being without eyes, without being able to see, it was impossible to see. That is very dangerous, because one can fall into a crevasse, one can fall toward the southern side of Lhotse, 3,000 meters straight down. I tried to go up, it was dark, I could not find the fixed line.

Some six hundred feet above the Col, Boukreev recognized the futility of his effort and returned to the tents, but, he admits, he very nearly became lost himself. In any case, it was just as well that he abandoned this rescue effort, because at that point his teammates were no longer on the peak above, where Boukreev had been headed—by the time he gave up his search, Beidleman's group was actually wandering around on the Col six hundred feet *below* the Russian.

When he arrived back at Camp Four around 9:00 P.M., Boukreev was worried about the nineteen climbers who were missing, but because he had no idea where they might be, there was nothing he could do except bide his time. Then, at 12:45 A.M., Beidleman, Groom, Schoening, and Gammelgaard hobbled into camp. "Klev and Neal had lost all power and could barely talk," Boukreev recalls. "They told me Charlotte, Sandy, and Tim need help, Sandy is close to dying. Then they give me general location where to find them."

Upon hearing the climbers arrive, Stuart Hutchison went out to assist Groom. "I got Mike into his tent," Hutchison recalled, "and saw that he was really, really exhausted. He was able to communicate clearly, but it required an agonal effort, like a dying man's last words. 'You have to get some Sherpas,' he told me. 'Send them out for Beck and Yasuko.' And then he pointed toward the Kangshung side of the Col."

Hutchison's efforts to organize a rescue team proved fruitless, however. Chuldum and Arita—Sherpas on Hall's team who hadn't accompanied the summit party and were waiting in reserve at Camp Four specifically for such an emergency—had been incapacitated with carbon monoxide poisoning from cooking in a poorly ventilated tent; Chuldum was actually vomiting blood. And the other four Sherpas on our team were too cold and debilitated from having gone to the summit.

After the expedition, I asked Hutchison why, once he learned the whereabouts of the missing climbers, he didn't attempt to wake Frank Fischbeck, Lou Kasischke, or John Taske—or make a second attempt to wake me—in order to request our help with the rescue effort. "It was so obvious that all of you were completely exhausted that I didn't even consider asking. You were so far past the point of ordinary fatigue that I thought if you attempted to help with a rescue you were only going to make the situation worse—that you would get out there and have to be rescued yourself." The upshot was that Stuart went out into the storm alone, but once again he turned around at the edge of camp when he became worried that he wouldn't be able to find his way back if he went farther.

At the same time, Boukreev was also trying to organize a rescue team, but he didn't contact Hutchison or come to my tent, so the efforts of Hutchison and Boukreev remained uncoordinated, and I never learned of either rescue plan. In the end Boukreev discovered, like Hutchison, that everybody he managed to rouse was too sick or exhausted or frightened to help. So the Russian resolved to bring back the group on his own. Bravely plunging into the maw of the hurricane, he searched the Col for nearly an hour but was unable to find anybody.

Boukreev didn't give up. He returned to camp, obtained a more detailed set of directions from Beidleman and Schoening, then went out into the storm again. This time he saw the faint glow of Madsen's fading headlamp and was thereby able to locate the missing climbers. "They were lying on the ice, without movement," says Boukreev. "They could not talk." Madsen was still conscious and largely able to take care of himself, but Pittman, Fox, and Weathers were utterly helpless, and Namba appeared to be dead.

After Beidleman and the others had set out from the huddle to get help, Madsen had gathered together the climbers who remained and hectored everybody to keep moving in order to stay warm. "I sat Yasuko down in Beck's lap," Madsen recalls, "but he was pretty unresponsive by that time, and Yasuko wasn't moving at all. A little later I saw that she'd laid down flat on her back, with snow blowing into her hood. Somehow she'd lost a glove—her right hand was bare, and her fingers were curled up so tightly you couldn't straighten them. It looked like they were pretty much frozen to the bone.

"I assumed she was dead," Madsen continues. "But then a while later she suddenly moved, and it freaked me out: she sort of arched her neck slightly, as if she was trying to sit up, and her right arm came up, then that was it. Yasuko lay back down and never moved again."

As soon as Boukreev found the group, it became obvious to him that he could bring only one climber in at a time. He was carrying an oxygen bottle, which he and Madsen hooked up to Pittman's mask. Then Boukreev indicated to Madsen that he'd be back as soon as possible and started helping Fox back toward the tents. "After they left," says Madsen, "Beck was crumpled in a fetal position, not moving a whole lot, and Sandy was curled up in my lap, not moving much, either. I screamed at her, 'Hey, keep wiggling your hands! Let me see your hands!' And when she sits up and pulls her hands out, I see she doesn't have any [mittens] on—that they were dangling from her wrists.

"So I'm trying to shove her hands back into her [mittens] when all of a sudden Beck mumbles, 'Hey, I've got this all figured out.' Then he kind of rolls a little distance away, crouches on a big rock, and stands up facing the wind with his arms stretched out to either side. A second later a gust comes up and just blows him over backward into the night, beyond the beam of my headlamp. And that was the last I saw of him.

"Toli came back a little bit after that and grabbed Sandy, so I just packed up my stuff and started waddling after them, trying to follow Toli's and Sandy's headlamps. By then I assumed Yasuko was dead and Beck was a lost cause." When they finally reached camp it was 4:30 A.M., and the sky was starting to brighten above the eastern horizon. Upon hearing from Madsen that Yasuko hadn't made it, Beidleman broke down in his tent and wept for forty-five minutes.

Chapter Sixteen

SOUTH COL 6:00 A.M., MAY 11, 1996 26,000 FEET

I distrust summaries, any kind of gliding through time, any too great a claim that one is in control of what one recounts; I think someone who claims to understand but is obviously calm, someone who claims to write with emotion recollected in tranquillity, is a fool and a liar. To understand is to tremble. To recollect is to re-enter and be riven. . . . I admire the authority of being on one's knees in front of the event.

Harold Brodkey
"Manipulations"

Stuart Hutchison finally managed to shake me awake at 6:00 A.M. on May 11. "Andy's not in his tent," he told me somberly, "and he doesn't seem to be in any of the other tents, either. I don't think he ever made it in."

"Harold's missing?" I asked. "No way. I saw him walk to the edge of camp with my own eyes." Shocked and confused, I pulled on my boots and rushed out to look for Harris. The wind was still fierce—strong enough to knock me down several times—but it was a bright, clear dawn, and the visibility was perfect. I searched the entire western half of the Col for more than an hour, peering behind boulders and poking under shredded, long-abandoned tents, but found no trace of Harris. Adrenaline surged through my veins. Tears welled in my eyes, instantly freezing my eyelids shut. How could Andy be gone? It couldn't be so.

I went to the place where Harris had slid down the ice just above the Col, and then methodically retraced the route he'd followed toward camp, which followed a broad, almost flat, ice gully. At the point where I last saw him when the clouds descended, a sharp left turn would have taken Harris forty or fifty feet up a rocky rise to the tents.

I realized, however, that if he hadn't turned left but instead continued straight down the gully—which would have been easy to do in the whiteout even if one wasn't exhausted and stupid with altitude sickness—he would have quickly come to the westernmost edge of the Col.

Below, the steep gray ice of the Lhotse Face dropped 4,000 vertical feet to the floor of the Western Cwm. Standing there, afraid to move any closer to the edge, I noticed a single set of faint crampon tracks leading past me toward the abyss. Those tracks, I feared, were Andy Harris's.

After getting into camp the previous evening, I'd told Hutchison that I'd seen Harris arrive safely at the tents. Hutchison had radioed this news to Base Camp, and from there it was passed along via satellite phone to the woman with whom Harris shared his life in New Zealand, Fiona McPherson. She'd been overcome with relief when she learned that Harris was safe at Camp Four. Now, however, Hall's wife back in Christchurch, Jan Arnold, would have to do the unthinkable: call McPherson back to inform her there had been a horrible mistake—that Andy was in fact missing and presumed dead. Imagining this phone conversation, and my role in the events leading up to it, I fell to my knees with dry heaves, retching over and over as the icy wind blasted against my back.

After spending sixty minutes searching in vain for Andy, I returned to my tent just in time to overhear a radio call between Base Camp and Rob Hall; he was up on the summit ridge, I learned, calling down for help. Hutchison then told me that Beck and Yasuko were dead and that Scott Fischer was missing somewhere on the peak above. Shortly after that, the batteries to our radio died, cutting us off from the rest of the mountain. Alarmed that they had lost contact with us, members of the IMAX team at Camp Two called the South African team, whose tents on the Col were a only few yards away from ours. David Breashears—the IMAX leader, and a climber I had known for twenty years—reports, "We knew the South Africans had a powerful radio and that it was working, so we got one of their team members at Camp Two to call up to Woodall on the South Col and say, 'Look, this is an emergency. People are dying up there. We need to be able to communicate with the survivors in Hall's team to coordinate a rescue. Please lend your radio to Jon Krakauer.' And Woodall said no. It was very clear what was at stake, but they wouldn't give up their radio."

| | |

Immediately after the expedition, when I was researching my article for *Outside* magazine, I interviewed as many of the people on Hall's and Fischer's summit teams as possible—I spoke with most of them several times. But Martin Adams, distrustful of reporters, kept a low profile in the aftermath of the tragedy and eluded my repeated attempts to interview him until after the *Outside* piece went to press.

When I eventually reached Adams by phone in mid-July and he consented to talk, I began by asking him to recount everything he remembered about the summit push. One of the stronger clients that day, he'd remained near the front of the pack and was either just ahead of me or just behind me for much of the climb. Because he possessed what seemed to be an unusually reliable memory, I was particularly interested to hear how his version of the events jibed with my own.

Very late in the afternoon, when Adams headed down from the Balcony at 27,600 feet, he said that I was still visible, perhaps fifteen minutes ahead of him, but that I was descending faster than he was and soon moved out of sight. "And the next time I saw you" he said, "it was almost dark and you were crossing the flats of the South Col, about a hundred feet from the tents. I recognized that it was you from your bright red down suit."

Shortly after that, Adams descended to a flat bench just above the steep ice incline that had given me so much trouble, and fell into a small crevasse. He managed to extricate himself, then fell into another, deeper, crevasse. "Lying in that crevasse, I was thinking, 'This may be it.' " he mused. "It took awhile, but eventually I managed to climb out of that one, too. When I got out, my face was covered with snow, which quickly turned to ice. Then I saw somebody sitting on the ice off to the left, wearing a headlamp, so I walked over in that direction. It wasn't pitch-black yet, but it was dark enough that I couldn't see the tents anymore.

"So I got to this fucker and said, 'Hey, where are the tents?' and the guy, whoever he was, pointed the way. So I said, 'Yeah, that's what I thought.' Then the guy said something like, 'Be careful. The ice here is steeper than it looks. Maybe we should go down and get a rope and some ice screws.' I thought, 'Fuck that. I'm out of here.' So I took two or three steps, tripped, and slid down the ice on my chest, headfirst.

As I was sliding, somehow the pick of my ice ax caught something and swung me around, then I came to a stop at the bottom. I got up, stumbled to the tent, and that's about the size of it."

As Adams described his encounter with the anonymous climber, and then sliding down the ice, my mouth went dry and the hairs on the back of my neck suddenly bristled. "Martin," I asked when he'd finished talking, "do you think that could have been me you ran into out there?"

"Fuck, no!" he laughed. "I don't know who it was, but it definitely wasn't you." But then I told him about my encounter with Andy Harris and the chilling series of coincidences: I had bumped into Harris about the same time Adams had encountered the cipher, and in about the same place. Much of the dialogue that transpired between Harris and me was eerily similar to the dialogue between Adams and the cipher. And then Adams had slid headfirst down the ice in much the same manner I remembered seeing Harris slide.

After talking for a few minutes more, Adams was convinced: "So that was you I talked to out there on the ice," he stated, astounded, acknowledging that he must have been mistaken when he saw me crossing the flats of the South Col just before dark. "And that was me you talked to. Which means it wasn't Andy Harris at all. Wow. Dude, I'd say you've got some explaining to do."

I was stunned. For two months I'd been telling people that Harris had walked off the edge of the South Col to his death, when he hadn't done that at all. My error had greatly and unnecessarily compounded the pain of Fiona McPherson; Andy's parents, Ron and Mary Harris; his brother, David Harris; and his many friends.

Andy was a large man, over six feet tall and 200 pounds, who spoke with a sharp Kiwi lilt; Martin was at least six inches shorter, weighed maybe 130 pounds, and spoke in a thick Texas drawl. How had I made such an egregious mistake? Was I really so debilitated that I had stared into the face of a near stranger and mistaken him for a friend with whom I'd spent the previous six weeks? And if Andy had never arrived at Camp Four after reaching the summit, what in the name of God had happened to him?

Chapter Seventeen

SUMMIT 3:40 P.M., MAY 10, 1996 29,028 FEET

[O]ur wreck is certainly due to this sudden advent of severe weather, which does not seem to have any satisfactory cause. I do not think human beings ever came through such a month as we have come through, and we should have got through in spite of the weather but for the sickening of a second companion, Captain Oates, and a shortage of fuel in our depots for which I cannot account, and finally, but for the storm which has fallen on us within 11 miles of the depot at which we hoped to secure our final supplies. Surely misfortune could scarcely have exceeded this last blow. . . . We took risks, we knew we took them; things have come out against us, and therefore we have no cause for complaint, but bow to the will of Providence, determined still to do our best to the last. . . .

Had we lived, I should have had a tale to tell of the hardihood, endurance, and courage of my companions which would have stirred the heart of every Englishman. These rough notes and our dead bodies must tell the tale.

Robert Falcon Scott,
in "Message to the Public,"
penned just prior to his death in
Antarctica on March 29, 1912,
from *Scott's Last Expedition*

Scott Fischer ascended to the summit around 3:40 on the afternoon of May 10 to find his devoted friend and sirdar, Lopsang Jangbu, waiting for him. The Sherpa pulled his radio from inside his down jacket, made contact with Ingrid Hunt at Base Camp, then handed the walkie-talkie to Fischer. "We all made it," Fischer told Hunt, 11,400 feet below. "God, I'm tired." A few minutes later Makalu Gau arrived with two Sherpas. Rob Hall was there, too, waiting impatiently for

Doug Hansen to appear as a rising tide of cloud lapped ominously at the summit ridge.

According to Lopsang, during the fifeen or twenty minutes Fischer spent on the summit, he complained repeatedly that he wasn't feeling well—something the congenitally stoic guide almost never did. "Scott tell to me, 'I am too tired. I am sick, also, need medicine for stomach,' " the Sherpa recalls. "I gave him tea, but he drank just a little bit, just half cup. So I tell to him, 'Scott, please, we go fast down.' So we come down then."

Fischer started down first, about 3:55. Lopsang reports that although Scott had used supplemental oxygen during the entire ascent and his third canister was more than three-quarters full when he left the summit, for some reason he took his mask off and stopped using it.

Shortly after Fischer left the top, Gau and his Sherpas departed as well, and finally Lopsang headed down—leaving Hall alone on the summit awaiting Hansen. A moment after Lopsang started down, about 4:00, Hansen at last appeared, toughing it out, moving painfully slowly over the last bump on the ridge. As soon as he saw Hansen, Hall hurried down to meet him.

Hall's obligatory turn-around time had come and gone a full two hours earlier. Given the guide's conservative, exceedingly methodical nature, many of his colleagues have expressed puzzlement at this uncharacteristic lapse of judgment. Why, they wondered, didn't he turn Hansen around much lower on the mountain, as soon as it became obvious that the American climber was running late?

Exactly one year earlier, Hall had turned Hansen around on the South Summit at 2:30 P.M., and to be denied so close to the top was a crushing disappointment to Hansen. He told me several times that he'd returned to Everest in 1996 largely as a result of Hall's advocacy—he said Rob had called him from New Zealand "a dozen times" urging him to give it another shot—and this time Doug was absolutely determined to bag the top. "I want to get this thing done and out of my life," he'd told me three days earlier at Camp Two. "I don't want to have to come back here. I'm getting too old for this shit."

It doesn't seem far-fetched to speculate that because Hall had talked Hansen into coming back to Everest, it would have been especially hard for him to deny Hansen the summit a second time. "It's very difficult to turn someone around high on the mountain," cautions Guy Cotter, a New Zealand guide who summitted Everest with Hall in 1992 and was guiding the peak for him in 1995 when Hansen made his first attempt. "If a client sees that the summit is close and they're dead-set on getting there, they're going to laugh in your face and keep going up." As the veteran American guide Peter Lev told *Climbing* magazine after the disastrous events on Everest, "We think that people pay us to make good decisions, but what people really pay for is to get to the top."

In any case, Hall did not turn Hansen around at 2:00 P.M.—or, for that matter, at 4:00, when he met his client just below the top. Instead, according to Lopsang, Hall placed Hansen's arm around his neck and assisted the weary client up the final forty feet to the summit. They stayed only a minute or two, then turned to begin the long descent.

When Lopsang saw that Hansen was faltering, he held up his own descent long enough to make sure Doug and Rob made it safely across a dangerously corniced area just below the top. Then, eager to catch Fischer, who was by now more than thirty minutes ahead of him, the Sherpa continued down the ridge, leaving Hansen and Hall at the top of the Hillary Step.

Just after Lopsang disappeared down the Step, Hansen apparently ran out of oxygen and foundered. He'd expended every last bit of his strength to reach the summit—and now there was nothing left in reserve for the descent. "Pretty much the same thing happened to Doug in '95," says Ed Viesturs, who, like Cotter, was guiding the peak for Hall that year. "He was fine during the ascent, but as soon as he started down he lost it mentally and physically; he turned into a zombie, like he'd used everything up."

At 4:30 P.M., and again at 4:41, Hall got on the radio to say that he and Hansen were in trouble high on the summit ridge and urgently needed oxygen. Two full bottles were waiting for them at the South Summit; if Hall had known this he could have retrieved the gas fairly quickly and then climbed back up to give Hansen a fresh tank. But Andy Harris, still at the oxygen cache, in the throes of his hypoxic dementia, overheard these radio calls and broke in to tell Hall—incorrectly, just as he'd told Mike Groom and me—that all the bottles at the South Summit were empty.

Groom heard the conversation between Harris and Hall on his radio as he was descending the Southeast Ridge with Yasuko Namba, just above the Balcony. He tried to call Hall to correct the misinformation and let him know that there were in fact full oxygen canisters waiting for him at the South Summit, but, Groom explains, "my radio was malfunctioning. I was able to receive most calls, but my outgoing calls could rarely be heard by anyone. On the couple of occasions that my calls were being picked up by Rob, and I tried to tell him where the full cylinders were, I was immediately interrupted by Andy, transmitting to say there was no gas at the South Summit."

Unsure whether there was oxygen waiting for him, Hall decided that the best course of action was to remain with Hansen and try to bring the nearly helpless client down without gas. But when they got to the top of the Hillary Step, Hall couldn't get Hansen down the 40-foot vertical drop, and their progress ground to a halt.

Shortly before 5:00, Groom finally managed to get through to Hall and communicate that there actually was oxygen at the South Summit. Fifteen minutes later, Lopsang arrived at the South Summit on his way down from the top and encountered Harris.* At this point, according to Lopsang, Harris must have finally understood that at least two of the oxygen canisters stashed there were full, because he pleaded with the Sherpa to help him carry the life-sustaining gas up to Hall and Hansen on the Hillary Step. "Andy says he will pay me five hundred dollars to bring oxygen to Rob and Doug," Lopsang recalls.

* It wasn't until I interviewed Lopsang in Seattle on July 25, 1996, that I learned he had seen Harris on the evening of May 10. Although I'd spoken briefly with Lopsang several times previously, I'd never thought to ask whether he'd encountered Harris on the South Summit, because at that point I was still certain I'd seen Harris at the South Col, 3,000 feet below the South Summit, at 6:30 P.M. Moreover, Guy Cotter *had* asked Lopsang if he'd seen Harris, and for some reason—perhaps a simple misunderstanding of the question—on that occasion Lopsang said no.

"But I am supposed to take care of just my group. I have to take care of Scott. So I say to Andy, no, I go fast down."

At 5:30, as Lopsang left the South Summit to resume his descent, he turned to see Harris—who must have been severely debilitated, if his condition when I'd seen him on the South Summit two hours earlier was any indication—plodding slowly up the summit ridge to assist Hall and Hansen. It was an act of heroism that would cost Harris his life.

| | |

A few hundred feet below, Scott Fischer was struggling down the Southeast Ridge, growing weaker and weaker. Upon reaching the top of the rock steps at 28,400 feet, he was confronted with a series of short but troublesome rappels that angled along the ridge. Too exhausted to cope with the complexities of the rope work, Fischer slid directly down an adjacent snow slope on his butt. This was easier than following the fixed lines, but once he was below the level of the rock steps it meant that he had to make a laborious 330-foot rising traverse through knee-deep snow to regain the route.

Tim Madsen, descending with Beidleman's group, happened to glance up from the Balcony around 5:20 and saw Fischer as he began the traverse. "He looked really tired," Madsen remembers. "He'd take ten steps, then sit and rest, take a couple more steps, rest again. He was moving real slow. But I could see Lopsang above him, coming down the ridge, and I figured, shoot, with Lopsang there to look after him, Scott would be O.K."

According to Lopsang, the Sherpa caught up with Fischer about 6:00 P.M., just above the Balcony: "Scott is not using oxygen, so I put mask on him. He says, 'I am very sick, too sick to go down. I am going to jump.' He is saying many times, acting like crazy man, so I tie him on rope, quickly, otherwise he is jumping down into Tibet."

Securing Fischer with a 75-foot length of rope, Lopsang persuaded his friend not to jump and then got him moving slowly toward the South Col. "The storm is very bad now," Lopsang recalls. "BOOM!

BOOM! Two times like sound of gun, there is big thunder. Two times lightning hit very close near me and Scott, very loud, very scared."

Three hundred feet below the Balcony, the gentle snow gully they'd been gingerly descending gave way to outcroppings of loose, steep shale, and Fischer was unable to handle the challenging terrain in his ailing condition. "Scott cannot walk now, I have big problem," says Lopsang. "I try to carry, but I am also very tired. Scott is big body, I am very small; I cannot carry him. He tell to me, 'Lopsang, you go down. You go down.' I tell to him. 'No, I stay together here with you.' "

About 8:00 P.M., Lopsang was huddling with Fischer on a snow-covered ledge when Makalu Gau and his two Sherpas appeared out of the howling blizzard. Gau was nearly as debilitated as Fischer and was likewise unable to descend the difficult bands of shale, so his Sherpas sat the Taiwanese climber beside Lopsang and Fischer and then continued down without him.

"I stay with Scott and Makalu one hour, maybe longer," says Lopsang. "I am very cold, very tired. Scott tell to me, 'You go down, send up Anatoli.' So I say, 'O.K., I go down, I send quick Sherpa up and Anatoli.' Then I make good place for Scott and go down."

Lopsang left Fischer and Gau on a ledge 1,200 feet above the South Col and fought his way down through the storm. Unable to see, he got far off route toward the west, ended up below the level of the Col before he realized his error, and was forced to climb back up the northern margin of the Lhotse Face* to locate Camp Four. Around midnight, nevertheless, he made it to safety. "I go to Anatoli tent," reported Lopsang. "I tell to Anatoli, 'Please, you go up, Scott is very sick, he cannot walk. Then I go to my tent, just fall asleep, sleep like dead person."

| | |

* Early the next morning while searching the Col for Andy Harris, I came across Lopsang's faint crampon tracks in the ice leading up from the lip of the Lhotse Face, and mistakenly believed they were Harris's tracks headed *down* the face—which is why I thought Harris had walked off the edge of the Col.

Guy Cotter, a longtime friend of both Hall's and Harris's, happened to be a few miles from Everest Base Camp on the afternoon of May 10, where he was guiding an expedition on Pumori, and had been monitoring Hall's radio transmissions throughout the day. At 2:15 P.M. he talked to Hall on the summit, and everything sounded fine. At 4:30 and 4:41, however, Hall called down to say that Doug was out of oxygen and unable to move, and Cotter became very alarmed. At 4:53 he got on the radio and strongly urged Hall to descend to the South Summit. "The call was mostly to convince him to come down and get some gas," says Cotter, "because we knew he wasn't going to be able to do anything for Doug without it. Rob said he could get himself down O.K., but not with Doug."

But forty minutes later, Hall was still with Hansen atop the Hillary Step, going nowhere. During radio calls from Hall at 5:36, and again at 5:57, Cotter implored his mate to leave Hansen and come down alone. "I know I sound like the bastard for telling Rob to abandon his client," confessed Cotter, "but by then it was obvious that leaving Doug was his only choice." Hall, however, wouldn't consider going down without Hansen.

There was no further word from Hall until the middle of the night. At 2:46 A.M., Cotter woke up in his tent below Pumori to hear a long, broken transmission, probably unintended: Hall had been wearing a remote microphone clipped to the shoulder strap of his backpack, which was occasionally keyed on by mistake. In this instance, says Cotter, "I suspect Rob didn't even know he was transmitting. I could hear someone yelling—it might have been Rob, but I couldn't be sure because the wind was so loud in the background. But he was saying something like, 'Keep moving! Keep going!' presumably to Doug, urging him on."

If this was indeed the case, it meant that in the wee hours of the morning Hall and Hansen—perhaps accompanied by Harris—were still struggling from the Hillary Step toward the South Summit through the gale. And if so, it also meant that it had taken them more than ten hours to move down a stretch of ridge that was typically covered by descending climbers in less than half an hour.

Of course, this is highly speculative. All that is certain is that Hall called down at 5:57 P.M. At that point, he and Hansen were still on the Step; and at 4:43 on the morning of May 11, when he next spoke to Base Camp, he had descended to the South Summit. And at that point neither Hansen nor Harris was with him.

In a series of transmissions over the next two hours, Rob sounded disturbingly confused and irrational. During the call at 4:43 A.M., he told Caroline Mackenzie, our Base Camp doctor, that his legs no longer worked, and that he was "too clumsy to move." In a ragged, barely audible voice, Rob croaked, "Harold was with me last night, but he doesn't seem to be with me now. He was very weak." Then, obviously befuddled, he asked, "Was Harold with me? Can you tell me that?"*

By this point Hall had possession of two full oxygen canisters, but the valves on his mask were so choked with ice that he couldn't get the gas to flow. He indicated, however, that he was attempting to de-ice the oxygen rig, "which," says Cotter, "made us all feel a little better. It was the first positive thing we'd heard."

At 5:00 A.M., Base Camp patched through a call on the satellite telephone to Jan Arnold, Hall's wife, in Christchurch, New Zealand. She had climbed to the summit of Everest with Hall in 1993, and she entertained no illusions about the gravity of her husband's predicament. "My heart really sank when I heard his voice," she recalls. "He was slurring his words markedly. He sounded like Major Tom or something, like he was just floating away. I'd been up there; I knew what it could be like in bad weather. Rob and I had talked about the impossibility of being rescued from the summit ridge. As he himself had put it, 'You might as well be on the moon.' "

At 5:31, Hall took four milligrams of oral dexamethasone and indicated he was still trying to clear his oxygen mask of ice. Talking to Base Camp, he asked repeatedly about the condition of Makalu Gau,

* I'd already reported with absolute certainty that I'd seen Harris on the South Col at 6:30 P.M., May 10. When Hall said that Harris was with him up on the South Summit—3,000 feet higher than where I said I'd seen him—most people, thanks to my error, wrongly assumed that Hall's statements were merely the incoherent ramblings of an exhausted, severely hypoxic man.

Fischer, Beck Weathers, Yasuko Namba, and his other clients. He seemed most concerned about Andy Harris and kept inquiring about his whereabouts. Cotter says they tried to steer the discussion away from Harris, who in all likelihood was dead, "because we didn't want Rob to have another reason for staying up there. At one point Ed Viesturs jumped on the radio from Camp Two and fibbed, 'Don't worry about Andy; he's down here with us.' "

A little later, Mackenzie asked Rob how Hansen was doing. "Doug," Hall replied, "is gone." That was all he said, and it was the last mention he ever made of Hansen.

On May 23, when David Breashears and Ed Viesturs reached the summit, they would find no sign of Hansen's body; they did, however, find an ice ax planted about fifty vertical feet above the South Summit, along a very exposed section of ridge where the fixed ropes came to an end. It's quite possible that Hall and/or Harris managed to get Hansen down the ropes to this point, only to have him lose his footing and fall 7,000 feet down the sheer Southwest Face, leaving his ice ax jammed into the ridge where he slipped. But this, too, is merely conjecture.

What might have happened to Harris remains even harder to discern. Between Lopsang's testimony, Hall's radio calls, and the fact that another ice ax found on the South Summit was positively identified as Andy's, we can be reasonably sure he was at the South Summit with Hall on the night of May 10. Beyond that, however, virtually nothing is known about how the young guide met his end.

At 6:00 A.M., Cotter asked Hall if the sun had reached him yet. "Almost," Rob replied—which was good, because he'd mentioned a moment earlier that he was shaking uncontrollably in the awful cold. In conjunction with his earlier revelation that he was no longer able to walk, this had been very upsetting news to the people listening down below. Nevertheless, it was remarkable that Hall was even alive after spending a night without shelter or oxygen at 28,700 feet in hurricane-force winds and windchill of one hundred degrees below zero.

During this same radio call, Hall asked after Harris yet again: "Did anyone see Harold last night except meself?" Some three hours later Rob was still obsessing over Andy's whereabouts. At 8:43 A.M. he mused over the radio, "Some of Andy's gear is still here. I thought he must have gone ahead in the nighttime. Listen, can you account for him or not?" Wilton attempted to dodge the question, but Rob persisted in his line of inquiry: "O.K. I mean his ice ax is here and his jacket and things."

"Rob," Viesturs replied from Camp Two, "if you can put the jacket on, just use it. Keep going down and worry only about yourself. Everybody else is taking care of other people. Just get yourself down."

After struggling for four hours to de-ice his mask, Hall finally got it to work, and by 9:00 A.M. he was breathing supplemental oxygen for the first time; by then he'd spent more than sixteen hours above 28,700 feet without gas. Thousands of feet below, his friends stepped up their efforts to cajole him to start down. "Rob, this is Helen at Base Camp," Wilton importuned, sounding as if she was on the brink of tears. "You think about that little baby of yours. You're going to see its face in a couple of months, so keep on going."

Several times Hall announced he was preparing to descend, and at one point we were sure he'd finally left the South Summit. At Camp Four, Lhakpa Chhiri and I shivered in the wind outside the tents, peering up at a tiny speck moving slowly down the upper Southeast Ridge. Convinced that it was Rob, coming down at last, Lhakpa and I slapped each other on the back and cheered him on. But an hour later my optimism was rudely extinguished when I noticed that the speck was still in the same place: it was actually nothing but a rock—just another altitude-induced hallucination. In truth, Rob had never even left the South Summit.

| | |

Around 9:30 A.M., Ang Dorje and Lhakpa Chhiri left Camp Four and started climbing toward the South Summit with a thermos of hot tea and two extra canisters of oxygen, intending to rescue Hall. They faced an exceedingly formidable task. As astounding and courageous as Boukreev's rescue of Sandy Pittman and Charlotte Fox had been the night before, it paled in comparison to what the two Sherpas were

proposing to do now: Pittman and Fox had been a twenty-minute walk from the tents over relatively flat ground; Hall was 3,000 vertical feet above Camp Four—an exhausting eight- or nine-hour climb in the best of circumstances.

And these were surely not the best of circumstances. The wind was blowing in excess of 40 knots. Both Ang Dorje and Lhakpa were cold and wasted from climbing to the summit and back just the day before. If they did somehow manage to reach Hall, moreover, it would be late afternoon before they got there, leaving only one or two hours of daylight in which to begin the even more difficult ordeal of bringing him down. Yet their loyalty to Hall was such that the two men ignored the overwhelming odds and set out toward the South Summit as fast as they could climb.

Shortly thereafter, two Sherpas from the Mountain Madness team—Tashi Tshering and Ngawang Sya Kya (a small, trim man, graying at the temples, who is Lopsang's father)—and one Sherpa from the Taiwanese team headed up to bring down Scott Fischer and Makalu Gau. Twelve hundred feet above the South Col the trio of Sherpas found the incapacitated climbers on the ledge where Lopsang had left them. Although they tried to give Fischer oxygen, he was unresponsive. Scott was still breathing, barely, but his eyes were fixed in their sockets, and his teeth were tightly clenched. Concluding that he was beyond hope, they left him on the ledge and started descending with Gau, who, after receiving hot tea and oxygen, and with considerable assistance from the three Sherpas, was able to move down to the tents on a short-rope under his own power.

The day had started out sunny and clear, but the wind remained fierce, and by late morning the upper mountain was wrapped in thick clouds. Down at Camp Two the IMAX team reported that the wind over the summit sounded like a squadron of 747s, even from 7,000 feet below. Meanwhile, high on the Southeast Ridge, Ang Dorje and Lhakpa Chhiri pressed on resolutely through the intensifying storm toward Hall. At 3:00 P.M., however, still 700 feet below the South Summit, the wind and subzero cold proved to be too much for them, and the Sherpas could go no higher. It was a valiant effort, but it had failed—and as they turned around to descend, Hall's chances for survival all but vanished.

Throughout the day on May 11, his friends and teammates incessantly begged him to make an effort to come down under his own power. Several times Hall announced that he was preparing to descend, only to change his mind and remain immobile at the South Summit. At 3:20 P.M., Cotter—who by now had walked over from his own camp beneath Pumori to the Everest Base Camp—scolded over the radio, "Rob, get moving down the ridge."

Sounding annoyed, Hall fired back, "Look, if I thought I could manage the knots on the fixed ropes with me frostbitten hands, I would have gone down six hours ago, pal. Just send a couple of the boys up with a big thermos of something hot—then I'll be fine."

"Thing is, mate, the lads who went up today encountered some high winds and had to turn around," Cotter replied, trying to convey as delicately as possible that the rescue attempt had been abandoned, "so we think your best shot is to move lower."

"I can last another night here if you send up a couple of boys with some Sherpa tea, first thing in the morning, no later than nine-thirty or ten," Rob answered.

"You're a tough man, Big Guy," said Cotter, his voice quavering. "We'll send some boys up to you in the morning."

At 6:20 P.M., Cotter contacted Hall to tell him that Jan Arnold was on the satellite phone from Christchurch and was waiting to be patched through. "Give me a minute," Rob said. "Me mouth's dry. I want to eat a bit of snow before I talk to her." A little later he came back on and rasped in a slow, horribly distorted voice, "Hi, my sweetheart. I hope you're tucked up in a nice warm bed. How are you doing?"

"I can't tell you how much I'm thinking about you!" Arnold replied. "You sound so much better than I expected.... Are you warm, my darling?"

"In the context of the altitude, the setting, I'm reasonably comfortable," Hall answered, doing his best not to alarm her.

"How are your feet?"

"I haven't taken me boots off to check, but I think I may have a bit of frostbite. . . ."

"I'm looking forward to making you completely better when you come home," said Arnold. "I just know you're going to be rescued. Don't feel that you're alone. I'm sending all my positive energy your way!"

Before signing off, Hall told his wife, "I love you. Sleep well, my sweetheart. Please don't worry too much."

These would be the last words anyone would hear him speak. Attempts to make radio contact with Hall later that night and the next day went unanswered. Twelve days later, when Breashears and Viesturs climbed over the South Summit on their way to the top, they found Hall lying on his right side in a shallow ice hollow, his upper body buried beneath a drift of snow.

Chapter Eighteen

NORTHEAST RIDGE MAY 10, 1996 28,550 FEET

Everest was the embodiment of the physical forces of the world. Against it he had to pit the spirit of man. He could see the joy in the faces of his comrades if he succeeded. He could imagine the thrill his success would cause among all fellow-mountaineers; the credit it would bring to England; the interest all over the world; the name it would bring him; the enduring satisfaction to himself that he had made his life worthwhile. . . . Perhaps he never exactly formulated it, yet in his mind must have been present the idea of "all or nothing." Of the two alternatives, to turn back a third time, or to die, the latter was for Mallory probably the easier. The agony of the first would be more than he as a man, as a mountaineer, and as an artist, could endure.

Sir Francis Younghusband
The Epic of Mount Everest, 1926

At 4:00 P.M. on May 10, around the same time a hurting Doug Hansen arrived on the summit supported by Rob Hall's shoulder, three climbers from the northern Indian province of Ladakh radioed down to their expedition leader that they, too, were on top of Everest. Members of a thirty-nine-person expedition organized by the Indo-Tibetan Border Police, Tsewang Smanla, Tsewang Paljor, and Dorje Morup had ascended from the Tibetan side of the peak via the Northeast Ridge—the route on which George Leigh Mallory and Andrew Irvine had so famously disappeared in 1924.

Leaving their high camp at 27,230 feet as a party of six, the Ladakhis did not get away from their tents until 5:45 A.M.* By mid-afternoon, still more than a thousand vertical feet below the top, they

* To avoid confusion, all times quoted in this chapter have been converted to Nepal time, even though the events I describe occurred in Tibet. Clocks in Tibet are set to reflect the Beijing time zone, which is two hours and fifteen minutes ahead of the Nepal time zone—e.g., 6:00 A.M. in Nepal is 8:15 in Tibet.

were engulfed by the same storm clouds that we encountered on the other side of the mountain. Three members of the team threw in the towel and went down at around 2:00 P.M., but Smanla, Paljor, and Morup pushed onward despite the deteriorating weather. "They were overcome by summit fever," explained Harbhajan Singh, one of the three who turned around.

The other three reached what they believed to be the summit at 4:00 P.M., by which time the clouds had become so thick that visibility was reduced to no more than 100 feet. They radioed their Base Camp on the Rongbuk Glacier to say they were on top, whereupon the leader of the expedition, Mohindor Singh, placed a satellite-telephone call to New Delhi and proudly reported the triumph to Prime Minister Narashima Rao. Celebrating their success, the summit team left an offering of prayer flags, katas, and climbing pitons on what appeared to be the highest point, and then descended into the fast-rising blizzard.

In truth, the Ladakhis were at 28,550 feet when they turned around, about two hours below the actual summit, which at that time still jutted above the highest clouds. The fact that they unwittingly stopped some 500 feet short of their goal explains why they didn't see Hansen, Hall, or Lopsang on top, and vice versa.

Later, shortly after dark, climbers lower on the Northeast Ridge reported seeing two headlamps in the vicinity of 28,300 feet, just above a notoriously problematic cliff known as the Second Step, but none of the three Ladakhis made it back to their tents that night, nor did they make further radio contact.

At 1:45 the next morning, May 11—around the same time Anatoli Boukreev was frantically searching the South Col for Sandy Pittman, Charlotte Fox, and Tim Madsen—two Japanese climbers, accompanied by three Sherpas, set out for the summit from the same high camp on the Northeast Ridge that the Ladakhis had used, despite the very high winds buffeting the peak. At 6:00 A.M., as they skirted a steep rock promontory called the First Step, twenty-one-year-old Eisuke Shigekawa and thirty-six-year-old Hiroshi Hanada were taken aback to see one of the Ladakhi climbers, probably Paljor, lying in the snow, horribly frostbitten but still alive after a night without shelter or oxygen, moaning unintelligibly. Not wanting to jeopardize their ascent by stopping to assist him, the Japanese team continued climbing toward the summit.

At 7:15 A.M. they arrived at the base of the Second Step, a dead-vertical prow of crumbling schist that is usually ascended by means of an aluminum ladder that had been lashed to the cliff by a Chinese team in 1975. To the dismay of the Japanese climbers, however, the ladder was falling apart and had become partially detached from the rock, so ninety minutes of strenuous climbing were required to surmount this 20-foot cliff.

Just beyond the top of the Second Step they came upon the other two Ladakhis, Smanla and Morup. According to an article in the *Financial Times* written by the British journalist Richard Cowper, who interviewed Hanada and Shigekawa at 21,000 feet immediately after their ascent, one of the Ladakhis was "apparently close to death, the other crouching in the snow. No words were passed. No water, food or oxygen exchanged hands. The Japanese moved on and 160 feet farther along they rested and changed oxygen cylinders."

Hanada told Cowper, "We didn't know them. No, we didn't give them any water. We didn't talk to them. They had severe high-altitude sickness. They looked as if they were dangerous."

Shigekawa explained, "We were too tired to help. Above 8,000 meters is not a place where people can afford morality."

Turning their backs on Smanla and Morup, the Japanese team resumed their ascent, passed the prayer flags and pitons left by the Ladakhis at 28,550 feet, and—in an astonishing display of tenacity—reached the summit at 11:45 A.M. in a screaming gale. Rob Hall was at that moment huddled on the South Summit, fighting for his life, a half hour's climb below them along the Southeast Ridge.

During their return down the Northeast Ridge to their high camp, the Japanese again came across Smanla and Morup above the Second Step. At this time Morup appeared to be dead; Smanla, though still alive, was hopelessly tangled in a fixed line. Pasang Kami, a Sherpa on the Japanese team, freed Smanla from the rope, then continued down the ridge. As they descended past the First Step—where on the way up they had climbed past Paljor, crumpled and raving in the snow—the Japanese party now saw no sign of the third Ladakhi.

Seven days later the Indo-Tibetan Border Police expedition launched another summit attempt. Departing their high camp at 1:15 on the morning of May 17, two Ladakhis and three Sherpas soon came upon the frozen bodies of their teammates. They reported that one of the men, in his death throes, had torn off most of his clothing before finally succumbing to the elements. Smanla, Morup, and Paljor were left on the mountain where they had fallen, and the five climbers continued to the top of Everest, which they reached at 7:40 A.M.

Chapter Nineteen

SOUTH COL 7:30 A.M., MAY 11, 1996 26,000 FEET

Turning and turning in the widening gyre
The falcon cannot hear the falconer;
Things fall apart; the center cannot hold;
Mere anarchy is loosed upon the world,
The blood-dimmed tide is loosed, and everywhere
The ceremony of innocence is drowned.

William Butler Yeats
"The Second Coming"

When I wobbled back to Camp Four around 7:30 Saturday morning, May 11, the actuality of what had happened—of what was still happening—began to sink in with paralyzing force. I was physically and emotionally wrecked after having just spent an hour scouring the South Col for Andy Harris; the search had left me convinced that he was dead. Radio calls my teammate Stuart Hutchison had been monitoring from Rob Hall on the South Summit made clear that our leader was in desperate straits and that Doug Hansen was dead. Members of Scott Fischer's team who'd spent most of the night lost on the Col reported that Yasuko Namba and Beck Weathers were dead. And Scott Fischer and Makalu Gau were believed to be dead or very near death, 1,200 feet above the tents.

Confronted with this tally, my mind balked and retreated into a weird, almost robotic state of detachment. I felt emotionally anesthetized yet hyperaware, as if I had fled into a bunker deep inside my skull and was peering out at the wreckage around me through a narrow, armored slit. As I gazed numbly at the sky, it seemed to have turned a preternaturally pale shade of blue, bleached of all but the faintest remnant of color. The jagged horizon was limned with a coronalike glow that flickered and pulsed before my eyes. I wondered if I had begun the downward spiral into the nightmarish territory of the mad.

After a night at 26,000 feet without supplemental oxygen, I was even weaker and more exhausted than I had been the previous evening after coming down from the summit. Unless we somehow acquired some more gas or descended to a lower camp, I knew that my teammates and I would continue to deteriorate rapidly.

The fast-track acclimatization schedule followed by Hall and most other modern Everesters is remarkably efficient: it allows climbers to embark for the summit after spending a relatively brief four-week period above 17,000 feet—including just a single overnight acclimatization excursion to 24,000 feet.* Yet this strategy is predicated on the assumption that everyone will have a continuous supply of bottled oxygen above 24,000 feet. When that ceases to be the case, all bets are off.

Searching out the rest of our crew, I found Frank Fischbeck and Lou Kasischke lying in a nearby tent. Lou was delirious and snow-blind, completely without sight, unable to do anything for himself, muttering incoherently. Frank looked as if he were in a severe state of shock, but he was doing his best to take care of Lou. John Taske was in another tent with Mike Groom; both men appeared to be asleep or unconscious. As rickety and feeble as I felt, it was obvious that everyone else except Stuart Hutchison was faring even worse.

As I went from tent to tent I tried to locate some oxygen, but all the canisters I found were empty. The ongoing hypoxia, coupled with my profound fatigue, exacerbated the sense of chaos and despair. Thanks to the relentless din of nylon flapping in the wind, it was impossible to communicate from tent to tent. The batteries in our one remaining radio were nearly depleted. An atmosphere of terminal entropy pervaded the camp, heightened by the fact that our team—which for the preceding six weeks had been encouraged to rely

* In 1996, Rob Hall's team spent just eight nights at Camp Two (21,300 feet) or higher before setting out for the summit from Base Camp, which is a pretty typical acclimatization period nowadays. Prior to 1990, climbers commonly spent considerably more time at Camp Two or higher—including at least one acclimatization sortie to 26,000 feet—before embarking for the top. Although the value of acclimatizing as high as 26,000 feet is debatable (the deleterious effects of spending extra time at such extreme altitude may well offset the benefits), there is little question that extending the current eight- or nine-night acclimatization period at 21,000 to 24,000 feet would provide a greater margin of safety.

thoroughly on our guides—was now suddenly and utterly without leadership: Rob and Andy were gone, and although Groom was present, the ordeal of the previous night had taken a terrible toll on him. Seriously frostbitten, lying insensate in his tent, at least for the time being he was unable even to speak.

With all our guides hors de combat, Hutchison stepped up to fill the leadership vacuum. A high-strung, self-serious young man from the upper crust of English-speaking Montreal society, he was a brilliant medical researcher who went on a big mountaineering expedition every two or three years but otherwise had little time for climbing. As the crisis mounted at Camp Four, he did his best to rise to the occasion.

While I tried to recover from my fruitless search for Harris, Hutchison organized a team of four Sherpas to locate the bodies of Weathers and Namba, who had been left on the far side of the Col when Anatoli Boukreev brought in Charlotte Fox, Sandy Pittman, and Tim Madsen. The Sherpa search party, headed by Lhakpa Chhiri, departed ahead of Hutchison, who was so exhausted and befuddled that he'd forgotten to put his boots on and had tried to leave camp in his light, smooth-soled liners. Only when Lhakpa pointed out the blunder did Hutchison return for his boots. Following Boukreev's directions, the Sherpas quickly found the two bodies on a slope of gray ice freckled with boulders near the lip of the Kangshung Face. Extremely superstitious about the dead, as many Sherpas are, they halted 60 or 70 feet away and waited for Hutchison.

"Both bodies were partially buried," Hutchison recalls. "Their backpacks were maybe 100 feet away, uphill from them. Their faces and torsos were covered with snow; only their hands and feet were sticking out. The wind was just screaming across the Col." The first body he came to turned out to be Namba, but Hutchison couldn't discern who it was until he knelt in the gale and chipped a three-inch-thick carapace of ice from her face. Stunned, he discovered that she was still breathing. Both her gloves were gone, and her bare hands appeared to be frozen solid. Her eyes were dilated. The skin on her face was the color of white porcelain. "It was terrible," Hutchison recalls. "I was overwhelmed. She was very near death. I didn't know what to do."

He turned his attention to Beck, who lay twenty feet away. Beck's head was also caked with a thick armor of frost. Balls of ice the size of grapes were matted to his hair and eyelids. After clearing the frozen detritus from Beck's face, Hutchison discovered that the Texan was still alive, too: "Beck was mumbling something, I think, but I couldn't tell what he was trying to say. His right glove was missing and he had terrible frostbite. I tried to get him to sit up but he couldn't. He was as close to death as a person can be and still be breathing."

Horribly shaken, Hutchison went over to the Sherpas and asked Lhakpa's advice. Lhakpa, an Everest veteran respected by Sherpas and sahibs alike for his mountain savvy, urged Hutchison to leave Beck and Yasuko where they lay. Even if they survived long enough to be dragged back to Camp Four, they would certainly die before they could be carried down to Base Camp, and attempting a rescue would needlessly jeopardize the lives of the other climbers on the Col, most of whom were going to have enough trouble getting themselves down safely.

Hutchison decided that Lhakpa was right—there was only one choice, however difficult: let nature take its inevitable course with Beck and Yasuko, and save the group's resources for those who could actually be helped. It was a classic act of triage. When Hutchison returned to camp he was on the verge of tears and looked like a ghost. At his urging we roused Taske and Groom and then crowded into their tent to discuss what to do about Beck and Yasuko. The conversation that ensued was anguished and halting. We avoided making eye contact. After five minutes, however, all four of us concurred: Hutchison's decision to leave Beck and Yasuko where they lay was the proper course of action.

We also debated heading down to Camp Two that afternoon, but Taske was insistent that we not descend from the Col while Hall was marooned on the South Summit. "I won't even consider leaving without him," he pronounced. It was a moot point, regardless: Kasischke and Groom were in such bad shape that going anywhere was out of the question for the time being.

"By then I was very worried that we were headed for a repeat of what happened on K2 in 1986," says Hutchison. On July 4 of that year, seven Himalayan veterans—including the legendary Austrian *bergsteiger* Kurt Diemberger—set out for the summit of the world's second-highest mountain. Six of the seven reached the top, but during the descent a severe storm struck the upper slopes of K2, pinning the climbers in their high camp at 26,250 feet. As the blizzard continued without letup for five days, they grew weaker and weaker. When the storm finally broke, only Diemberger and one other person made it down alive.

| | |

Saturday morning, as we discussed what to do about Namba and Weathers and whether to descend, Neal Beidleman was mustering Fischer's team from their tents and hectoring them to start down from the Col. "Everyone was so messed up from the night before that it was really hard getting our group up and out of the tents—I practically had to punch some people to get them to put their boots on," he says. "But I was adamant that we leave immediately. In my view, staying at twenty-six thousand feet longer than absolutely necessary is asking for trouble. I could see that rescue efforts were under way for Scott and Rob, so I turned my full attention to getting our clients off the Col and down to a lower camp."

While Boukreev remained behind at Camp Four to wait for Fischer, Beidleman herded his group slowly down from the Col. At 25,000 feet he paused to give Pittman another injection of dexamethasone, and then everyone stopped for a long time at Camp Three to rest and rehydrate. "When I saw those guys," says David Breashears, who was at Camp Three when Beidleman's crew arrived, "I was astounded. They looked like they'd been through a five-month war. Sandy started to break down—she was crying, 'It was terrible! I just gave up and lay down to die!' All of them appeared to be in severe shock."

Just before dark, the last of Beidleman's group was working their way down the steep ice of the lower Lhotse Face, when, 500 feet from the bottom of the fixed ropes, they were met by some Sherpas from a

Nepali cleanup expedition who'd come up to assist them. As they resumed their descent, a volley of grapefruit-sized stones came whizzing down from the upper mountain and one of them struck a Sherpa in the back of the head. "The rock just creamed him," says Beidleman, who observed the incident from a short distance above.

"It was sickening," Klev Schoening recalls. "It sounded like he'd been hit with a baseball bat." The force of the blow chipped a divot as large as a silver dollar from the Sherpa's skull, knocked him unconscious, and sent him into cardiopulmonary arrest. As he flopped over and started sliding down the rope, Schoening jumped in front of him and managed to halt his fall. But a moment later, as Schoening cradled the Sherpa in his arms, a second rock came down and smashed into the Sherpa; once again the man took the impact squarely on the back of his head.

Despite this second blow, after a few minutes the stricken man gasped violently and began breathing again. Beidleman managed to lower him to the bottom of the Lhotse Face, where a dozen of the Sherpa's teammates met them and carried the injured man to Camp Two. At that point, says Beidleman, "Klev and I just stared at each other in disbelief. It was like, 'What's going on here? What have we done to make this mountain so angry?' "

| | |

Throughout April and early May, Rob Hall had expressed his concern that one or more of the less competent teams might blunder into a bad jam, compelling our group to rescue them, thereby ruining our summit bid. Now, ironically, it was Hall's expedition that was in grave trouble, and other teams were in the position of having to come to our aid. Without rancor, three such groups—Todd Burleson's Alpine Ascents International expedition, David Breashears's IMAX expedition, and Mal Duff's commercial expedition—immediately postponed their own summit plans in order to assist the stricken climbers.

The day before—Friday, May 10—while we in Hall's and Fischer's teams were climbing from Camp Four toward the top, the Alpine Ascents International expedition headed by Burleson and Pete

Athans was arriving at Camp Three. On Saturday morning, as soon as they learned of the disaster that was unfolding above, Burleson and Athans left their clients at 24,000 feet in care of their third guide, Jim Williams, and rushed up to the South Col to help.

Breashears, Ed Viesturs, and the rest of the IMAX team happened to be in Camp Two at that time; Breashears immediately suspended filming in order to direct all of his expedition's resources toward the rescue effort. First, he relayed a message to me that some spare batteries were stashed in one of the IMAX tents on the Col; by midafternoon I'd found them, allowing Hall's team to re-establish radio contact with the lower camps. Then Breashears offered his expedition's supply of oxygen—fifty canisters that had been laboriously carried to 26,000 feet—to the ailing climbers and would-be rescuers on the Col. Even though this threatened to put his $5.5 million film project in jeopardy, he made the crucial gas available without hesitation.

Athans and Burleson arrived at Camp Four in midmorning, immediately began distributing IMAX gas bottles to those of us starved for oxygen, then waited to see what came of the Sherpas' efforts to rescue Hall, Fischer, and Gau. At 4:35 P.M., Burleson was standing outside the tents when he noticed someone walking slowly toward camp with a peculiar, stiff-kneed gait. "Hey, Pete," he called to Athans. "Check this out. Somebody's coming into camp." The person's bare right hand, naked to the frigid wind and grotesquely frostbitten, was outstretched in a kind of odd, frozen salute. Whoever it was reminded Athans of a mummy in a low-budget horror film. As the mummy lurched into camp, Burleson realized that it was none other than Beck Weathers, somehow risen from the dead.

The previous night, huddling with Groom, Beidleman, Namba, and the other members of that group, Weathers had felt himself "growing colder and colder. I'd lost my right glove. My face was freezing. My hands were freezing. I felt myself growing really numb and then it got really hard to stay focused, and finally I just sort of slid off into oblivion."

Through the rest of the night and most of the following day, Beck lay out on the ice, exposed to the merciless wind, cataleptic and barely alive. He has no recollection of Boukreev coming for Pittman, Fox, and Madsen. Nor does he remember Hutchison finding him in the morning and chipping the ice from his face. He remained comatose for more than twelve hours. Then, late Saturday afternoon, for some unknowable reason a light went on in the reptilian core of Beck's inanimate brain and he floated back to consciousness.

"Initially I thought I was in a dream," Weathers recalls. "When I first came to, I thought I was laying in bed. I didn't feel cold or uncomfortable. I sort of rolled onto my side, got my eyes open, and there was my right hand staring me in the face. Then I saw how badly frozen it was, and that helped bring me around to reality. Finally I woke up enough to recognize that I was in deep shit and the cavalry wasn't coming so I better do something about it myself."

Although Beck was blind in his right eye and able to focus his left eye within a radius of only three or four feet, he started walking directly into the wind, deducing correctly that camp lay in that direction. Had he been mistaken, he would have stumbled immediately down the Kangshung Face, the edge of which lay just thirty feet in the opposite direction. About ninety minutes later he encountered "some unnaturally smooth, bluish-looking rocks," which turned out to be the tents of Camp Four.

Hutchison and I were in our tent monitoring a radio call from Rob Hall on the South Summit when Burleson came rushing over. "Doctor! We need you bad!" he yelled to Stuart from just outside the door. "Grab your stuff. Beck just walked in, and he's in bad shape!" Struck dumb by Beck's miraculous resurrection, an exhausted Hutchison crawled outside to answer the call.

He, Athans, and Burleson placed Beck in an unoccupied tent, bundled him into two sleeping bags with several hot-water bottles, and put an oxygen mask over his face. "At that point," Hutchison confesses, "none of us thought Beck was going to survive the night. I could barely detect his carotid pulse, which is the last pulse you lose before you die. He was critically ill. And even if he did live until morning, I couldn't imagine how we were going to get him down."

By now the three Sherpas who had gone up to rescue Scott Fischer and Makalu Gau were back in camp after bringing down Gau; they'd left Fischer on a ledge at 27,200 feet after concluding that he was beyond saving. Having just seen Beck walk into camp after being given up for dead, however, Anatoli Boukreev was unwilling to write Fischer off. At 5:00 P.M., as the storm intensified, the Russian headed up alone to attempt to save him.

"I find Scott at seven o'clock, maybe it is seven-thirty or eight," says Boukreev. "By then it is dark. Storm is very strong. His oxygen mask is around face, but bottle is empty. He is not wearing mittens; hands completely bare. Down suit is unzipped, pulled off his shoulder, one arm is outside clothing. There is nothing I can do. Scott is dead." With a heavy heart, Boukreev lashed Fischer's backpack across his face as a shroud and left him on the ledge where he lay. Then he collected Scott's camera, ice ax, and favorite pocketknife—which Beidleman would later give to Scott's nine-year-old son in Seattle—and descended into the tempest.

The gale that struck on Saturday evening was even more powerful than the one that had lashed the Col the night before. By the time Boukreev made it back down to Camp Four the visibility was down to a few yards, and he almost failed to find the tents.

Breathing bottled oxygen (thanks to the IMAX team) for the first time in thirty hours, I fell into a tortured, fitful sleep despite the racket produced by the furiously flapping tent. Shortly after midnight, I was in the midst of a nightmare about Andy—he was falling down the Lhotse Face trailing a rope, demanding to know why I hadn't held onto the other end—when Hutchison shook me awake. "Jon," he shouted above the roar of the storm, "I'm concerned about the tent. Do you think it's going to be O.K.?"

As I struggled groggily up from the depths of my troubled reverie like a drowning man rising to the ocean's surface, it took me a minute to notice why Stuart was so worried: the wind had flattened half our shelter, which rocked violently with each successive gust. Several of the poles were badly bent, and my headlamp revealed that two of the main seams were in imminent danger of being ripped asunder. Flurries of fine snow particles filled the air inside the tent, blanketing everything with frost. The wind was blowing harder than anything I'd ever experienced anywhere, even on the Patagonian Ice Cap, a place reputed to be the windiest on the planet. If the tent disintegrated before morning, we would be in grave trouble.

Stuart and I gathered up our boots and all our clothing and then positioned ourselves on the windward side of the shelter. Bracing our backs and shoulders against the damaged poles, for the next three hours we leaned into the hurricane, despite our surpassing fatigue, holding up the battered nylon dome as if our lives depended on it. I kept imagining Rob up on the South Summit at 28,700 feet, his oxygen gone, exposed to the full savagery of this storm with no shelter whatsoever—but it was so disturbing that I tried not to think about it.

Just before dawn on Sunday, May 12, Stuart's oxygen ran out. "Without it I could feel myself becoming really cold and hypothermic," he says. "I began to lose feeling in my hands and feet. I worried that I was slipping over the edge, that I might not be able to get down from the Col. And I worried that if I didn't get down that morning, I might never get down." Giving Stuart my oxygen bottle, I rooted around until I found another one with some gas left in it, and then we both began packing for the descent.

When I ventured outside, I saw that at least one of the unoccupied tents had blown completely off the Col. Then I noticed Ang Dorje, standing alone in the appalling wind, sobbing inconsolably over the loss of Rob. After the expedition, when I told his Canadian friend Marion Boyd about his grief, she explained that "Ang Dorje sees his role on this earth as keeping people safe—he and I have talked about it a lot. It's all-important for him in terms of his religion, and preparing for the next go-around in life.* Even though Rob was the

* Devout Buddhists believe in *sonam*—an accounting of righteous deeds that, when large enough, enables one to escape the cycle of birth and rebirth and transcend forever this world of pain and suffering.

expedition leader, Ang Dorje would see it as his responsibility to ensure the safety of Rob and Doug Hansen and the others. So when they died, he couldn't help but blame himself."

Worried that Ang Dorje was so distraught that he might refuse to go down, Hutchison beseeched him to descend from the Col immediately. Then, at 8:30 A.M.—believing that by now Rob, Andy, Doug, Scott, Yasuko, and Beck were all surely dead—a badly frostbitten Mike Groom forced himself out of his tent, gamely assembled Hutchison, Taske, Fischbeck, and Kasischke, and started leading them down the mountain.

In the absence of any other guides, I volunteered to fill that role and bring up the rear. As our despondent group filed slowly away from Camp Four toward the Geneva Spur, I braced myself to make one last visit to Beck, whom I assumed had died in the night. I located his tent, which had been blasted flat by the hurricane, and saw that both doors were wide open. When I peered inside, however, I was shocked to discover that Beck was still alive.

He was lying on his back across the floor of the collapsed shelter, shivering convulsively. His face was hideously swollen; splotches of deep, ink-black frostbite covered his nose and cheeks. The storm had blown both sleeping bags from his body, leaving him exposed to the subzero wind, and with his frozen hands he'd been powerless to pull the bags back over himself or zip the tent closed. "Jesus fucking Christ!" he wailed when he saw me, his features twisted into a rictus of agony and desperation. "What's a guy have to do to get a little help around here!" He'd been screaming for help for two or three hours, but the storm had smothered his cries.

Beck had awakened in the middle of the night to find that "the storm had collapsed the tent and was blowing it apart. The wind was pressing the tent wall so hard against my face that I couldn't breathe. It would let up for a second, then come slamming back down into my face and chest, knocking the wind out of me. On top of everything else, my right arm was swelling up, and I had this stupid wristwatch on, so as my arm got bigger and bigger, the watch got tighter and tighter until it was cutting off most of the blood supply to my hand. But with my hands messed up so badly, there was no way I could get the damn thing off. I yelled for help, but nobody came. It was one hell of a long night. Man, I was glad to see your face when you stuck your head inside the door."

Upon first finding Beck in the tent, I was so shocked by his hideous condition—and by the unforgivable way that we'd let him down yet again—I nearly broke into tears. "Everything's going to be O.K.," I lied, choking back my sobs as I pulled the sleeping bags over him, zipped the tent doors shut, and tried to re-erect the damaged shelter. "Don't worry, pal. Everything's under control now."

As soon as I made Beck as comfortable as possible, I got on the radio to Dr. Mackenzie at Base Camp. "Caroline!" I begged in a hysterical voice. "What should I do about Beck? He's still alive, but I don't think he can survive much longer. He's in really bad shape!"

"Try to remain calm, Jon," she replied. "You need to go down with Mike and the rest of the group. Where are Pete and Todd? Ask them to look after Beck, then start down." Frantic, I roused Athans and Burleson, who immediately rushed over to Beck's tent with a canteen of hot tea. As I hurried out of camp to rejoin my teammates, Athans was getting ready to inject four milligrams of dexamethasone into the dying Texan's thigh. These were praiseworthy gestures, but it was hard to imagine that they would do him much good.

Chapter Twenty

THE GENEVA SPUR 9:45 A.M., MAY 12, 1996 25,900 FEET

The one great advantage which inexperience confers on the would-be mountaineer is that he is not bogged down by tradition or precedence. To him, all things appear simple, and he chooses straightforward solutions to the problems he faces. Often, of course, it defeats the success he is seeking, and sometimes it has tragic results, but the man himself doesn't know this when he sets out on his adventure. Maurice Wilson, Earl Denman, Klavs Becker-Larsen—none of them knew much about mountain climbing or they would not have set out on their hopeless quests, yet, untrammelled by techniques, determination carried them a long way.

Walt Unsworth
Everest

Fifteen minutes after leaving the South Col on Sunday morning, May 12, I caught up to my teammates as they were descending from the crest of the Geneva Spur. It was a pathetic sight: we were all so debilitated that it took the group an incredibly long time just to descend the few hundred feet to the snow slope immediately below. The most wrenching thing, however, was our shrunken size: three days earlier, when we had ascended this terrain we'd numbered eleven; now there were only six of us.

Stuart Hutchison, at the back of the pack, was still atop the Spur when I reached him, preparing to rappel down the fixed lines. I noticed that he wasn't wearing his goggles. Even though it was a cloudy day, the vicious ultraviolet radiation at this altitude would render him snow-blind very quickly. "Stuart!" I yelled over the wind, pointing at my eyes. "Your goggles!"

"Oh yeah," he replied in a weary voice. "Thanks for reminding me. Hey, as long as you're here, would you mind checking my harness? I'm so tired that I'm not thinking clearly any more. I'd appreciate it if you'd keep an eye on me." Examining his harness, I saw immediately that the buckle was only half-fastened. Had he clipped into the rope with his safety tether it would have opened under his body weight and sent him tumbling down the Lhotse Face. When I pointed this out, he said, "Yeah, that's what I thought, but my hands were too cold to do it right." Yanking off my gloves in the bitter wind, I hurriedly cinched the harness tightly around his waist and sent him down the Spur after the others.

As he clipped his safety tether onto the fixed rope he tossed his ice ax down, then left it lying on the rocks as he embarked on the first rappel. "Stuart!" I shouted. "Your ax!"

"I'm too tired to carry it," he shouted back. "Just leave it there." I was so knackered myself that I didn't argue with him. I left the ax where it lay, clipped the rope, and followed Stuart down the steep flank of the Geneva Spur.

An hour later we arrived atop the Yellow Band, and a bottleneck ensued as each climber cautiously descended the vertical limestone cliff. As I waited at the back of the queue, several of Scott Fischer's Sherpas caught up to us. Lopsang Jangbu, half-crazed with grief and exhaustion, was among them. Placing a hand on his shoulder, I told him that I was sorry about Scott. Lopsang pounded his chest and tearfully blurted, "I am very bad luck, very bad luck. Scott is dead; it is my fault. I am very bad luck. It is my fault. I am very bad luck."

| | |

I dragged my haggard ass into Camp Two around 1:30 P.M. Although by any rational standard I was still at high altitude—21,300 feet—this place felt manifestly different from the South Col. The murderous wind had completely abated. Instead of shivering and worrying about frostbite, I was now sweating heavily beneath a scorching sun. No longer did it seem as though I were clinging to survival by a fraying thread.

Our mess tent, I saw, had been transformed into a makeshift field hospital, staffed by Henrik Jessen Hansen, a Danish physician on Mal Duff's team, and Ken Kamler, an American client and physician on

Todd Burleson's expedition. At 3:00 P.M., as I was drinking a cup of tea, six Sherpas hustled a dazed-looking Makalu Gau into the tent and the doctors sprang into action.

They immediately laid him down, removed his clothing, and stuck an IV tube into his arm. Examining his frozen hands and feet, which had a dull whitish sheen like a dirty bathroom sink, Kamler observed grimly, "This is the worst frostbite I've ever seen." When he asked Gau if he could photograph his limbs for the medical record, the Taiwanese climber consented with a broad smile; like a soldier displaying battle wounds, he seemed almost proud of the gruesome injuries he'd sustained.

Ninety minutes later, the doctors were still working on Makalu when David Breashears's voice barked over the radio: "We're on our way down with Beck. We'll have him to Camp Two by dark."

A long beat passed before I realized that Breashears wasn't talking about hauling a body off the mountain; he and his companions were bringing Beck down alive. I couldn't believe it. When I'd left him on the South Col seven hours earlier, I was terrified that he wasn't going to survive through the morning.

Given up for dead yet again, Beck had simply refused to succumb. Later I learned from Pete Athans that shortly after he had injected Beck with dexamethasone, the Texan experienced an astonishing recovery. "Around ten-thirty we got him dressed, put his harness on, and discovered that he was actually able to stand up and walk. We were all pretty amazed."

They started descending from the Col with Athans directly in front of Beck, telling him where to place his feet. With Beck draping an arm over Athans's shoulders and Burleson grasping the Texan's climbing harness tightly from behind, they shuffled carefully down the mountain. "At times we had to help him pretty substantially," says Athans, "but really, he moved surprisingly well."

At 25,000 feet, arriving above the limestone cliffs of the Yellow Band, they were met by Ed Viesturs and Robert Schauer, who efficiently lowered Beck down the steep rock. At Camp Three they were assisted by Breashears, Jim Williams, Veikka Gustafsson, and Araceli

Segarra; the eight healthy climbers actually brought the severely crippled Beck down the Lhotse Face in considerably less time than my teammates and I had managed to descend earlier that morning.

When I heard that Beck was on his way down, I made my way to my tent, wearily pulled on my mountaineering boots, and started plodding up to meet the rescue party, expecting to encounter them on the lower reaches of the Lhotse Face. Just twenty minutes above Camp Two, however, I was amazed to run into the entire crew. Although he was being assisted with a short-rope, Beck was moving under his own power. Breashears and company hustled him down the glacier at such a fast pace that in my own woeful state, I could barely keep up with them.

Beck was placed beside Gau in the hospital tent, and the physicians began stripping off his clothing. "My God!" Dr. Kamler exclaimed when he saw Beck's right hand. "His frostbite is even worse than Makalu's." Three hours later, when I crawled into my sleeping bag, the doctors were still gingerly thawing Beck's frozen limbs in a pot of lukewarm water, working by the glow of their headlamps.

The next morning—Monday, May 13—I left the tents at first light and walked two and a half miles through the deep cleft of the Western Cwm to the lip of the Icefall. There, acting on instructions radioed up from Guy Cotter at Base Camp, I scouted for a level area that could serve as a helicopter landing pad.

Over the preceding days, Cotter had been doggedly working the satellite phone to arrange a helicopter evacuation from the lower end of the Cwm, so that Beck wouldn't have to descend the treacherous ropes and ladders of the Icefall, which would have been difficult and very hazardous with such severely injured hands. Helicopters had landed in the Cwm previously, in 1973, when an Italian expedition used a pair of them to ferry loads from Base Camp. It was nevertheless extremely dangerous flying, at the limit of the aircraft's range, and one of the Italian machines had crashed on the glacier. In the twenty-three years since, nobody had attempted to land above the Icefall again.

Cotter was persistent, however, and thanks to his efforts the American Embassy persuaded the Nepalese army to attempt a helicopter rescue in the Cwm. Around 8:00 Monday morning, as I searched in vain for an acceptable helipad among the jumbled seracs at the lip of the Icefall, Cotter's voice crackled over my radio: "The helicopter's on the way, Jon. He should be there any minute. You better find a place for him to land pretty quickly." Hoping to find level terrain higher on the glacier, I promptly ran into Beck being short-roped down the Cwm by Athans, Burleson, Gustafsson, Breashears, Viesturs, and the rest of the IMAX crew.

Breashears, who had worked around many helicopters during the course of a long and distinguished film career, immediately found a landing pad bordered by two gaping crevasses at 19,860 feet. I tied a silk kata to a bamboo wand to serve as a wind indicator, while Breashears—using a bottle of red Kool-Aid as dye—marked a giant X in the snow at the center of the landing zone. A few minutes later Makalu Gau appeared, having been dragged down the glacier on a piece of plastic by a half-dozen Sherpas. A moment after that we heard the THWOCK-THWOCK-THWOCK of a helicopter's rotors thrashing furiously at the thin air.

Piloted by Lieutenant Colonel Madan Khatri Chhetri of the Nepalese army, the olive-drab B2 Squirrel helicopter—stripped of all unnecessary fuel and equipment—made two passes, but on each occasion aborted at the last moment. On Madan's third attempt, however, he settled the Squirrel shakily onto the glacier with its tail hanging over a bottomless crevasse. Keeping the rotors revving at full power, never taking his eyes off the control panel, Madan raised a single finger, indicating that he could take only one passenger; at this altitude, any additional weight might cause him to crash while taking off.

Because Gau's frostbitten feet had been thawed at Camp Two, he could no longer walk or even stand, so Breashears, Athans, and I agreed that the Taiwanese climber should be the one to go. "Sorry," I yelled to Beck above the scream of the chopper's turbines. "Maybe he'll be able to make a second flight." Beck nodded philosophically.

We hoisted Gau into the rear of the helicopter, and the machine labored tentatively into the air. As soon as Madan's skids lifted from the glacier, he nosed the aircraft forward, dropped like a stone over the lip of the Icefall, and disappeared into the shadows. A dense silence now filled the Cwm.

Thirty minutes later we were standing around the landing zone, discussing how to get Beck down, when a faint THWOCK-THWOCK-THWOCK-THWOCK sounded from the valley below. Slowly the noise grew louder and louder, and finally the small green helicopter popped into view. Madan flew a short distance up the Cwm before bringing the aircraft around, so that its snout pointed downhill. Then, without hesitation, he set the Squirrel down once more on the Kool-Aid crosshatch, and Breashears and Athans hustled Beck aboard. A few seconds later the helicopter was airborne, flitting past the West Shoulder of Everest like a freakish metal dragonfly. An hour later Beck and Makalu Gau were receiving treatment in a Kathmandu hospital.

After the rescue team dispersed, I sat in the snow for a long while by myself, staring at my boots, endeavoring to get a grip on what had happened over the preceding seventy-two hours. How could things have gone so haywire? How could Andy and Rob and Scott and Doug and Yasuko really be dead? But try as I might, no answers were forthcoming. The magnitude of this calamity was so far beyond anything I'd ever imagined that my brain simply shorted out and went dark. Abandoning my hope of comprehending what had transpired, I shouldered my backpack and headed down into the frozen witchery of the Icefall, nervous as a cat, for one last trip through the maze of decaying seracs.

Chapter Twenty-one

EVEREST BASE CAMP MAY 13, 1996 17,600 FEET

I shall inevitably be asked for a word of mature judgement on the expedition of a kind that was impossible when we were all up close to it. . . . On the one hand, Amundsen going straight there, getting there first, and returning without the loss of a single man, and without having put any greater strain on himself and his men than was all in the day's work of polar exploration. On the other hand, our expedition, running appalling risks, performing prodigies of superhuman endurance, achieving immortal renown, commemorated in august cathedral sermons and by public statues, yet reaching the Pole only to find our terrible journey superfluous, and leaving our best men dead on the ice. To ignore such a contrast would be ridiculous: to write a book without accounting for it a waste of time.

Apsley Cherry-Garrard
The Worst Journey in the World,
an account of Robert Falcon
Scott's doomed 1912 expedition
to the South Pole

Arriving at the bottom of the Khumbu Icefall on Monday morning, May 13, I came down the final slope to find Ang Tshering, Guy Cotter, and Caroline Mackenzie waiting for me at the edge of the glacier. Guy handed me a beer, Caroline gave me a hug, and the next thing I knew I was sitting on the ice with my face in my hands and tears streaking my cheeks, weeping like I hadn't wept since I was a small boy. Safe now, the crushing strain of the preceding days lifted from my shoulders, I cried for my lost companions, I cried because I was grateful to be alive, I cried because I felt terrible for having survived while others had died.

On Tuesday afternoon, Neal Beidleman presided over a memorial service at the Mountain Madness encampment. Lopsang Jangbu's father, Ngawang Sya Kya—an ordained lama—burned juniper incense and chanted Buddhist scripture beneath a metallic gray sky. Neal said a few words, Guy spoke, Anatoli Boukreev mourned the loss of Scott Fischer. I got up and stammered out some memories of Doug Hansen. Pete Schoening tried to raise everyone's spirits by urging us to look forward, not back. But when the service ended and we all dispersed to our tents, a funereal gloom hung over Base Camp.

Early the next morning, a helicopter arrived to evacuate Charlotte Fox and Mike Groom, both of whom had frostbitten feet that needed immediate medical attention. John Taske, who was a doctor, flew out as well to treat Charlotte and Mike en route. Then, shortly before noon, while Helen Wilton and Guy Cotter stayed behind to oversee the dismantling of the Adventure Consultants compound, Lou Kasischke, Stuart Hutchison, Frank Fischbeck, Caroline, and I walked out of Base Camp, bound for home.

On Thursday, May 16, we were helicoptered from Pheriche to the village of Syangboche, just above Namche Bazaar. As we walked across the dirt landing strip to await a second flight into Kathmandu, Stuart, Caroline, and I were approached by three ashen-faced Japanese men. The first said that his name was Muneo Nukita—he was an accomplished Himalayan climber who'd twice reached the top of Everest—and then politely explained that he was acting as a guide and an interpreter for the other two, whom he introduced as Yasuko Namba's husband, Kenichi Namba, and her brother. Over the next forty-five minutes they asked many questions, few of which I could answer.

By then Yasuko's death had become headline news across Japan. Indeed, on May 12—less than twenty-four hours after she perished on the South Col—a helicopter had touched down in the middle of Base Camp, and two Japanese journalists had hopped out wearing oxygen masks. Accosting the first person they saw—an American climber named Scott Darsney—they had demanded information about Yasuko. Now, four days later, Nukita warned us that a similarly predacious swarm of print and television reporters lay in wait for us in Kathmandu.

Late that afternoon we jammed aboard a gigantic Mi-17 helicopter and lifted off through a gap in the clouds. An hour later the chopper set down at Tribhuvan International Airport, and we stepped out the door into a thicket of microphones and television cameras. As a journalist, I found it edifying to experience things from the other side of the fence. The throng of reporters, mostly Japanese, wanted a neatly scripted version of the calamity, replete with villains and heroes. But the chaos and suffering I'd witnessed were not easily reduced to sound bites. After twenty minutes of grilling on the tarmac, I was rescued by David Schensted, the consul from the American Embassy, who delivered me to the Garuda Hotel.

More difficult interviews followed—by other reporters, and then by a gauntlet of scowling officials at the Ministry of Tourism. Friday evening, wandering through the alleys of Kathmandu's Thamel district, I sought refuge from a deepening depression. I handed a scrawny Nepalese boy a fistful of rupees and received a tiny, paper-covered packet in return, emblazoned with a snarling tiger. Unwrapping it back in my hotel room, I crumbled the contents across a leaf of cigarette paper. The pale green buds were sticky with resin and redolent of rotting fruit. I rolled a joint, smoked it down to nothing, rolled a second fatty, and smoked nearly half of that one, too, before the room began to spin and I stubbed it out.

I lay naked across the bed and listened to the sounds of the night drift through the open window. The jingle of ricksha bells blended with car horns, the come-ons of street peddlers, a woman's laughter, music from a nearby bar. Flat on my back, too high to move, I closed my eyes and let the glutinous premonsoon heat cover me like a balm; I felt as though I were melting into the mattress. A procession of intricately etched pinwheels and big-nosed cartoon figures floated across the backs of my eyelids in neon hues.

As I turned my head to the side, my ear brushed against a wet spot; tears, I realized, were running down my face and soaking the sheets. I felt a gurgling, swelling bubble of hurt and shame roll up my spine from somewhere deep inside. Erupting out of my nose and mouth in a flood of snot, the first sob was followed by another, then another and another.

| | |

On May 19 I flew back to the States, carrying two duffels of Doug Hansen's belongings to return to the people who loved him. At the Seattle airport I was met by his children, Angie and Jaime; his girlfriend, Karen Marie; and other friends and family members. I felt stupid and utterly impotent when confronted by their tears.

Breathing thick marine air that carried the scent of a minus tide, I marveled at the fecundity of the Seattle spring, appreciating its damp, mossy charms as never before. Slowly, tentatively, Linda and I began the process of becoming reacquainted. The twenty-five pounds I'd shed in Nepal came back with a vengeance. The ordinary pleasures of life at home—eating breakfast with my wife, watching the sun go down over Puget Sound, being able to get up in the middle of the night and walk barefoot to a warm bathroom—generated flashes of joy that bordered on rapture. But such moments were tempered by the long penumbra cast by Everest, which seemed to recede little with the passage of time.

Stewing over my culpability, I put off calling Andy Harris's partner, Fiona McPherson, and Rob Hall's wife, Jan Arnold, for such a long time that they finally phoned me from New Zealand. When the call came, I was able to say nothing to diminish Fiona's anger or bewilderment. During my conversation with Jan, she spent more time comforting me than vice versa.

I'd always known that climbing mountains was a high-risk pursuit. I accepted that danger was an essential component of the game—without it, climbing would be little different from a hundred other trifling diversions. It was titillating to brush up against the enigma of mortality, to steal a glimpse across its forbidden frontier. Climbing was a magnificent activity, I firmly believed, not in spite of the inherent perils, but precisely because of them.

Until I visited the Himalaya, however, I'd never actually seen death at close range. Hell, before I went to Everest, I'd never even been to a funeral. Mortality had remained a conveniently hypothetical concept, an idea to ponder in the abstract. Sooner or later the divestiture of such a privileged innocence was inevitable, but when it finally happened the shock was magnified by the sheer superfluity of the carnage: all told, Everest killed twelve men and women in the spring of 1996, the worst single-season death toll since climbers first set foot on the peak seventy-five years ago.

Of the six climbers on Hall's expedition who reached the summit, only Mike Groom and I made it back down: four teammates with whom I'd laughed and vomited and held long, intimate conversations lost their lives. My actions—or failure to act—played a direct role in the death of Andy Harris. And while Yasuko Namba lay dying on the South Col, I was a mere 350 yards away, huddled inside a tent, oblivious to her struggle, concerned only with my own safety. The stain this has left on my psyche is not the sort of thing that washes off after a few months of grief and guilt-ridden self-reproach.

Eventually I spoke of my lingering disquietude to Klev Schoening, whose home was not far from mine. Klev said that he, too, felt awful about the loss of so many lives, but unlike me, he had no "survivor's guilt." He explained, "Out on the Col that night, I used up everything I had trying to save myself and the people with me. By the time we made it back to the tents I had absolutely nothing left. I'd frostbitten one cornea and was practically blind. I was hypothermic, delirious, and shivering uncontrollably. It was terrible losing Yasuko, but I've make peace with myself over it, because I know in my heart that there was nothing more I could have done to save her. You shouldn't be so hard on yourself. It was a bad storm. In the condition you were in at the time, what could you have possibly done for her?"

Perhaps nothing, I concurred. But in contrast to Schoening, I'll never be sure. And the enviable peace of which he speaks eludes me.

| | |

With so many marginally qualified climbers flocking to Everest these days, a lot of people believe that a tragedy of this magnitude was overdue. But nobody imagined that an expedition led by Rob Hall would be at the center of it. Hall ran the tightest, safest operation on the mountain, bar none. A compulsively methodical man, he had elaborate systems in place that were supposed to prevent such a catastrophe. So what happened? How can it be explained, not only to the loved ones left behind, but to a censorious public?

Hubris probably had something to do with it. Hall had become so adept at running climbers of all abilities up and down Everest that he got a little cocky, perhaps. He'd bragged on more than one occasion that he could get almost any reasonably fit person to the summit, and his record seemed to support this. He'd also demonstrated a remarkable ability to prevail over adversity.

In 1995, for instance, Hall and his guides not only had to cope with Hansen's problems high on the peak, but they also had to deal with the complete collapse of another client named Chantal Mauduit, a celebrated French alpinist, who was making her seventh stab at Everest without oxygen. Mauduit passed out stone cold at 28,700 feet and had to be dragged and carried all the way down from the South Summit to the South Col "like a sack of spuds," as Guy Cotter put it. After everybody came out of that summit attempt alive, Hall may well have thought there was little he couldn't handle.

Before this year, however, Hall had had uncommonly good luck with the weather, and it might have skewed his judgment. "Season after season," confirmed David Breashears, who has been on more than a dozen Himalayan expeditions and has himself climbed Everest three times, "Rob had brilliant weather on summit day. He'd never been caught by a storm high on the mountain." In fact, the gale of May 10, though violent, was nothing extraordinary; it was a fairly typical Everest squall. If it had hit two hours later, it's likely that nobody would have died. Conversely, if it had arrived even one hour earlier, the storm could easily have killed eighteen or twenty climbers—me among them.

Certainly time had as much to do with the tragedy as the weather, and ignoring the clock can't be passed off as an act of God. Delays at the fixed lines were foreseeable and eminently preventable. Predetermined turn-around times were egregiously ignored.

Extending the turn-around times may have been influenced to some degree by the rivalry between Fischer and Hall. Fischer had never guided Everest before 1996. From a business standpoint, there was tremendous pressure on him to be successful. He was exceedingly motivated to get clients to the summit, especially a celebrity client like Sandy Hill Pittman.

Likewise, having failed to get anybody to the top in 1995, it would have been bad for Hall's business if he failed again in 1996—especially if Fischer succeeded. Scott had a charismatic personality, and that charisma had been aggressively marketed by Jane Bromet. Fischer was trying very hard to eat Hall's lunch, and Rob knew it. Under the circumstances, the prospect of turning his clients around while his rival's clients were pushing toward the summit may have been sufficiently distasteful to cloud Hall's judgment.

It can't be stressed strongly enough, moreover, that Hall, Fischer, and the rest of us were forced to make such critical decisions while severely impaired with hypoxia. In pondering how this disaster could have occurred, it is imperative to remember that lucid thought is all but impossible at 29,000 feet.

Wisdom comes easily after the fact. Shocked by the toll in human life, critics have been quick to suggest policies and procedures to ensure that the catastrophes of this season won't be repeated. It has been proposed, for example, that a guide-to-client ratio of one to one be established as the standard on Everest—i.e., each client would climb with his or her own personal guide and remain roped to that guide at all times.

Perhaps the simplest way to reduce future carnage would be to ban bottled oxygen except for emergency medical use. A few reckless souls might perish trying to reach the summit without gas, but the great bulk of marginally competent climbers would be forced to turn back by their own physical limitations before they ascended high enough to get into serious trouble. And a no-gas regulation would have the corollary benefit of automatically reducing trash and crowding because considerably fewer people would attempt Everest if they knew supplemental oxygen was not an option.

But guiding Everest is a very loosely regulated business, administered by byzantine Third World bureaucracies spectacularly ill-equipped to assess qualifications of guides or clients. Moreover, the two nations that control access to the peak—Nepal and China—are staggeringly poor. Desperate for hard currency, the governments of both countries have a vested interest in issuing as many expensive climbing permits as the market will support, and both are unlikely to enact any policies that significantly limit their revenues.

Analyzing what went wrong on Everest is a useful enough enterprise; it might conceivably prevent some deaths down the road. But to believe that dissecting the tragic events of 1996 in minute detail will actually reduce the future death rate in any meaningful way is wishful thinking. The urge to catalog the myriad blunders in order to "learn from the mistakes" is for the most part an exercise in denial and self-deception. If you can convince yourself that Rob Hall died because he made a string of stupid errors and that you are too clever to repeat those same errors, it makes it easier for you to attempt Everest in the face of some rather compelling evidence that doing so is injudicious.

In fact, the murderous outcome of 1996 was in many ways simply business as usual. Although a record number of people died in the spring climbing season on Everest, the 12 fatalities amounted to only 3 percent of the 398 climbers who ascended higher than Base Camp—which is actually slightly below the historical fatality rate of 3.3 percent. Or here's another way to look at it: between 1921 and May 1996, 144 people died and the peak was climbed some 630 times—a ratio of one in four. Last spring, 12 climbers died and 84 reached the summit—a ratio of one in seven. Compared to these historical standards, 1996 was actually a safer-than-average year.

Truth be told, climbing Everest has always been an extraordinarily dangerous undertaking and doubtless always will be, whether the people involved are Himalayan neophytes being guided up the peak or world-class mountaineers climbing with their peers. It is worth noting that before the mountain claimed the lives of Hall and Fischer, it had already wiped out a whole corps of elite climbers, including Peter Boardman, Joe Tasker, Marty Hoey, Jake Breitenbach, Mick Burke, Michel Parmentier, Roger Marshall, Ray Genet, and George Leigh Mallory.

In the case of the guided ilk, it rapidly became clear to me in 1996 that few of the clients on the peak (myself included) truly appreciated the gravity of the risks we faced—the thinness of the margin by which human life is sustained above 25,000 feet. Walter Mittys with Everest dreams need to bear in mind that when things go wrong up in the Death Zone—and sooner or later they always do—the strongest guides in the world may be powerless to save a client's life; indeed, as the events of 1996 demonstrated, the strongest guides in the world are sometimes powerless to save even their own lives. Four of my teammates died not so much because Rob Hall's systems were faulty—indeed, nobody's were better—but because on Everest it is the nature of systems to break down with a vengeance.

In the midst of all the postmortem ratiocination, it is easy to lose sight of the fact that climbing mountains will never be a safe, predictable, rule-bound enterprise. This is an activity that idealizes risk-taking; the sport's most celebrated figures have always been those who stick their necks out the farthest and manage to get away with it. Climbers, as a species, are simply not distinguished by an excess of prudence. And that holds especially true for Everest climbers: when presented with a chance to reach the planet's highest summit, history shows, people are surprisingly quick to abandon good judgment. "Eventually," warns Tom Hornbein, thirty-three years after his ascent of the West Ridge, "what happened on Everest this season is certain to happen again."

For evidence that few lessons were learned from the mistakes of May 10, one need look no farther than what happened on Everest in the weeks that immediately followed.

| | |

On May 17, two days after Hall's team quit Base Camp, over on the Tibetan side of the mountain an Austrian named Reinhard Wlasich and a Hungarian teammate, climbing without supplemental oxygen, ascended to the high camp at 27,230 feet on the Northeast Ridge, where they occupied a tent abandoned by the ill-fated Ladakhi expedition. The following morning Wlasich complained that he felt ill and then lost consciousness; a Norwegian doctor who happened to be present determined that the Austrian was suffering from both pulmonary and cerebral edema. Although the doctor administered oxygen and medication, by midnight Wlasich was dead.

Meanwhile, over on the Nepalese side of Everest, David Breashears's IMAX expedition regrouped and considered their options. Since $5.5 million dollars had been invested in their film project, they had a big incentive to remain on the mountain and undertake a summit attempt. With Breashears, Ed Viesturs, and Robert Schauer, they were without question the strongest, most competent team on the mountain. And despite giving away half of their supply of oxygen to assist rescuers and climbers in need, they were subsequently able to scrounge enough gas from expeditions leaving the mountain to replace most of what they'd lost.

Paula Barton Viesturs, Ed's wife, had been monitoring the radio as Base Camp manager for the IMAX crew when disaster struck on May 10. A friend of both Hall's and Fischer's, she was devastated; Paula assumed that after such a horrifying tragedy the IMAX team would automatically fold up their tents and go home. Then she overheard a radio call between Breashears and another climber, in which the IMAX leader nonchalantly declared that the team intended to take a short break at Base Camp and then go for the summit.

"After all that had happened, I couldn't believe they'd really go back up there," Paula admits. "When I heard the radio call, I just lost it." She was so upset that she left Base Camp and walked down to Tengboche for five days to collect herself.

On Wednesday, May 22, the IMAX team arrived on the South Col, in perfect weather, and set out for the top that night. Ed Viesturs, who had the starring role in the film, reached the summit at 11:00

Thursday morning, without using supplemental oxygen.* Breashears arrived twenty minutes later, followed by Araceli Segarra, Robert Schauer, and Jamling Norgay Sherpa—the son of the first ascender, Tenzing Norgay, and the ninth member of the Norgay clan to climb the peak. All told, sixteen climbers summitted that day, including the Swede who'd ridden his bike to Nepal from Stockholm, Göran Kropp, and Ang Rita Sherpa, whose ascent marked his tenth visit to the top of Everest.

On the way up, Viesturs had climbed past the frozen bodies of Fischer and Hall. "Both Jean [Fischer's wife] and Jan [Hall's wife] had asked me to bring some personal effects back for them," Viesturs says sheepishly. "I knew Scott wore his wedding ring around his neck, and I wanted to bring it down to Jeannie, but I couldn't force myself to go digging around his body. I just didn't have it in me." Instead of collecting any keepsakes, Viesturs sat down next to Fischer during the descent and spent a few minutes alone with him. "Hey, Scott, how you doing?" Ed sadly inquired of his friend. "What happened, man?"

On Friday afternoon, May 24, as the IMAX team was descending from Camp Four to Camp Two, they encountered what remained of the South African Team—Ian Woodall, Cathy O'Dowd, Bruce Herrod, and three Sherpas—at the Yellow Band, on their way to the South Col to make their own summit attempt. "Bruce looked strong, his face looked good," recalls Breashears. "He shook my hand really hard, congratulated us, said he felt great. Half an hour behind him were Ian and Cathy, collapsed over their ice axes, looking like hell—really out of it.

"I made a point of spending a little time with them," Breashears continues. "I knew they were very inexperienced, so I said, 'Please be careful. You saw what happened up here earlier this month. Remember that getting to the summit is the easy part; it's getting back down that's hard.' "

* Viesturs had previously ascended Everest in 1990 and '91 without gas. In 1994 he climbed it a third time, with Rob Hall; on that ascent he used bottled oxygen because he was guiding the peak and thought it would be irresponsible to do so without it.

The South Africans set out for the summit that night. O'Dowd and Woodall left the tents twenty minutes after midnight with Sherpas Pemba Tendi, Ang Dorje,* and Jangbu carrying oxygen for them. Herrod seems to have left camp within minutes of the main group, but he fell farther and farther behind as the ascent dragged on. On Saturday, May 25, at 9:50 A.M., Woodall called Patrick Conroy, the Base Camp radio operator, to report that he was on the summit with Pemba and that O'Dowd would be on top in fifteen minutes with Ang Dorje and Jangbu. Woodall said that Herrod, who wasn't carrying a radio, was some unknown distance below.

Herrod, whom I'd met several times on the mountain, was an amiable thirty-seven-year-old of bearish build. Although he had no previous high-altitude experience, he was a competent mountaineer who'd spent eighteen months in the frigid wastes of Antarctica working as a geophysicist—he was far and away the most accomplished climber remaining on the South African team. Since 1988 he'd been working hard to make a go of it as a freelance photographer, and he hoped reaching the summit of Everest would give his career a needed boost.

When Woodall and O'Dowd were on the summit, as it turned out, Herrod was still far below, struggling up the Southeast Ridge by himself at a dangerously slow pace. Around 12:30 P.M. he passed Woodall, O'Dowd, and the three Sherpas on their way down. Ang Dorje gave Herrod a radio and described where an oxygen bottle had been stashed for him, then Herrod continued alone toward the top. He didn't reach the summit until just after 5:00 P.M., seven hours after the others, by which time Woodall and O'Dowd were already back in their tent at the South Col.

Coincidentally, at the same moment Herrod radioed down to Base Camp to report that he was on top, his girlfriend, Sue Thompson, happened to call Conroy on the Base Camp satellite phone from her London home. "When Patrick told me that Bruce was on the sum-

* A reminder: the Sherpa named Ang Dorje on the South African team is not the same person as the Sherpa named Ang Dorje on Rob Hall's team.

mit," Thompson recalls, "I said, 'Fuck! He can't be on the summit this late—it's five-fifteen! I don't like this.' "

A moment later Conroy patched Thompson's phone call through to Herrod on top of Everest. "Bruce sounded compos mentis," she says. "He was aware that he'd taken a long time to get there, but he sounded as normal as one can sound at that altitude, having taken his oxygen mask off to speak. He didn't even seem particularly breathless."

Nevertheless, it had taken Herrod seventeen hours to climb from the South Col to the summit. Although there was little wind, clouds now enveloped the upper mountain, and darkness was fast approaching. Completely alone on the roof of the world, extremely fatigued, he must have been out of oxygen, or nearly out. "That he was up there that late, with nobody else around, was crazy," says his former teammate, Andy de Klerk. "It's absolutely boggling."

Herrod had been up on the South Col from the evening of May 9 through May 12. He'd felt the ferocity of that storm, heard the desperate radio calls for help, seen Beck Weathers crippled with horrible frostbite. Early on during his ascent of May 25, Herrod climbed right past the corpse of Scott Fischer, and several hours later at the South Summit he would have had to step over Rob Hall's lifeless legs. Apparently, the bodies made little impression on Herrod, however, for despite his lagging pace and the lateness of the hour he pressed onward to the top.

There was no further radio transmission from Herrod after his 5:15 call from the summit. "We sat waiting for him at Camp Four with the radio on," O'Dowd explained in an interview published in the Johannesburg *Mail & Guardian.* "We were terribly tired and eventually fell asleep. When I woke up the next morning at about 5:00 A.M., and he hadn't radioed, I realised we had lost him."

Bruce Herrod is now presumed dead, the twelfth casualty of the season.

Epilogue

SEATTLE NOVEMBER 29, 1996 270 FEET

Now I dream of the soft touch of women, the songs of birds, the smell of soil crumbling between my fingers, and the brilliant green of plants that I diligently nurture. I am looking for land to buy and I will sow it with deer and wild pigs and birds and cottonwoods and sycamores and build a pond and the ducks will come and fish will rise in the early evening light and take the insects into their jaws. There will be paths through this forest and you and I will lose ourselves in the soft curves and folds of the ground. We will come to the water's edge and lie on the grass and there will be a small, unobtrusive sign that says, THIS IS THE REAL WORLD, MUCHACHOS, AND WE ARE ALL IN IT.—B. TRAVEN. . . .

Charles Bowden
Blood Orchid

Several people who were on Everest last May have told me they've managed to move beyond the tragedy. In mid-November I received a letter from Lou Kasischke in which he wrote,

> It took a few months in my case for the positive aspects to begin to develop. But they have. Everest was the worst experience in my life. But that was then. Now is now. I'm focusing on the positive. I learned some important things about life, others, and myself. I feel I now have a clearer perspective on life. I see things today I never saw before.

Lou had just returned from spending a weekend with Beck Weathers in Dallas. Following his helicopter evacuation from the Western Cwm, Beck had his right arm amputated halfway below the elbow. All four fingers and the thumb on his left hand were removed. His nose was amputated and reconstructed with tissue from his ear and forehead. Lou mused that visiting Beck

> was both sad and triumphant. It hurts to see Beck like this: rebuilt nose, facial scars, disabled for life, Beck wondering if he can practice medicine again, and the like. But it was also remarkable to see how a man can accept all this and be ready to move on in life. He is conquering this. He will be victorious.
>
> Beck had only nice things to say about everyone. Beck doesn't play the blame game. You may not have shared political views with Beck, but you would share my pride in seeing how he has handled this. Somehow, some day, this will net out in a positive way for Beck.

I'm heartened that Beck, Lou, and others are apparently able to look at the positive side of the experience—and envious. Perhaps after more time has passed I, too, will be able to recognize some greater good that's resulted from so much suffering, but right now I can't.

As I write these words, half a year has passed since I returned from Nepal, and on any given day during those six months, no more than two or three hours have gone by in which Everest hasn't monopolized my thoughts. Not even in sleep is there respite: imagery from the climb and its aftermath continues to permeate my dreams.

After my article about the expedition was published in the September issue of *Outside,* the magazine received an unusually large volume of mail about the piece. Much of the correspondence offered support and sympathy for those of us who had returned, but there was also an abundance of scathingly critical letters. For example, a lawyer from Florida admonished,

> All I can say is that I agree with Mr. Krakauer when he said, "My actions—or failure to act—played a direct role in the death of Andy Harris." I also agree with him when he says, "[He was] a mere 350 yards [away], lying inside a tent, doing absolutely nothing. . . ." I don't know how he can live with himself.

Some of the angriest letters—and by far the most disturbing to read—came from relatives of the deceased. Scott Fischer's sister, Lisa Fischer-Luckenbach, wrote,

> Based on your written word, YOU certainly seem now to have the uncanny ability to know precisely what was going on in the minds and hearts of every individual on the expedition. Now that YOU are home, alive and well, you have judged the judgments of others, analyzed their intentions, behaviors, personalities and motivations. You have commented on what SHOULD have been done by the leaders, the Sherpas, the clients, and have made arrogant accusations of their wrongdoing. All according to Jon Krakauer, who after sensing the doom brewing, scrambled back to his tent for his own safety and survival. . . .
>
> Perhaps catch a glimpse of what you are doing by seeming to KNOW EVERYTHING. You have already been wrong with your SPECULATION of what happened to Andy Harris causing much grief and anguish to his family and friends. And now you have repudiated the character of Lopsang with your "tattle tale" accounts of him.
>
> What I am reading is YOUR OWN ego frantically struggling to make sense out of what happened. No amount of your analyzing, criticizing, judging, or hypothesizing will bring the peace you are looking for. There are no answers. No one is at fault. No one is to blame. Everyone was doing their best at the given time under the given circumstances.
>
> No one intended harm for one another. No one wanted to die.

This latter missive was especially upsetting because I received it soon after learning that the list of victims had grown to include Lopsang

Jangbu. In August, after the retreat of the monsoon from the high Himalaya, Lopsang had returned to Everest to guide a Japanese client up the South Col and Southeast Ridge route. On September 25, as they were ascending from Camp Three to Camp Four to launch their summit assault, a slab avalanche engulfed Lopsang, another Sherpa, and a French climber just below the Geneva Spur and swept them down the Lhotse Face to their deaths. Lopsang left behind a young wife and a two-month-old baby in Kathmandu.

There has been other bad news as well. On May 17, after resting for just two days at Base Camp after coming down from Everest, Anatoli Boukreev climbed alone to the summit of Lhotse. "I am tired," he told me, "but I go for Scott." Continuing his quest to ascend all fourteen of the world's 8,000-meter peaks, in September Boukreev traveled to Tibet and climbed both Cho Oyu and 26,291-foot Shisha Pangma. But in mid-November, during a visit to his home in Kazakhstan, a bus he was riding in crashed. The driver was killed and Anatoli received severe head injuries, including grave and possibly permanent damage to one of his eyes.

On October 14, 1996, the following message was posted on the Internet as part of a South African discussion forum about Everest:

> I am a Sherpa orphan. My father was killed in the Khumbu Icefall while load-ferrying for an expedition in the late sixties. My mother died just below Pheriche when her heart gave out under the weight of the load she was carrying for another expedition in 1970. Three of my siblings died from various causes, my sister and I were sent to foster homes in Europe and the U.S.
>
> I never have gone back to my homeland because I feel it is cursed. My ancestors arrived in the Solo-Khumbu region fleeing from persecution in the lowlands. There they found sanctuary in the shadow of "Sagarmathaji,"

"mother goddess of the earth." In return they were expected to protect that goddesses' sanctuary from outsiders.

But my people went the other way. They helped outsiders find their way into the sanctuary and violate every limb of her body by standing on top of her, crowing in victory, and dirtying and polluting her bosom. Some of them have had to sacrifice themselves, others escaped through the skin of their teeth, or offered other lives in lieu. . . .

So I believe that even the Sherpas are to blame for the tragedy of 1996 on "Sagarmatha." I have no regrets of not going back, for I know the people of the area are doomed, and so are those rich, arrogant outsiders who feel they can conquer the world. Remember the Titanic. Even the unsinkable sank, and what are foolish mortals like Weathers, Pittman, Fischer, Lopsang, Tenzing, Messner, Bonington in the face of the "Mother Goddess." As such I have vowed never to return home and be part of that sacrilege.

| | |

Everest seems to have poisoned many lives. Relationships have foundered. The wife of one of the victims has been hospitalized for depression. When I last spoke to a certain teammate, his life had been thrown into turmoil. He reported that the strain of coping with the expedition's aftereffects was threatening to wreck his marriage. He couldn't concentrate at work, he said, and he had received taunts and insults from strangers.

Upon her return to Manhattan, Sandy Pittman found that she'd become a lightning rod for a great deal of public anger over what had happened on Everest. *Vanity Fair* magazine published a withering article about her in its August 1996 issue. A camera crew from the tabloid television program *Hard Copy* ambushed her outside her apartment. The writer Christopher Buckley used Pittman's high-altitude tribulations as the punchline of a joke on the back page of *The New Yorker.* By autumn, things had gotten so bad that she confessed tearfully to a friend that her son was being ridiculed and ostracized by classmates at his exclusive private school. The blistering intensity of the collective wrath over Everest—and the fact that so much of that wrath was directed at her—took Pittman completely by surprise and left her reeling.

For Neal Beidleman's part, he helped save the lives of five clients by guiding them down the mountain, yet he remains haunted by a death he was unable to prevent, of a client who wasn't on his team and thus wasn't even officially his responsibility.

I chatted with Beidleman after we'd both re-acclimated to our home turf, and he recalled what it felt like to be out on the South Col, huddling with his group in the awful wind, trying desperately to keep everyone alive. "As soon as the sky cleared enough to give us an idea where camp was," he recounted, "it was like, 'Hey, this break in the storm may not last long, so let's *GO!*' I was screaming at everyone to get moving, but it became clear that some people didn't have enough strength to walk, or even stand.

"People were crying. I heard someone yell, 'Don't let me die here!' It was obvious that it was now or never. I tried to get Yasuko on her feet. She grabbed my arm, but she was too weak to get up past her knees. I started walking, and dragged her for a step or two, then her grip loosened and she fell away. I had to keep going. Somebody had to make it to the tents and get help or everybody was going to die."

Beidleman paused. "But I can't help thinking about Yasuko," he said when he resumed, his voice hushed. "She was so little. I can still feel her fingers sliding across my biceps, and then letting go. I never even turned to look back."

Author's Note

My article in *Outside* angered several of the people I wrote about, and hurt the friends and relatives of some Everest victims. I sincerely regret this—I did not set out to harm anyone. My intent in the magazine piece, and to an even greater degree in this book, was to tell what happened on the mountain as accurately and honestly as possible, and to do it in a sensitive, respectful manner. I believe quite strongly that this story needed to be told. Obviously, not everyone feels this way, and I apologize to those who feel wounded by my words.

Additionally, I would like to express my profound condolences to Fiona McPherson, Ron Harris, Mary Harris, David Harris, Jan Arnold, Sarah Arnold, Eddie Hall, Millie Hall, Jaime Hansen, Angie Hansen, Bud Hansen, Tom Hansen, Steve Hansen, Diane Hansen, Karen Marie Rochel, Kenichi Namba, Jean Price, Andy Fischer-Price, Katie Rose Fischer-Price, Gene Fischer, Shirley Fischer, Lisa Fischer-Luckenbach, Rhonda Fischer Salerno, Sue Thompson, and Ngawang Sya Kya Sherpa.

In assembling this book I received invaluable assistance from many people, but Linda Mariam Moore and David S. Roberts deserve special mention. Not only was their expert advice crucial to this volume, but without their support and encouragement I would never have attempted the dubious business of writing for a living, or stuck with it over the years.

On Everest I benefited from the companionship of Caroline Mackenzie, Helen Wilton, Mike Groom, Ang Dorje Sherpa, Lhakpa

Chhiri Sherpa, Chhongba Sherpa, Ang Tshering Sherpa, Kami Sherpa, Tenzing Sherpa, Arita Sherpa, Chuldum Sherpa, Ngawang Norbu Sherpa, Pemba Sherpa, Tendi Sherpa, Beck Weathers, Stuart Hutchison, Frank Fischbeck, Lou Kasischke, John Taske, Guy Cotter, Nancy Hutchison, Susan Allen, Anatoli Boukreev, Neal Beidleman, Jane Bromet, Ingrid Hunt, Ngima Kale Sherpa, Sandy Hill Pittman, Charlotte Fox, Tim Madsen, Pete Schoening, Klev Schoening, Lene Gammelgaard, Martin Adams, Dale Kruse, David Breashears, Robert Schauer, Ed Viesturs, Paula Viesturs, Liz Cohen, Araceli Segarra, Sumiyo Tsuzuki, Laura Ziemer, Jim Litch, Peter Athans, Todd Burleson, Scott Darsney, Brent Bishop, Andy de Klerk, Ed February, Cathy O'Dowd, Deshun Deysel, Alexandrine Gaudin, Philip Woodall, Makalu Gau, Ken Kamler, Charles Corfield, Becky Johnston, Jim Williams, Mal Duff, Mike Trueman, Michael Burns, Henrik Jessen Hansen, Veikka Gustafsson, Henry Todd, Mark Pfetzer, Ray Door, Göran Kropp, Dave Hiddleston, Chris Jillet, Dan Mazur, Jonathan Pratt, and Chantal Mauduit.

I am very grateful to my matchless editors at Villard Books/Random House, David Rosenthal and Ruth Fecych. Thanks, as well, to Adam Rothberg, Annik LaFarge, Dan Rembert, Diana Frost, Kirsten Raymond, Jennifer Webb, Melissa Milsten, Dennis Ambrose, Bonnie Thompson, Brian McLendon, Beth Thomas, Caroline Cunningham, Dianne Russell, Katie Mehan, and Suzanne Wickham. Randy Rackliff created the remarkable woodcuts.

This book originated as an assignment from *Outside* magazine. Special gratitude is owed to Mark Bryant, who has edited my work with uncommon intelligence and sensitivity for some fifteen years now, and Larry Burke, who has been publishing my work even longer. Also contributing to my Everest piece were Brad Wetzler, John Alderman, Katie Arnold, John Tayman, Sue Casey, Greg Cliburn, Hampton Sides, Amanda Stuermer, Lorien Warner, Sue Smith, Cricket Lengyel, Lolly Merrell, Stephanie Gregory, Laura Hohnhold, Adam Horowitz, John Galvin, Adam Hicks, Elizabeth Rand, Chris Czmyrid, Scott Parmalee, Kim Gattone, and Scott Mathews.

I'm indebted to John Ware, my superb agent. Thanks, also, to David Schensted and Peter Bodde of the American Embassy in Kathmandu, Lisa Choegyal of Tiger Mountain, and Deepak Lama of Wilderness Experience Trekking for their assistance in the wake of the tragedy.

For providing inspiration, hospitality, friendship, information, and sage advice, I'm grateful to Tom Hornbein, Bill Atkinson, Madeleine David, Steve Gipe, Don Peterson, Martha Kongsgaard, Peter Goldman, Rebecca Roe, Keith Mark Johnson, Jim Clash, Muneo Nukita, Helen Trueman, Steve Swenson, Conrad Anker, Alex Lowe, Colin Grissom, Kitty Calhoun, Peter Hackett, David Shlim, Brownie Schoene, Michael Chessler, Marion Boyd, Graem Nelson, Stephen P. Martin, Jane Tranel, Ed Ward, Sharon Roberts, Matt Hale, Roman Dial, Peggy Dial, Steve Rottler, David Trione, Deborah Shaw, Nick Miller, Dan Cauthorn, Greg Collum, Dave Jones, Fran Kaul, Dielle Havlis, Lee Joseph, Pat Joseph, Pierret Vogt, Paul Vogt, David Quammen, Tim Cahill, Paul Theroux, Charles Bowden, Alison Lewis, Barbara Detering, Lisa Anderheggen-Leif, Helen Forbes, and Heidi Baye.

I was aided by the efforts of fellow writers and journalists Elizabeth Hawley, Michael Kennedy, Walt Unsworth, Sue Park, Dile Seitz, Keith McMillan, Ken Owen, Ken Vernon, Mike Loewe, Keith James, David Beresford, Greg Child, Bruce Barcott, Peter Potterfield, Stan Armington, Jennet Conant, Richard Cowper, Brian Blessed, Jeff Smoot, Patrick Morrow, John Colmey, Meenakshi Ganguly, Jennifer Mattos, Simon Robinson, David Van Biema, Jerry Adler, Rod Nordland, Tony Clifton, Patricia Roberts, David Gates, Susan Miller, Peter Wilkinson, Claudia Glenn Dowling, Steve Kroft, Joanne Kaufman, Howie Masters, Forrest Sawyer, Tom Brokaw, Audrey Salkeld, Liesl Clark, Jeff Herr, Jim Curran, Alex Heard, and Lisa Chase.

Selected Bibliography

Armington, Stan. *Trekking in the Nepal Himalaya.* Oakland, CA: Lonely Planet, 1994.
Bass, Dick, and Frank Wells with Rick Ridgeway. *Seven Summits.* New York: Warner Books, 1986.
Baume, Louis C. *Sivalaya: Explorations of the 8,000-Metre Peaks of the Himalaya.* Seattle: The Mountaineers, 1979.
Cherry-Garrard, Apsley. *The Worst Journey in the World.* New York: Carroll & Graf, 1989.
Dyrenfurth, G. O. *To the Third Pole.* London: Werner Laurie, 1955.
Fisher, James F. *Sherpas: Reflections on Change in Himalayan Nepal.* Berkeley: University of California, 1990.
Holzel, Tom, and Audrey Salkeld. *The Mystery of Mallory and Irvine.* New York: Henry Holt, 1986.
Hornbein, Thomas F. *Everest: The West Ridge.* San Francisco: The Sierra Club, 1966.
Hunt, John. *The Ascent of Everest.* Seattle: The Mountaineers, 1993.
Long, Jeff. *The Ascent.* New York: William Morrow, 1992.
Messner, Reinhold. *The Crystal Horizon: Everest—the First Solo Ascent.* Seattle: The Mountaineers, 1989.
Morris, Jan. *Coronation Everest: The First Ascent and the Scoop That Crowned the Queen.* London: Boxtree, 1993.
Roberts, David. *Moments of Doubt.* Seattle: The Mountaineers, 1986.
Shipton, Eric. *The Six Mountain-Travel Books.* Seattle: The Mountaineers, 1985.
Unsworth, Walt. *Everest.* London: GraftonBooks, 1991.

About the Author

Jon Krakauer is a contributing editor of *Outside* magazine and the author of *Eiger Dreams: Ventures Among Men and Mountains* and the acclaimed *Into the Wild*. His writing also appears in *Smithsonian*, *National Geographic*, *Playboy*, *Rolling Stone*, and *Architectural Digest*. He lives in Seattle.